RESTRAINING EQUALITY
HUMAN RIGHTS COMM
IN CANADA

R. Brian Howe and David Johnson

Restraining Equality addresses the contemporary financial, social, legal, and policy pressures currently experienced by human rights commissions across Canada. Through a combination of public policy analysis, historical research, and legal analysis, R. Brian Howe and David Johnson trace the evolution of human rights policy within this country and explore the stresses placed on human rights commissions resulting from greater fiscal restraints and society's rising expectations for equality rights over the past two decades.

The book analyses sources of these tensions in relation to the delivery of equality rights in both federal and provincial jurisdictions since the Second World War. Through a series of interviews with human rights commission officials and a survey of advocacy groups, business organizations, and human rights staff Howe and Johnson explore the performance and the internal workings of these commissions. The authors also analyse human rights commissions in light of the theoretical literature and empirical data, and discuss the political and legal contexts in which the commissions operate and the reform measures that have been implemented.

R. BRIAN HOWE and DAVID JOHNSON are professors in the Department of Politics, Government, and Public Administration at University College of Cape Breton, Nova Scotia.

R. BRIAN HOWE AND DAVID JOHNSON

Restraining Equality: Human Rights Commissions in Canada

UNIVERSITY OF TORONTO PRESS
Toronto Buffalo London

© University of Toronto Press Incorporated 2000
Toronto Buffalo London
Printed in Canada

ISBN 0-8020-4482-4 (cloth)
ISBN 0-8020-8263-7 (paper)

Printed on acid-free paper

Canadian Cataloguing in Publication Data

Howe, Robert Brian
  Restraining equality : human rights commissions in Canada

  Includes bibliographical references and index.
  ISBN 0-8020-4482-4 (bound)   ISBN 0-8020-8263-7 (pbk.)

  1. Civil rights – Government policy – Canada. 2. Administrative agencies – Canada. I. Johnson, David, 1957– . II. Title.

  JC599.C3H68 1999   353.4′8225′0971   C99-931551-X

University of Toronto Press acknowledges the financial assistance to its publishing program of the Canada Council for the Arts and the Ontario Arts Council.

This book has been published with the help of a grant from the Humanities and Social Sciences Federation of Canada, using funds provided by the Social Sciences and Humanities Research Council of Canada.

University of Toronto Press acknowledges the financial support for its publishing activities of the Government of Canada through the Book Publishing Industry Development Program (BPIDP).

Canadä

To Katherine, Tim, and Chris Covell
and
To Blanche and Charles Johnson

Contents

ACKNOWLEDGMENTS xi
INTRODUCTION xiii

Chapter 1: The Evolution of Human Rights Legislation 3
Ground Zero 3
Pioneering Legislation 6
The Dawn of Human Rights Commissions 9
Expansionary Developments: Legislative Change 12
Expansionary Developments: Judicial Interpretation 22
Why Human Rights Legislation? 25

Chapter 2: The Public Administration of Human Rights 37
Commission Foundations: The Institutional Perspective 37
Human Rights Commissions and Institutional Design: The Critique of the Courts 39
The Administrative Rationale for Human Rights Commissions 42
The Legal Rationale for Human Rights Commissions 44
The Organizational Design of Commissions 48
General Agency Structure 49
Organizational Design and Procedure: The Ontario Model 52
Commission Structure 52
Case Procedure 54
Organizational Design and Procedure: The Federal Model 58
Organizational Design and Procedure: The Quebec Model 61
Organizational Design and Procedure: The British Columbia Model 65
Conclusion: Administrative Options, Legal Constraints 68

viii   Contents

Chapter 3: Fiscal Restraint   70

Expanding Commission Workloads   71
The Contraction of Resources   75
The Impact of Restraint   79
Variations in Restraint   82
Revenue Availability   84
The Size of Minorities   84
Interest Group Pressures   86
Administrative Structure   89
Women in Power   90
Political Party in Office   91
Why Human Rights Restraint?   95

Chapter 4: Coping with Restraint   101

The Context of Contemporary Rights Administration   101
The Reconfiguration of Public Administration: Reinvention or Reform?   103
Human Rights Commissions and Reinvention   106
Human Rights Commissions: Coping with Restraint   107
Rethinking Case Management   109
Case Screening   112
Investigation and Conciliation   113
Caseflow and Management Information Systems   115
Boards of Inquiry and Adjudication   116
Public Education   120
Systemic Discrimination   124
Restraint and Reform   127
Commissions and Organizational Models   132
Conclusion   133

Chapter 5: The Paradox of Human Rights Policy   135

Great Expectations   137
A Human Rights Report Card   138
The Overall Results   141
The Perspective of Advocacy Groups   142
The Perspective of Employers and Business Groups   145
The Perspective of Human Rights Staff and Officials   147

The Grand Paradox 150
The Paradox, Part One: Rights Consciousness 150
The Paradox, Part Two: Rights Restraint 153
The Paradox Constructed: Incompatible Expectations, Limited
    Capacities 157
Viewpoints: 1. Crisis 159
Viewpoints: 2. Balance 160
The Pluralist Perspective: An Assessment 162
Conclusion: The Paradox Continues 166

NOTES 169
INDEX 189

Acknowledgments

We thank the anonymous reviewer and the final evaluator from the University of Toronto Press for very constructive criticisms of the manuscript, which were invaluable in preparing the final version. For the time they spent carefully reading the manuscript and for their ideas, we are very grateful.

We thank the Social Sciences and Humanities Research Council of Canada for their support of our research through a standard research grant. This provided us with assistance in collecting material and in interviewing officials of the human rights commissions and of organizations familiar with human rights policy and the work of the commissions.

We are grateful to the officials and staff of the human rights commissions, who provided us with the information and material we were seeking. All of Canada's commissions were generous with their time, and helped us without hesitation.

We thank our research assistants, Angela MacKinnon, Tara King, Gerald Davis, and Ken MacDonald, who were all students at the University College of Cape Breton. They gathered information, summarized research, and discussed the material with us over the course of the project. Without their energy, the project would have taken much longer.

We are grateful to Virgil Duff, Siobhan McMenemy, and Matthew Kudelka of the University of Toronto Press for their sound judgment and for their efficiency in publishing this book. We are very grateful to Virgil Duff for his faith in our ideas and for his continued support of this project.

We thank our colleagues and the librarians at the University College of Cape Breton. Dr Katherine Covell helped with the survey and the statistical part of our research. Laura Syms of the University College Library came to our rescue several times when we thought we could never get the material we were seeking. Finally, we greatly appreciate the support and encouragement given by Dr Robert Morgan, Director of Research and Development, and Dr Jacquelyn Thayer Scott, President of the University College of Cape Breton.

Introduction

Since the Second World War, human rights policies have been established in Canada to provide protection against discrimination and to advance equality rights. These policies have been given legal and institutional effect through provincial, federal, and territorial human rights legislation (or antidiscrimination legislation) and through special human rights commissions established to administer and enforce that legislation. The chief responsibilities assigned to these commissions have been to settle complaints of discrimination and to develop programs and launch initiatives in areas such as public education, race relations, and – more recently – systemic discrimination and affirmative action. Their core task has been to advance equality rights in the areas of employment, housing, and the provision of public services.

But in this new era of fiscal restraint, commissions are under enormous stress. In the context of society's expanding awareness of equality rights, equality-seeking groups have been pressuring the commissions to take more vigorous action in the pursuit of equality and to adopt stronger policies, procedures, and programs. Yet at these same time, the commissions are enjoying fewer resources relative to their growing responsibilities, and are thus constrained in their capacity to meet the rising expectations for equality. Funding and staffing restrictions have made it much more difficult for commissions to 'deliver' human rights. This situation has been complicated further by demands from business groups and social conservatives that the commissions show more balance, restraint, and procedural fairness. In this new environment of fiscal restraint, rising expectations, and contradictory pressures, commissions are finding it harder to be effective agents of equality rights.

The purpose of this book is to examine the forces that led to the development of human rights legislation, and to assess the response of human rights commissions to the challenges of fiscal restraint. Like other government agencies, human rights commissions have been asked to do more with less. Our questions are these: What forces have been responsible for restraining human rights commissions? What has been the impact on human rights procedures and programs? How have commissions responded to the challenge, and how are their responses to be assessed?

In contrast to studies of public policies that focus on societal pressures as the main force driving policy development, we will highlight forces *within* the state. In accounting for the origins and development of human rights legislation, we will point to the key role played by state actors and to the dynamic relationship between state and societal forces. Since the Second World War, interest groups have played an important role in raising equality rights issues, but it has been state actors, and forces *within* the state, that have done most to develop and expand the legislation. It also has been state actors who have been responsible for developing responses and initiating reforms in times of fiscal restraint. We do not dispute that societal forces and interest groups are important in the development of human rights legislation and policies. But we do put state actors on centre stage.

In our analysis of the challenges posed by fiscal restraint, we highlight the tensions between rising equality rights consciousness and the administrative structure of the commissions. The rise of human rights interest groups and advocates, influenced and encouraged by equality rights consciousness, has been a key source of pressure for more vigorous commissions and policies. Yet the very rationale behind human rights commissions ultimately poses important practical difficulties for commissions and for the people they are designed to serve. As we will show, the commissions were created as means to promote human rights policy within society. In that respect, they were to be administrative alternatives to the traditional courts. Thus it was anticipated that human rights commissions would be better defenders and promoters of rights policies, in that their administration of this important policy field would be marked by the values of economy, efficiency, and effectiveness. But these same commissions were also designed to be law enforcement bodies with important responsibilities regarding how the law was applied and legal disputes were adjudicated. In other words, they were expected to carry out their duties in accordance with long-established legal principles of due process and natural justice.

For commissions and for those touched by their work, this constitutes an important source of tension. These agencies are designed to be accessible and comprehensible, and to do their work expeditiously; yet at the same time they are semijudicial bodies charged with deciding cases in full accordance with all legal requirements and legal rights. Unavoidably, these legal requirements have made commission procedures relatively complex, time-consuming, and costly. This has embittered many who have found themselves needing to deal with the commissions.

The commissions have struggled with these tensions since they were first formed, and the economic restraints of the 1980s and 1990s have only heightened them. All government institutions have been hurt by the fiscal restraints of recent decades, and human rights commissions have not come away unscathed. The federal and provincial governments have cut their budgets and told them that even though they have more to do, they have to find ways to do it with less. The commissions have tried to adapt to these cross-pressures by reforming their own procedures. Often they have adapted successfully. But a number of commissions are still plagued by organizational problems, many of which have to do with cases being delayed. This in turn leads to public criticisms that damage their reputation.

Yet at least potentially, the commissions may benefit from the restraints of the present day. The pressure to do more with less has compelled them to reassess their priorities and review how they accomplish them; this is helping them to remember their core responsibilities and to concentrate on those tasks which the public most demands of them. From this perspective the pressures of fiscal restraint, coupled with those arising from the demands of legal due process, may help the commissions redesign their policies to meet the needs of contemporary society. Strict adherence to the administrative law rules of natural justice may have brought about higher costs and more case delays, but it has also reinforced the legitimacy of human rights procedures. That legal rights and procedural safeguards have been incorporated into the human rights system has helped legitimize that system in the eyes of Canada's legal and political communities. Also, fiscal restraint may have slowed down the process of assessing and resolving cases, and sometimes stalled program development; but it has also forced commissions to innovate, and thwarted programs that the public would not have broadly supported. That commissions have been compelled for fiscal reasons to consider their initiatives in areas such as systemic discrimination and affirmative action can be seen as a good thing, and one that helps foster legitimacy among the broad public.

The first two chapters deal with the historical background of human rights commissions and their institutional structure. In Chapter 1 we discuss the origins and expansion of human rights legislation in Canada. We account for expansionary developments in terms of the growing public awareness of human rights and the relationship between state and societal forces. We show how human rights commissions both reflect equality rights consciousness and at the same time fuel social and political pressures for still more human rights legislation. By the 1980s the commissions were deeply embedded in Canadian society as protectors of, and vehicles for, equality rights.

In Chapter 2 we discuss how commissions administer and enforce human rights legislation. We focus on the Ontario model, which is the one most commonly used in this country; but we also consider variants, including those found in Quebec and British Columbia and at the federal level. We explain how due process and legal formalities came to be built into complaint procedures. This has important implications, for at a time of growing rights consciousness, the legal framework fosters procedures that are slower, more expensive, and more complex.

In Chapter 3 we discuss how fiscal restraint policies by various governments in the 1980s and 1990s have affected human rights procedures and programs. We explain not only why fiscal restraint is applied to field of human rights, but also why this restraint varies between provinces. To this end, we analyse how different provinces fund commissions, and how the differences are linked to left–right differences in ideology. Parties of the left generally provide more funding than parties of the right; but in this era of globalization and fiscal restraints, parties across the spectrum are cutting or limiting the budgets of human rights commissions.

In Chapter 4 we discuss how human rights commissions are attempting to cope with fiscal restraint. In their efforts to do more with less, most commissions are practising self-reform: redesigning their structures, introducing new case management techniques, and altering their educational programming. Contrary to theorists who see in such development the reinvention of government, we point to the change as representing necessary reform.

Finally, in Chapter 5, we assess the impact of the reforms. We begin by describing and analysing the perspectives of the key players in the human rights policy community: advocacy and human rights interest groups, business and employer organizations, and human rights officers and officials. What we find is an expression of general dissatisfaction, suggesting that human rights policies and the administrative reforms are not working. But we conclude that, once past the expressions of dissatisfaction, the system is in fact working. Serious problems remain, but in general terms, restraint has forced innovation while maintaining the legitimacy of human rights commissions in the eyes of the broader community.

RESTRAINING EQUALITY

1. The Evolution of Human Rights Legislation

The concept of using human rights legislation as a tool for opposing discrimination first emerged in Canada during the 1940s. It did so against the background of the Second World War, which had done much to generate a surge of egalitarian idealism. This expansion of idealism and equality rights consciousness was not unique to Canada: in varying degrees the concept was taking root in liberal societies everywhere, stimulated by the international struggle against fascism and state-sanctioned racism, and by new postwar standards of human rights. And in Canada, as elsewhere, it created a new principle: that the state had a responsibility, through legal and administrative means, to counter discrimination and to secure equality rights in such areas as employment, education, housing, and the provision of services. Based on that principle, a broad movement for human rights legislation emerged in Canada. The result was that policies, laws, and programs against discrimination were established and steadily expanded.

We now review this development as it took place in Canada, focusing on provincial legislation because civil rights and property are in the provincial jurisdiction under the Canadian constitution. It follows that the control of discrimination is largely the responsibility of the provinces.

Ground Zero

Until the Second World War, human rights received scant attention in Canada, and little political support. Small consideration was given to the principle of equality rights or to legislative protection against discrimination in key areas such as employment, housing, and the provision of services; and there was little interest in establishing such rights. The issue seldom arose in public policy debates, political writings, or party platforms.[1] And when the idea of legislation against discrimination did rear its head, it was resisted – sometimes fiercely. As a result, discrimination continued to be practised in Canada, not only in private social and economic relations but also in legislation and public policy.

There were many reasons why discrimination was practised and why the public did not support human rights legislation. First of all, discriminatory attitudes and beliefs were widespread. In Canada as elsewhere, prejudice, bigotry, and intolerance, together with racism, sexism, and other exclusionary 'isms,' were all too common. These attitudes and beliefs were responsible not only for discrimination against minorities and women in social and economic relations (e.g., employers against job applicants), but also for discrimination by the state, reflecting the will of legislators and majorities. Examples of state-sponsored and legislative discrimination were many: the denial of voting rights to women, Asian Canadians, and native peoples; the highly restrictive federal Indian Act, which barred native people from political and other activities; exclusionary immigration policies that discriminated against nonwhites; segregate schools in Nova Scotia and Ontario that disadvantaged black communities; and restrictive labour and employment laws, especially in British Columbia, that prohibited Asian Canadians from employment in certain sectors of the economy.[2] So great was the prejudice that even in Saskatchewan and Ontario there were laws prohibiting white women from working for Chinese employers.

Another reason why human rights legislation was resisted was the widespread belief in social *laissez-faire* and voluntarism in social relations. This belief can be summarized as follows: While prejudice and discrimination might be morally wrong or socially undesirable, human rights legislation or legal action against discrimination would to more harm than good. It would involve unwanted state interference with individual freedom, property rights, and the right of contract. The state would thereby be constraining the freedom of individuals, employers, and businesspeople. A new, legalistic approach not only would erode liberty but also might undermine harmony in social and ethnic relations. As cases came forward, resentment and backlash would build. Thus, while equality of opportunity without discrimination might be a positive goal, human rights law was not the best approach to take. Rather, the approach should be one of social *laissez-faire* in which the prime focus was on education and voluntarism. It followed that discrimination was best dealt with not through public policy but rather through the private means of moral suasion and education. Much more would be achieved through moral suasion than through legal compulsion, and it would be achieved without interference with individual freedom and property rights.[3]

This widespread belief in social *laissez-faire* was reflected in legislative debates and court decisions of the 1930s and 1940s. For example, in 1933 in Ontario a private member's bill was introduced into the legislature that would have prohibited the public display of discriminatory signs, notices, and advertisements.[4] At this time signs such as WHITES ONLY, GENTILES ONLY, and NO JEWS OR BLACKS ALLOWED were not uncommon in store windows, on beaches, and in resort areas. The bill was soundly defeated on grounds that it was impractical and would interfere with freedom. In line with social *laissez-faire*, critics said that while racial and religious prejudice may be morally indesireable, an overriding principle in the law should be individual freedom and property rights. The best way to combat prejudice was through moral disapproval and education rather than legislation.

In the 1940 Quebec case *Christie v. York Corporation*, the priority of individual freedom over equality rights was made very clear.[5] The case involved a black man, Frederick Christie, who was refused service in a Montreal tavern. The Supreme Court of Canada ruled against Christie on the ground that 'the general principle of the law of Quebec was that of complete freedom of commerce.' In the words of Justice Rinfret, 'any merchant is free to deal with as he may choose with any member of the public. It is not a question of motives or reasons ... he is free to do either.' Again, it was the view that individual freedom was (and should be) the overriding principle. Discrimination should be answered not by the law but by moral suasion.

Social *laissez-faire* found favour even among minority leaders and ethnocultural organizations. For example, in Ontario's Jewish community during the 1930s, community leaders were reluctant to campaign for human rights legislation.[6] They preferred to promote self-help within their community while trying to persuade anti-Semitic employers and landlords to refrain from discrimination. It was felt that pressuring legislators for antidiscrimination laws might do more harm than good. Such a cautious approach was illustrated in 1939, when the Jewish community formed a committee to study the general issue of prejudice and discrimination against Jews in employment. The committee concluded that the problem was best dealt with through a friendly educational approach whereby employers were persuaded that it was in their own best interests not to discriminate. A more openly political approach of pressuring government for legislation might easily invite a Gentile backlash.[7]

Pioneering Legislation

Before the Second World War, legislation against discrimination hardly existed in Canada. There were minor exceptions: Ontario amended its insurance legislation in 1932 to prohibit discrimination in the assessment of insurance risks based on race and religion.[8] The same year, British Columbia amended its unemployment insurance relief legislation to ban discrimination in relief work projects based on race, religion, and political affiliation. But beyond this, little was done. However, change – and the momentum for more change – began to occur during and immediately after the war.

The Second World War was a pivotal event in the evolution of human rights legislation. The nature of this global struggle against fascism, and the realization after the war ended of the true extent of the Holocaust, changed the way people thought. The war, by mobilizing Canadians against state-sanctioned racism, by illustrating the evil consequences to which racism can lead, and by demonstrating – through the mistreatment of Japanese Canadians – the shortcomings of Canadian society itself, served as a catalyst for human rights awareness and for legislation against discrimination. The experience led policymakers, judges, and community leaders to rethink social *laissez-faire* and become more supportive of the principle of human rights legislation. Other postwar events promoted this new consciousness. One was Canada's participation in establishing the United Nations and its signing of the Universal Declaration of Human Rights.[9] This participation added legitimacy to proposals for enacting human rights laws in Canada. Another factor was the apparently successful implementation of antidiscrimination laws in the United States, especially in New York State during the 1940s,[10] which boosted support for similar laws in Canada. But it was the experience of war that was the main stimulus of change. To a great extent, American developments and the establishment of the Universal Declaration of Human Rights were themselves a product of the war experience.

Pioneering legislation against discrimination began to be enacted during and immediately after the war. In 1944, Ontario's Conservative government enacted the Racial Discrimination Act, which banned the public display of discriminatory signs and notices.[11] Although the statute was brief and quite limited in scope, it was the first piece of modern human rights legislation in Canada. In 1947, Saskatchewan under the CCF enacted much more comprehensive legislation, the Saskatchewan Bill of Rights Act. This statute was relatively broad in scope, and provided not only for equality rights but also for fundamental freedoms and political rights. As the first major piece of antidiscrimination legislation in Canada, it provided protection against discrimination in a wide range of areas, including employment, housing, the workplace, land transactions, and education.

The early Ontario and Saskatchewan statutes were quasi-criminal pieces of legislation and had certain weaknesses.[12] They approached discrimination as a crime to be dealt with by the police and through the courts. As one result, victims of discrimination were often reluctant to initiate criminal proceedings, because police generally were unwilling to act, because in order for there to be a successful prosecution under the criminal standard of proof, discrimination had to be proven beyond a reasonable doubt. This was highly problematic in that it was relatively easy for defence lawyers to argue that a job opportunity (for example) had been denied for reasons other than discrimination. Another problem with the approach was that many judges were reluctant to convict even if the evidence was substantial. Many senior judges were still committed to the older social values of individual freedom and freedom of contract, and refused to recognize discrimination as a real crime. Thus they tended not to take discrimination cases seriously. Yet another problem was the outcome of the cases that did come to trial. Even when there was a conviction, the legal sanction – usually a small fine against the discriminator – was of little help to the victim. Victims of discrimination required a remedy, not knowledge of a conviction.

To overcome these problems, during the 1950s and 1960s a new enforcement approach was adopted. This 'fair practices' legislation,[13] as it was called, was modelled on legislation first introduced in North America in New York in 1945. In Canada it first appeared in the 1950s, in Ontario.[14] There were two main types of such legislation: fair employment practices acts, and fair accommodation practices acts. As the terms suggest, these acts prohibited discrimination in employment, housing, and services. The grounds of discrimination were at first lim-

TABLE 1.1
Pioneering human rights legislation in Canada

Year	Jurisdiction	Legislation	Party in office
1944	Ontario	Racial Discrimination Act	Conservative
1947	Saskatchewan	Bill of Rights Act	CCF
1951	Ontario	Fair Employment Practices	Conservative
1951	Ontario	Equal Pay Act	Conservative
1952	Saskatchewan	Equal Pay Act	CCF
1953	Manitoba	Fair Employment Practices	Liberal Prog.
1954	Ontario	Fair Accommodation Practices	Conservative
1956	Saskatchewan	Fair Accommodation Practices	CCF

ited to race and religion but were later extended to include sex and age.

The first province to enact fair employment practices legislation was Ontario (1951), followed by Manitoba (in 1953, the same year as the federal government), Nova Scotia (1955), and New Brunswick, BC, and Saskatchewan (1956). Ontario was also the first government to enact a fair accommodation practices act. It did so in 1954, followed by Saskatchewan (1956), Nova Scotia and New Brunswick (1959), and Manitoba (1960). By the 1960s most jurisdictions in Canada had passed fair practices laws. Also by the 1960s, most had passed equal pay acts, which are another type of fair practices legislation. These acts prohibited wage discrimination against women who were doing the same work as men in the same workplace. Again, the pioneering province was Ontario, which passed an equal pay act in 1951, followed by Saskatchewan (1952), BC (1953), and Nova Scotia, New Brunswick, and Manitoba (1956, the same year as the federal government).

Fair practices legislation emphasized conciliation and the settlement of complaints, and in that sense was based on methods and procedures used in labour relations. This proved to be a considerable improvement over the criminal approach. Under the new system, victims of discrimination brought complaints to administrative officials (usually in the Department of Labour), who then investigated and tried to negotiate a settlement agreeable to both the complainant and the respondent. A settlement, for example, might involve a job offer. If conciliation failed, a board of inquiry might be set up to hear the case; as a last resort, the case might be referred for criminal prosecution. This approach made it easier for victims of discrimination to file complaints. And because the civil law standard of proof was used, in order to prove discrimination it was necessary only to show a balance of probabilities. Thus, victims knew they stood a more reasonable chance of success. They also had the benefit of administrative support, in that government officials were now responsible for investigating the complaint and attempting a resolution. This eliminated the legal costs associated with a criminal proceeding. As well, the system was an improvement in terms of outcomes. If the complainant had a strong case, the outcome might include a job offer or financial compensation. In practical terms, this was more valuable than a criminal conviction.

But a serious problem remained in the system. The officials responsible for investigation and conciliation were civil servants in a regular government department, and had to deal with a wide variety of duties on a daily basis.[15] For them, human rights cases were only one responsibility among many. Administration and enforcement were conducted on a part-time basis, under the constraints of both time and bureaucratic hierarchy. And public awareness of the available antidiscrimination procedures was virtually nonexistent. The result was that many victims of discrimination still did not come forward, as they were either unaware of the procedure, or aware that complaints were received only grudgingly by part-time officials. Consequently, few complaints were made. Arguments began to be made for the creation of permanent human rights commissions that would address this problem. Such commissions would be staffed by full-time professionals who would be responsible for administering complaint procedures and for educating the public.

The Dawn of Human Rights Commissions

The year 1961 marked a major advance in the history of Canadian human rights legislation, and the pioneering province was again Ontario. This was the creation of Canada's first human rights commission, the Ontario Human Rights Commission, to administer the new Ontario Human Rights Code of 1962.[16] Previously separate fair practices laws were consolidated in the new code, under which the commission was assigned the following functions and responsibilities: to administer a complaint procedure; to develop a program to educate the public about the new legislation; to advise the government on the future development of the code; and in general to forward the cause of equality rights in the province.[17]

In some respects this was a modest development. Under the code, discrimination was prohibited only on the most basic grounds (race, creed, colour), and only in the most fundamental areas (employment, housing), and fines for violating the code were minuscule ($100 for individuals, $500 for employers). Yet in other respects the change was significant. The consolidation of legislation into a single code meant that issues of discrimination were now to be approached as part of a general problem. This helped raise the profile of discrimination issues; it also invited victims of discrimination of come forward. That a permanent human rights commission had been established was of special importance in providing support to victims of discrimination.[18] The commission was mandated to publicize the equality rights of Ontario citizens and to administer more user-friendly procedures; to this end, it was assigned a full-time director, a full-time professional staff, and a permanent office. The administrative machinery of the state was thus made available to victims of discrimination.

Why was Ontario at the forefront in fair practices legislation and human rights codes? There were a number of reasons. One was the effort and skill of human rights activists and interest groups during the 1950s and early and 1960s.[19] These players – many of them from labour organizations, ethnocultural groups, and civil liberties associations – developed an incrementalist strategy whereby they pressured Queen's Park not for comprehensive change but rather for specific laws that were limited in scope, clearly defined, and reasonably attainable. Once these laws had been put into effect, further pressure was applied for yet more change. The strategy worked. Step by step, separate fair practices laws were enacted, and these led to the creation of the code and a commission to oversee it.

But this was not the only factor. Another was the structural change taking place in Ontario. After the war, immigrants (many of them minorities) were flooding into the province; at the same time, the labour movement was growing and more and more women were entering the workforce. All of this helped create a social basis for anti-discrimination legislation. As a result of the concerns held by minorities and women about discrimination, and the desire of politicians to gain votes and of union leaders to gain the support of their members, the momentum for legislation was heightened. Yet another factor was that the legislation posed little threat to business. The business community soon realized that it had little reason to fear the legislation: the grounds of discrimination were relatively narrow, maximum fines were small, and the role of the commission was limited largely to responding to complaints and settling these complaints through conciliation. A final factor was the role played by state actors. Conservative politicians like Allan Grossman and John Yaremko applied pressure within the party for the legislation, senior policy advisors such as Thomas Eberlee and Alexander MacLeod encouraged the legislation within government, and Ontario premiers Leslie Frost (1949–61) and John Robarts (1961–71), while known to be pragmatic and cautious, gave approval to the legislation beyond what was electorally called for.

The system for enforcing the legislation operated in roughly the following manner, referred to by Walter Tarnopolsky as the 'velvet glove' and the 'iron hand.' Conciliation, persuasion, and education were all perceived as vital to the process if it was to work.[20] An alleged victim of discrimination registered a formal complaint with the commission. A human rights officer then investigated the complaint. If preliminary evidence supported the complainant, the officer responded first with the velvet glove. At this point, strong albeit informal efforts were made to bring the complainant and respondent together, conciliate the dispute, and reach an amicable settlement. The assumption followed was that most people who discriminate are less evil than misguided and are acting on the basis of faulty stereotypes or ignorance. These people require persuasion and education to change their behaviour – not accusation and judgment. Thus, a velvet glove should be used. Strong law enforcement would be counterproductive and might arouse resistance and even strengthen prejudice. If conciliation failed – for example, if the respondent was determined not to co-operate – the commission might then turn to tougher law enforcement, putting an iron hand in the velvet glove. Here, the commission could recommend that a board of inquiry or human rights tribunal be appointed to decide the case. In a particularly severe case, it could even recommend criminal prosecution. But this would be exceptional. The main focus was always on conciliation, negotiation, and settlement.

This was the system established in Ontario. Other provinces soon followed Ontario's lead, and human rights commissions and consolidated human rights codes (or acts or charters) spread across the country.[21] As indicated in Table 1.2, by the late 1970s legislation and commissions had been established in every province and at the federal level. At the territorial level, a human rights act and commission were created in 1987. (The Northwest Territories still awaits a commission

12 Restraining Equality

TABLE 1.2
The spread of human rights codes and commissions

Year	Legislation	Commission	Party
1962	Ontario Human Rights Code	1961	Conservative
1963	Nova Scotia Human Rights Act	1967	Conservative
1966	Alberta Human Rights Act	1972	Social Credit
1967	New Brunswick Human Rights Act	1967	Liberal
1968	PEI Human Rights Code	1975	Liberal
1969	BC Human Rights Act	1969	Social Credit
1969	Newfoundland Human Rights Code	1969	Liberal
1970	Manitoba Human Rights Act	1970	NDP
1975	Quebec Charter of Human Rights	1975	Liberal
1977	Canada Human Rights Act	1977	Liberal
1979	Saskatchewan Human Rights Code	1972	NDP
1987	Yukon Human Rights Act	1987	NDP

Notes: Party refers to the party responsible for enacting the legislation. In Ontario and Saskatchewan, commissions were established before codes came into effect.

and code or act, relying on a fair practices act first established in 1988.) These different pieces of human rights legislation are essentially the same in the types of protection they provide, except that Saskatchewan and Quebec provide broader categories of protection. Saskatchewan includes fundamental freedoms and political rights in its coverage (as it has since the Bill of Rights Act of 1947); and Quebec includes social and economic rights as well as fundamental freedoms and legal rights. We discuss differences in organizational design and procedures in Chapter 2.

Expansionary Developments: Legislative Change

Canada's early human rights legislation was relatively limited in scope and capacity. The definition of discrimination was narrow; human rights protections were quite restricted, and so were the ways they were applied; and the powers and responsibilities of commissions and boards of inquiry were limited, as was the redress available to victims of discrimination. But between the 1960s and the 1990s, with revisions and amendments to the legislation and with generally liberal judicial interpretations, the legislation was greatly expanded and strengthened.[22] The major steps in this expansion are summarized in Table 1.3. The general pattern of legislative development was one of widening

TABLE 1.3
The expansion of Canadian human rights legislation

Year	Jurisdiction	Legislation	Party
1973	British Columbia	Human Rights Code	NDP
1973	New Brunswick	Human Rights Act	Conservative
1981	Ontario	Human Rights Code	Conservative
1987	Manitoba	Human Rights Code	NDP
1988	Newfoundland	Human Rights Code	Conservative
1988	Prince Edward Island	Human Rights Act	Liberal
1991	Nova Scotia	Human Rights Act	Conservative
1996	Federal	Human Rights Act	Liberal
1996	British Columbia	Human Rights Code	NDP

protections and increasing powers for commissions, but there was one notable exception: in 1983, British Columbia's Social Credit government dismantled the BC Human Rights Code and commission, replacing them with a more restrictive and smaller-scale Human Rights Act and human rights council, which lasted until 1996.[23]

The BC exception warrants elaboration. In 1973 the NDP had enacted a remarkable piece of legislation, the BC Human Rights Code. What made this code remarkable was its provisions for the mandatory investigation of complaints and for reasonable cause in the determination of discrimination. Under the mandatory investigation provision, human rights officers were required to investigate and to attempt to settle every complaint filed. BC's system differed from most systems in Canada, which gave officials a measure of discretion to screen out frivolous complaints. Under the reasonable cause provision, discrimination was prohibited not only on specified grounds but also in general, unless 'reasonable cause' existed as determined by human rights officials. Again, this differed from all other systems in Canada, which specified the grounds of discrimination. The impact of the reasonable cause provision was that discrimination was defined not according to specific grounds but on the basis of the judgments of officials – in effect, all discrimination was banned unless it was deemed by officials to be reasonable. Under this open-ended clause, officials could and did extend protections into new and controversial areas such as sexual orientation. From the perspective of critics in the business community, the media, and the Social Credit Party, the system was much too liberal. Mandatory investigation encouraged too many trivial cases, and reasonable cause invited too much subjectivity and placed too much power in the hands of human rights officials.

In 1983, under a program of severe fiscal restraint, the Social Credit government acted against the NDP-created system. The system was dismantled and replaced in 1984 by the new Human Rights Act and BC Human Rights Council. In many ways the new system was a throwback to much earlier times of antidiscrimination protection: the scope of human rights protections was diminished; provisions for affirmative action were taken away; the conciliation function was reduced; administrative support for victims of discrimination was removed; and a new human rights council was created that would deal with complaints much more quickly and on a quasi-judicial basis. The burden of responsibility for proving discrimination was shifted back to complainants, who once again were required to get witnesses, acquire documents, and hire their own lawyers. When assistance was provided, it was by part-time officials from other agencies – a common practice in the 1950s – rather than by full-time, experienced professionals. Complainants who were able to get enough evidence could present their cases before the council. But unlike commissions in other jurisdictions, the BC council was not a party to the proceedings. Complainants were left virtually on their own, and their cases were decided in a summary manner. All of this is instructive in showing how a counterstrike against human rights legislation is possible. But the events in BC were an exception to the general trend of expansion.

The pattern of expansion in Canada can be seen by comparing the situation of the early 1960s with that of the late 1990s. In the beginning, the scope of human rights protection was quite narrow. In Ontario's 1962 code, the only prohibited grounds of discrimination were race and religion, and application was restricted mainly to private sector employment (larger employers) and housing (larger landlords).[24] Apart from providing for equal pay for the same work, the code did not even prohibit sex discrimination. But by the 1990s, as indicated in Tables 1.4 and 1.5, there had been a significant enlargement of protections both in employment and in the provision of goods and services. With some variation across the country, prohibited grounds of discrimination were expanded to include age, disability, political belief, sexual orientation, record of criminal conviction, dependence on alcohol or drugs, and even source of income. Concurrent with this, the scope of the application of the legislation was enlarged to include such areas as contracts, employment agencies, sexual harassment, hate literature, the employment of domestic workers, and reasonable accommodation by employers to religious minorities and persons with disabilities. Even in BC there was an expansionary trend. In 1996 the NDP government there replaced the Human Rights Act with a new and expanded Human Rights Code, to be administered by a new and strengthened human rights commission that would again perform conciliation and education functions. This change put British Columbia again at the forefront of human rights development in Canada.

Expansion included administrative reforms as well as broadened protection. In Ontario's original 1962 code, the role of the human rights commission was mainly to respond to individual complaints. The commission had little proactive power, and few positive functions apart from a general public education and advisory role. But by the late 1990s, legislation across the country had been altered to provide for a stronger and more proactive system. This involved such key areas as affirmative action, the investigation of systemic discrimination, and the ordering of remedies. In the area of affirmative action, commissions in virtually all jurisdictions (led by New Brunswick and Saskatchewan in the 1970s) were given the power to recommend, approve, or initiate special programs as a remedy for systemic or indirect discrimination.[25] Furthermore, boards of inquiry or tribunals were given the power to order affirmative action as apart of a remedy. Alberta was (and remains) the only jurisdiction in Canada not to provide specifically for affirmative action. Also, in some jurisdictions – Quebec, the Yukon, federal – commissions were given the power to receive complaints based on the principle of equal pay for work of equal value, or pay equity.[26] In most other jurisdictions – Ontario, Manitoba, PEI, New Brunswick, Nova Scotia – pay equity is dealt with under specialized pay equity legislation and pay equity commissions or bureaux.[27]

Commissions also were given the authority to initiate complaints themselves, and in some jurisdictions to investigate patterns of systemic discrimination. This was the case in Ontario, Quebec, Manitoba, Saskatchewan, Nova Scotia, BC, and the federal jurisdiction.[28] Before this change, only the grieved person could initiate a complaint of discrimination. Moreover, in the jurisdictions mentioned above and in Alberta, amendments allowed for complaints by persons other than the alleged victims (e.g., friends, relatives). In the key area of systemic discrimination, legislative reforms in Ontario, Nova Scotia, and BC allowed commissions to investigate not only direct discrimination but

TABLE 1.4
Employment: Prohibited grounds of discrimination

Prohibited ground	Jurisdiction	Comments
Race or colour	All jurisdictions	
Religion	All jurisdictions	Yukon's Act reads: 'religion or creed, or religious belief, religious association or religious activity'
Physical or mental disability	All jurisdictions	Quebec uses the phrase 'handicap or use of any means to palliate a handicap'
Dependence on alcohol or drugs	All *except* Yukon and NWT	Policy to accept complaints in BC, alcohol or drugs Alberta, Saskatchewan, Manitoba, Ontario, New Brunswick, and PEI
Quebec: included in 'handicap' ground
Previous dependence only in New Brunswick and Nova Scotia
Age	All jurisdictions	BC 19–65
Alberta 18
Saskatchewan 18–64
Ontario 18–65
Newfoundland 19–65
Quebec: except as provided for by law
Sex (includes pregnancy and childbirth)	All jurisdictions	BC includes breast feeding
Alberta uses the term 'gender'
Manitoba includes gender-determined characteristics
Ontario recognizes the protection of transgendered persons and accepts complaints related to 'gender identity'; Ontario policy to accept complaints related to female genital mutilation
In Quebec, pregnancy as such is considered a ground of discrimination

TABLE 1.4 *(Continued)*

Prohibited ground	Jurisdiction	Comments
Marital status	All jurisdictions	Quebec uses the term 'civil status'
Family status	All *except* New Brunswick and Newfoundland	Saskatchewan defines as being in a parent–child relationship Quebec uses the term 'civil status'
Sexual orientation	All *except* NWT	The Supreme Court of Canada read ground into the Alberta Human Rights, Citizenship and Multiculturalism Act in 1998
National or ethnic origin (including linguistic background)	All *except* BC and Alberta	Saskatchewan and NWT use the term 'nationality' Ontario's code includes both 'ethnic origin' and 'citizenship'
Ancestry or place of origin	Yukon, BC, Alberta, Saskatchewan, Manitoba, NWT, Ontario, and New Brunswick	
Language	Yukon, Ontario, and Quebec	Ontario accepts complaints under the grounds of ancestry, ethnic origin, place of origin, and race Although not an enumerated ground in New Brunswick, it will accept language-related complaints filed on the basis of ancestry
Social condition or origin	Quebec and Newfoundland	
Source of income	Alberta, Saskatchewan, Manitoba, Quebec, PEI, and Nova Scotia	Defined as 'receipt of public assistance' in Saskatchewan Quebec: included under social condition
Assignment, attachment, or seizure of pay	Newfoundland	Quebec: included under social condition

TABLE 1.4 (Concluded)

Prohibited ground	Jurisdiction	Comments
Based on association	Yukon, Manitoba, Ontario, New Brunswick, Nova Scotia, and PEI	
Political belief	Yukon, BC, Manitoba, Quebec, Nova Scotia, PEI, and Newfoundland	Newfoundland has prohibition on basis of 'political opinion'
Record of criminal conviction	Yukon, BC, Quebec, and PEI	Yukon's Act reads: 'criminal charges or criminal record'
Pardoned conviction	Federal, BC, NWT, Ontario, and Quebec	

Source: Canadian Human Rights Commission, *Prohibited Grounds of Discrimination in Canada*, 1998. Reproduced with the permission of the Minister of Public Works and Government Services Canada.
Note: Under the Canadian Human Rights Act, it is a discriminatory practice for a person against whom a complaint has been filed to retaliate or threaten retaliation against the individual who filed the complaint or the alleged victim.

TABLE 1.5
Provision of goods, services, facilities, and accommodation: Prohibited grounds of discrimination

Prohibited ground	Jurisdiction	Comments
Race or colour	All jurisdictions	
Religion	All jurisdictions	Yukon's Act reads: 'religion or creed, or religious belief, religious association, or religious activity'
Physical or mental disability	All jurisdictions	Quebec uses the phrase 'handicap or use of any means to palliate a handicap'
Dependence on alcohol or drugs	All *except* Yukon, NWT, and Quebec	Previous dependence only in New Brunswick and Nova Scotia Quebec: included in 'handicap' ground
Age	All *except* BC, Alberta, and Newfoundland	For tenancy only in BC Saskatchewan does not include accommodation In Ontario, applies to those 18 years and older, although 16- and 17-year-olds who have left the care of parents or guardians are protected regarding accommodation Quebec: except as provided for by law
Sex (includes pregnancy and childbirth)	All jurisdictions	Alberta uses the term 'gender' Manitoba includes gender-determined characteristics Ontario recognizes the protection of transgendered persons and accepts complaints related to 'gender identity'; Ontario policy to accept complaints related to female genital mutilation In Quebec, pregnancy as such is considered a ground of discrimination
Marital status	All jurisdictions	Quebec uses the term 'civil status'

TABLE 1.5 *(Continued)*

Prohibited ground	Jurisdiction	Comments
Family status	All *except* New Brunswick and Newfoundland	Saskatchewan defines as being in a parent–child relationship Quebec uses the term 'civil status'
Sexual orientation	All *except* NWT	The Supreme Court of Canada read sexual orientation into the Alberta Human Rights, Citizenship and Multiculturalism Act in 1998
National or ethnic origin (including linguistic background)	All *except* BC and Alberta	Saskatchewan and NWT use the term 'nationality' Ontario's code includes both 'ethnic origin' and 'citizenship'
Ancestry or place of origin	All jurisdictions	
Language	Ontario and Quebec	Ontario accepts complaints under the grounds of ancestry, ethnic origin, place of origin, and race Although not an enumerated ground in New Brunswick, it will accept language-related complaints filed on the basis of ancestry
Social condition or origin	Quebec and Newfoundland	
Source of income	BC, Alberta, Saskatchewan, Manitoba, Ontario, PEI, and Nova Scotia	Applies to tenancy only (not public services or facilities) in BC Defined as 'receipt of social assistance' in Saskatchewan Ontario bans discrimination in accommodation on the grounds of receipt of public assistance Quebec: included under social condition Nova Scotia: is only for occupancy or accommodation
Assignment, attachment, or seizure of pay	Newfoundland	Quebec: included under social condition

TABLE 1.5 (Concluded)

Prohibited ground	Jurisdiction	Comments
Based on association	Yukon, Manitoba, Ontario, New Brunswick, Nova Scotia, and PEI	Yukon includes political activity and political association
Political belief	Yukon, Manitoba, Quebec, Nova Scotia, PEI, and Newfoundland	Newfoundland has prohibition on basis of 'political opinion'
Record of criminal conviction	Yukon and Quebec	Yukon's Act reads: 'criminal charges or criminal record'
Pardoned conviction	Federal, Yukon, and NWT	

Source: Canadian Human Rights Commission, *Prohibited Grounds of Discrimination in Canada*, 1998. Reproduced with the permission of the Minister of Public Works and Government Services Canada.
Note: Under the Canadian Human Rights Act, it is a discriminatory practice for a person against whom a complaint has been filed to retaliate or threaten retaliation against the individual who filed the complaint or the alleged victim.

also discrimination in which rule or practice – apparently neutral on its face – had a disparate impact on a person or group protected under the legislation. Such authority in the area of systemic discrimination was a major development, and led to pressures in other jurisdictions for similar change. Finally, in the area of financial penalties and remedies, legislation was altered to allow for larger fines and for higher levels of monetary compensation. In Ontario's 1962 code, boards lacked the power to award general damages and the maximum fine for contravening the legislation was only $100. But by the 1980s and 1990s, across the country, maximum fines had been increased significantly (to $25,000 in Ontario) and boards had been authorized to order damages for mental anguish. Boards could award damages for hurt feelings and mental distress without a financial limit (except in Saskatchewan, Ontario, and the federal jurisdiction); they could also order financial compensation without a limit for lost earnings due to discrimination.[29]

Expansionary Developments: Judicial Interpretation

Judicial decisions by boards of inquiry, human rights tribunals, and the courts also played a key role in the expansion of human rights legislation. In deciding human rights cases where the law was unclear or imprecise, even when there were restrictive interpretations and reversals, boards and courts often interpreted the law liberally in favour of extending equality rights. These liberal interpretations frequently contributed to pressures for explicit legislation. One example of this involved sexual harassment. Until new legislation was established to cover sexual harassment, boards of inquiry, beginning with the 1980 *Cherie Bell* case in Ontario, interpreted sex discrimination as including sexual harassment.[30] When Ontario revised its code in 1981, in an effort to clarify the law it made explicit sexual harassment a form of discrimination. Quebec followed suit in 1982, and the federal government and Newfoundland in 1983. By 1994, sexual harassment was illegal in all jurisdictions. Another example of expansive judicial interpretation was in the area of reasonable accommodation. In *Froese*, decided by a Manitoba board of adjudication in 1978, and in reasoning affirmed by an Ontario board of inquiry in 1981 and by the Supreme Court of Canada in 1985 in *O'Malley*, it was determined that reasonable accommodation by employers to members of religious minorities was an extension of a person's right to be free from discrimination.[31] It was ruled that in employment situations, employers must accommodate religious minorities unless undue hardship is involved. This judicial interpretation was followed by explicit legislation providing for the duty of reasonable accommodation, first in Ontario in 1981 and then in other jurisdictions in the 1980s and 1990s.

Boards and courts did not always provide liberal interpretations. An example was in the area of sexual orientation. Following an early BC board of inquiry decision in *Gay Alliance* (1975),[32] in which it was ruled that discrimination against gays and lesbians was illegal under the BC code's reasonable cause provision, boards and courts adopted a generally conservative approach. In the absence of explicit legislative protection for gays and lesbians, complainants argued that sexual orientation was included within the meaning of discrimination on the basis of sex. But in *University of Saskatchewan* (1976), decided by the Saskatchewan Court of Queen's Bench, and in *Vogel* (1983), decided by a Manitoba board of adjudication, it was ruled that sex discrimination refers only to gender and therefore could not include sexual orientation.[33] But even these rulings had some expansive effect. They helped raise the issues and fostered pressures in the direction of explicit legislative protection. As a result, sexual orientation was included explicitly as a ground on discrimination in Quebec in 1977, in Ontario in 1986, and in Manitoba and the Yukon in 1987.[34] By the mid-1990s, all jurisdictions provided protection on the basis of sexual orientation except Alberta, PEI, and the Northwest Territories.

Judicial interpretation also played a key role in expanding the legal definition of discrimination. The term was originally understood to mean intentional acts of unjustified differential conduct by individuals motivated by prejudice. This understanding meant that in providing a case of discrimination, it was up to the complainant and the commission to show intent on the part of the respondent. But in the 1970s, in line with American developments, boards of inquiry and courts began to adopt a wider, systemic concept of discrimination.[35] For discrimination to exist under this concept, there need not be intent. It could also arise on the basis of results or adverse effects, such as through apparently neutral policies or practices (e.g., word-of-mouth hiring). This board interpretation was first made in law by the U.S. Supreme Court in the landmark *Griggs* case of 1971. In Canada, the concept of systemic discrimination was applied first by the Alberta Supreme Court in *Gares* (1976) and, soon after, by an Ontario board of inquiry in *Singh* (1977).[36] While a series of later judicial decisions opposed the concept, the systemic definition was finally upheld by the Supreme Court of Canada in

1985 in *O'Malley* and *Bhinder*.[37] The systemic definition was also made explicit in human rights legislation, beginning in Ontario in 1981.[38] But whether it has been given legislative recognition or not, through judicial interpretation human rights law now deals with two forms of discrimination: the direct, intention type, and the systemic, adverse-effect type. Each category of discrimination has it own burdens of proof, means of proof, and legal defence.[39]

Finally, judicial interpretation played an important role in elevating the legal status of human rights legislation. In some provinces, such as Ontario in 1981, a 'primacy clause' was inserted into human rights legislation. This meant that in the event of a conflict, human rights legislation had primacy over all other statutes or regulations. In most jurisdictions, however, the primacy of human rights legislation was not made this clear. In British Columbia, following *Heerspink* (1977), this issue came before the courts.[40] The question was whether British Columbia's Human Rights Code took precedence over newer insurance legislation (normally, newer legislation takes precedence over older legislation). The lower courts were divided. The Supreme Court of Canada finally ruled in 1982 that human rights legislation in Canada was 'fundamental law,' and thus took precedence over other legislation.[41] Similarly, in *Craton* (1985), the Supreme Court ruled that human rights legislation takes precedence because it is fundamental and of a 'special nature.'[42] Finally, the Supreme Court declared that same year in *O'Malley* that although human rights legislation is not quite constitutional, it does have primacy over ordinary legislation.[43] As quasi-constitutional law, said the Supreme Court, the courts are obligated to grant human rights legislation a broad liberal interpretation.

With such a view of the status of human rights legislation, the Supreme Court did indeed provide liberal interpretations in key cases. In *O'Malley* (1985), as previously discussed, the Supreme Court ruled that systemic discrimination can be considered a form of discrimination in human rights legislation and that an employer has a duty of reasonable accommodation. In *Robichaud* (1987), the Court ruled not only that sexual harassment is a form of sex discrimination and thus part of human rights legislation, but also that employers may be liable for acts of sexual harassment in the workplace.[44] Finally, in *Vriend* (1988), an Alberta case, the Court ruled that in light of the equality rights protection in the Charter of Rights, protection on the basis of sexual orientation must be read into human rights legislation whether that protection was explicit or not.[45] With the judicial expansion of human rights legislation in *Vriend*, basic protection for gays and lesbians was complete. With Alberta forced to provide protection, the last two jurisdictions without coverage – PEI and the Northwest Territories – must do so as well.

Why Human Rights Legislation?

What are the principle forces behind the development of human rights legislation and policy? In searching for an account of the origins and development of the legislation in Canada, reference can be made at a general level to society-centred and state-centred explanations of public policy formation.[46] In society-centred explanations, policy is seen as largely the result of forces emanating from society itself. There are different versions of this theory. In the pluralist version, these forces are individuals, broad public opinion, and especially organized interests and interest groups applying pressure on the state for material and nonmaterial ends. In the neopluralist version, the key pressures are those of business groups who, with their immense economic power, enjoy a privileged position in the policy process. Finally, in the neo-Marxist or political economy version, the chief force is the capitalist or business class, which because of its dominant position in a class-divided capitalist society, is also dominant in the political system. But regardless of which particular theory is accepted, the overall explanation assumes that what happens in public policy and legislation is ultimately a reflection of what happens in society. Directly or indirectly, the state and its officials respond to the strongest and most compelling of societal forces for reasons of power and politics. State officials may have a degree of autonomy in setting policies, but overall, public policy bears the stamp of pressures from society rather than the beliefs and preferences of state policymakers or the structure of the state.

In state-centred explanations the perspective is very different. Public policy is seen as reflecting less societal pressures than forces within the state. In the stronger version of the theory, sometimes referred to as the theory of the autonomous state, public policy over a wide range of fields is seen as largely the product of the preferences, beliefs, and inclinations of state authorities.[47] These authorities enjoy substantial autonomy from society and set policy largely as they see fit, apart from the pressures of interest groups or economic classes. Pressures from society are not unimportant but they tend to play a secondary role, often serving to justify what state officials (especially senior bureaucrats and cabinet ministers) want to do anyway. Due to the immense legal and financial resources at the command of the state and to divided pressures from society, these officials are able and willing to impose their particular stamp on public policy. In the softer version of this theory, more allowance is made for the influence of societal pressures.[48] Societal and state forces are seen to interact in a dynamic manner in the formation and development of public policy. Notwithstanding this interaction, forces within the state have the leadership role in ongoing policy development. Policy is driven largely by the state in the form not only of the beliefs and preferences of state actors but also of the structure of the state. Rules, institutions, and structures such as federalism and a charter of rights have a major impact in constraining and creatively influencing policy outcomes.[49] Whichever version of this theory is accepted, the key assumption is that public policy is shaped more by forces within the state than by ones in society.

Both theories – society-centred and state-centred – have support in explaining the evolution of human rights legislation. First, support for the pluralist version of society-centred theory can be seen in the spread of equality rights consciousness in Canadian society during and after the Second World War, the growth of women and ethnocultural minorities in the labour force, and the rise of human rights interest groups pressuring for antidiscrimination legislation. Before the war, in a society lacking in equality rights consciousness and in support of social *laissez-faire*, there was little desire and thus little pressure for legislation against discrimination. The result was that virtually no legislation was enacted. Indeed, when public pressure did develop, as it did in regard to Asian minorities in BC, it was in the opposite direction – for the enactment of discriminatory laws.[50] As noted by Walter Tarnopolsky, from Confederation to the Second War not only were human rights laws absent, but discriminatory laws actually increased.[51] However, with the growth of equality rights consciousness during and after the war, public pressure began to emerge for an end to existing discrimination laws and to laws against discrimination. As a result, major policy developments occurred in both directions. For instance, between the 1940s and 1960s discriminatory provisions were removed from franchise laws and immigration policies. And during the same period, pioneering laws against discrimination were set in place and human rights commissions were created. As equality rights consciousness expanded between the 1960s and the 1990s, so too did human rights legislation.

The exact origins of equality rights consciousness are not easy to pinpoint. But the liberalism that had been a prevailing feature of Canada's early political culture in producing rights consciousness undoubtedly played a role. While it did not produce such an intense rights consciousness as American liberalism did in the United States, Canada's liberal culture nevertheless put high value on individual rights and freedoms. These rights and freedoms did not extend to social rights such as rights to equal opportunity without discrimination. Before the 1940s, the main concerns were the traditional ones: political rights such as the right to vote and freedom of expression; economic rights such as property rights and freedom of commerce; and legal rights such as procedural fairness in the legal system. In part because of the strong belief in social *laissez-faire* and property rights, equality rights did not become part of core Canadian values. At the same time, however, the fact that rights consciousness did exist helped prepare the way for equality rights consciousness. If a person's dignity was reason for the right to vote in the political system, and for the right to procedural fairness in the legal system, then a person's dignity should also be reason for the right to equality without discrimination. Thus, in Canada's early political culture the soil did exist for equality rights consciousness to take root. And in the 1940s that soil proved to be productive. In a rights-oriented political culture, the experience of the Second World War stimulated the growth of equality rights consciousness. By focusing attention on the evils of racism and discrimination, the importance of human dignity, and the importance of human rights – including the right to be free from discrimination – the wartime experience brought out what was latent in the political culture.

While liberalism and the experience of the war did much to foster equality rights consciousness, other factors were also at work. The American civil rights movement of the 1950s and 1960s and the women's movement of the 1960s and 1970s were sources of inspiration for many social activists and human rights groups in Canada. Many American developments in human rights law were quickly replicated in Canada after a period of interest group pressure. But there was a deeper cultural influence at work: the shift from materialist to postmaterialist values, not only in the United States and Canada but in all economically advanced countries after the war. This shift is best explained in the work of Ronald Inglehart.[52] According to Inglehart, who was building on the human needs theory of Abraham Maslow,[53] a public's value priorities are shaped by the degree to which human needs are met and at the same time by the effects of socialization. In an environment of insecurity, when basic material needs are unmet and when people are socialized in materialist values during their formative years, public attention is given largely to materialist values such as economic growth, social order, and individual economic improvement. This focus on materialism and individual self-interest largely described Canada and other nations before the Second World War. Conversely, during more comfortable times, when basic needs are reasonably met and when socialization is directed at broader social values, public attention shifts to postmaterialist values such a cleaner environment, wider democracy, and the pursuit of equality rights. According to Inglehart, such a shift, which inolved the spread of equality rights consciousness, occurred in Canada and other economically advanced countries after the war. In a new postwar era of relative affluence and economic prosperity, socialization was directed at instilling broader social values, and Canadians became increasingly supportive of equality rights.

Societal pressure for human rights legislation was boosted, as well, by structural changes in Canadian postwar society. Key changes here were the growing number of ethnocultural minorities in Canada and the labour force, and the entry of more and more women into the labour force. Mainly because of greatly increased immigration after the Second World War, and changes in immigration patterns, the ethnic composition of Canada and of the Canadian workforce changed significantly. In 1941, 80 per cent of Canadians were of British or French origin; this proportion had decreased to 74 per cent by 1961 and to 67 per cent by 1981 (by which time human rights codes or acts were well established across the country).[54] By the mid-1980s, almost 38 per cent of Canadians were neither British nor French in origin, and with increasing immigration from non-European countries, 6 per cent of Canadians belonged to visible minorities.[55] As the ethnic structure was changing, so too was the labour force participation of women. Before the Second World War a minority of women were in the workforce; by the 1980s a majority of women were working. In 1931 the labour force participation rate for single women was 44 per cent, and for married women 4 per cent; in 1961 the figures were respectively 54 per cent and 22 per cent; and in 1981 they were 65 per cent and 51 per cent.[56] This structural change did much to reinforce societal pressures for human rights legislation. As women and minorities encountered discrimination and unequal opportunities in the workforce, they lent their support to legislation that would provide for equality rights. Thus, as the numbers of minorities and women in the workforce expanded, politicians and labour leaders increasingly found it in their interests to press for legislation.

In Ontario, interest groups played a pivotal role after the war in raising the issue of discrimination, mobilizing public support for legislation, and prompting policymakers into legislative action.[57] During the early stages of legislative development (the 1940s and 1950s), the leading groups were labour organizations, ethnocultural groups (Ontario Jewish organizations played a major role), and civil liberties associations. Later on, in the 1960s to the 1980s, the movement broadened to include (among others) organizations representing women, the disabled, and gays and lesbians. Across Canada, any major revisions or amendments to human rights legislation were always preceded by activity and lobbying by human rights interest groups. This indicates how close a correspondence there is between societal pressures and the development of human rights legislation. It also indicates that society-centred theory is applicable.

However, there is also evidence of the applicability of state-centred theory. On many occasions, state policymakers went further in developing legislation than public opinion or interest groups pressures demanded. A prime example was in Saskatchewan, when in 1947 the CCF government enacted the first major piece of human rights legislation in Canada, the Bill of Rights Act, before public pressure for the legislation had a chance to develop. The key factor here was the ideological commitment of Premier T.C. Douglas and senior CCF politicians and policymakers (the CCF had shown strong support for the principle of antidiscrimination laws as far back as the early 1930s).[58] While after the war virtually all political parties came out in favour of human rights legislation (Social Credit was an exception), it was the CCF/NDP that demonstrated the strongest support. This was indicated not only by the early Bill of Rights Act in Saskatchewan but also by pressure from NDP opposition parties in other provinces for expansive legislation, and by the strong human rights legislation that NDP governments enacted in British Columbia in 1973 and 1996. This support was not surprising, given that the NDP, as a leftist party, believed fervently in the concept of equality and in a strong role for the state in regulating society and the economy.

That said, ideological differences cannot be taken too far. To varying degrees, all parties after the war adopted a belief in equality, social welfare, and greater state regulation of society. This was part of the new Keynesian, welfare state consensus. Though from different ideological perspectives, all parties came to endorse the principle of human rights legislation. Progressive Conservatives became much more equality-minded and state-oriented, and soon adapted to human rights legislation their old red tory belief that the state has a paternalistic role to play in supporting disadvantaged groups. Liberals became more committed to the concept of state-supported social equality. Here they were moving away from classical liberalism, and the strong belief in individual freedom, toward the ideology of reform liberalism, which emphasized the state's key role in providing social welfare and promoting greater equality. Thus socialists and social democrats may have had an earlier and stronger commitment to equality rights, but they were not alone. This was reflected in the fact that governing parties of all ideologies played a role in developing human rights legislation. The Progressive Conservatives were responsible for pioneering legislation in Ontario and Nova Scotia during the 1950s and 1960s. The Liberals were responsible for the Canadian Human Rights Act at the federal level and for the Charter of Rights and Freedoms in Quebec during the 1970s. Thus, while a case can be made that the CCF/NDP was more strongly committed to human rights legislation, virtually all parties shared that commitment. From that commitment, legislation followed.

Besides politicians, other state officials helped develop the legislation. As discussed earlier, boards of inquiry, human rights tribunals, and judges played a major role, through judicial interpretation, in widening and strengthening human rights law. For example, during the 1970s and 1980s they were responsible for expanding the legal definition of discrimination to include systemic as well as direct discrimination. Here they were influenced less by interest group and societal pressures than by American jurisprudence and their own values and beliefs in equality rights. Similarly, their values and beliefs motivated them to include in human rights law a positive duty of reasonable accommodation by employers to religious minorities and persons with disabilities, and a positive duty of preventative action by employers against sexual and racial harassment. In the area of harassment they determined, as part of this same liberal belief system, that sexual harassment and racial harassment were a part of sex discrimination and racial discrimination (respectively). In the area of gay and lesbian rights, after a series of reversals the Supreme Court of Canada ultimately ruled that protection on the basis of sexual orientation must be read into human rights legislation whether such protection is explicit in the legislation or not. Finally, as a key interpretative principle the Supreme Court ruled that Canadian human rights legislation has the status of quasi-constitutional law and requires a broad and liberal interpretation because of that special nature.

That the judges and boards played such a key role was due partly to their liberal beliefs and to the influence of equality rights consciousness. Judicial rulings before the Second World War had expressed sympathy for social *laissez-faire*; rulings after the war, and especially after the 1970s, expressed wide support for equality rights. That the Supreme Court of Canada ruled that human rights legislation must be given a broad and liberal interpretation, and that judges and boards generally provided such interpretations, was a reflection of equality rights consciousness. However, the importance of the state was related not only to the beliefs of state actors but also to the rules and structure of the state. One profound change in institutional rules was the establishment of the Charter of Rights and Freedoms in 1982. As a result of the Charter, the traditional principles of parliamentary supremacy and of judicial deference to the legislature were replaced by the principle of judicially enforced constitutional rights. Before the Charter, Parliament and the provincial legislatures were supreme (within the rule of law and within their jurisdiction) in determining legislation, including legislation concerning rights; after the Charter, the courts had a mandate to uphold constitutional charter rights against government and against ordinary legislation. Before the Charter, societal pressures (through interest groups and public opinion) could have considerable influence over politicians in determining legislation involving rights; after the Charter, these societal pressures were weakened, because the courts were relatively immune from these pressures. Issues of constitutional rights and the validity of legislation could now be determined, much more than before, by state actors in relative isolation from societal forces. Judges now were able to provide liberal interpretations on the basis of a constitutional rule change.

This change in the structure of the state greatly affected the development of human rights legislation. Given a clear constitutional mandate to guard basic rights, the courts were emboldened to strike down legislation that infringed on the Charter, including the section 15 equality rights of the Charter. Human rights legislation was no exception. In *Re Blainey and the Ontario Hockey Association* (1986), the Ontario

Court of Appeal struck down a section of the Ontario Human Rights Code that allowed for restrictive membership in athletic organizations on the basis of gender.[59] The exclusion of girls from a hockey league, which had been permitted under the Code was not permitted under the Charter. Clearly, the Charter was going to have an expansionary effect on human rights legislation. Realizing this, many governments amended their human rights legislation so as to avoid challenges under the Charter. For example, Ontario in 1986 introduced amendments that prohibited discrimination on the basis of sexual orientation and of pregnancy and in the area of adults-only housing. The stated rationale was to ensure that the legislation conformed with the Charter of Rights.[60] However, some governments chose not to take action. Alberta, for example, refused to amend its legislation to extend protection to gays and lesbians. But eventually, in *Vriend* (1998), the expansionary effect of the Charter was revealed again. The Supreme Court ordered such protection on the basis that human rights legislation must conform with equality rights protected by the Charter. Furthermore, the Supreme Court, emboldened by the Charter, was inspired not only to broaden human rights legislation but also to declare the legislation special and quasi-constitutional law requiring a generous interpretation. Human rights legislation was thus expanded not only by a liberal belief system of judges but by the structure of the state.

Finally, a major contribution to the expansion of the legislation was made by human rights commission officials, especially commissioners, executive directors, senior managers, and case officers. This was possible because of the advisory role that commissions played in the development of legislation. In virtually every jurisdiction, commissions were given the general mandate to forward the cause of human rights. These officials, like the judges, were motivated to expand the legislation by their generally liberal beliefs and equality rights consciousness. They often recommended to government legislative changes that would enlarge human rights protections, and they occasionally brought forward test cases to tribunals and the courts intended to stretch the law. As part of the expansionary developments from the 1960s through to the 1980s, commission officials were particularly assertive in testing the law, pushing the envelope, and pressuring for wider protections. Interest group pressures certainly played a role in these developments. But these pressures often were used as justifications for changes that officials themselves wanted undertaken.[61] And in the absence of interest group demands or where such demands were small, commissions occasionally recommended to governments legislative amendments they perceived as desirable. And governments often responded, especially when it came to less popular protections such as in the areas of sexual orientation and past criminal record. The influence of commission officials was also reflected in the development of particular policies that accepted complaints of discrimination not explicit in the legislation. Such policies were developed with respect to discrimination based on pregnancy (Newfoundland and PEI), sexual orientation (Newfoundland), dependence on alcohol or drugs (BC, Alberta, Saskatchewan, Manitoba, Ontario, New Brunswick, and PEI), and language (Ontario).[62]

Thus there is evidence for both society-centred and state-centred theories of public policy development. A more complete explanation of human rights development may be obtained in reference to Alan Cairns's theory of the embedded state.[63] This is representative of the more moderate version of state-centred theory, which combines societal and statist forces in an explanation but which also perceives the state as taking on an increasingly important role as policy becomes developed. According to Cairns, policy development – especially in the area of constitutional policy – is the product not simply of societal pressures or autonomous state forces but of a dynamic relationship between the two over time. In the early stages of policy development, social forces and interest group pressures play a major role in establishing state policy. Issues are raised, public support is mobilized, and pressure is applied. If the pressure is compelling, authorities in the state respond by making policy.

But in the later stages of policy development, according to Cairns, the state and its leading officials play an increasingly important role. Not only do state actors (ministers, senior bureaucrats, judges, and so on) set policy independently from societal pressures, but the very existence of the state (including its policies, programs, and structure) also plays a leading role. It does this by helping develop an increasingly politicized society and by encouraging interest groups and greater public pressure for more or stronger public policy. Policy, once set, leads to more policy. Eventually the state becomes the 'embedded state': a state embedded in society, closely connected to society, and interdependent with society. The embedded state politicizes society and groups within, and in turn is subject to increasing political demands by the politicized society and organized interest groups.

Such dynamism becomes a major driving force for much public policy, especially policy dealing with constitutional rights.

Cairns's main focus is on the evolution of constitutional policy, including the very important movement toward the Charter of Rights after the Second World War. According to his analysis in this area, growing ethnic and gender consciousness after the war fuelled demands for change in Canada's constitutional order. Women's groups and ethnocultural minorities began to challenge the gender division of power in the Canadian state and the unequal ethnic distribution of power and status. Such politicization of ethnicity and gender led the state to establish the Canadian Bill of Rights and later proposals and initiatives during the 1960s and 1970s on route to the Charter of the Rights. But in the course of these changes, state activity was not without effect. It encouraged further politicization and further constitutional demands, including those from aboriginal groups, organizations for the disabled, and gay and lesbian organizations. Such groups see advantages in making constitutional claims and improving their situation through constitutional politics and through closer links with the state. Thus, the constitutional policy development that resulted in the establishment of the Charter of Rights must not be seen simply as the product of a state initiative or of societal pressures. Rather, it was the product of a dynamic interpenetration of state and society and the role of the embedded state.

But Cairns's theory also may be applied to policy development in the area of human rights legislation. Accordingly, at the very early stages (up to the Second World War), Canada was at ground zero in antidiscrimination protection. In a political culture enamoured of social *laissez-faire* and property rights, women and members of minority groups had very little protection from discriminatory action in private social relations. Indeed, they had good reason to fear that discriminatory laws and policies would be enacted against them. Then, during and immediately after the war, major change took place. Pressures for public policy and legislation against discrimination emerged through social and cultural forces coming out of the war – in particular, the forces of growing equality rights consciousness. Leading carriers of this consciousness were minority activists and human rights interest groups, who pressured governments for human rights laws and commissions. A handful of politicians and governments did play a leading role in some of this development, the CCF government in Saskatchewan being a case in point. But generally, interest groups were at the forefront in the early stages. In incremental fashion, they mobilized public opinion, publicized the need for legislation, and applied pressure until politicians found it in their electoral and political self-interest to respond. This resulted during the 1950s in the drive toward fair practices laws and during the 1960s and 1970s in the creation of human rights codes and commissions.

Once established, the policy itself and forces within the state played a pivotal role in the further development of the legislation. This is not to minimize the importance of interest groups. They continued to raise issues and mobilize pressure for ever wider human rights protections. But the state and state officials took on an increasingly influential role. As discussed earlier, boards of inquiry and judges generally provided liberal and equality-expanding interpretations of human rights law, while commission officials continuously urged expansive legislation and brought test cases forward to stretch the law. But in addition, the educational programs of commissions and the very existence of the legislation and the complaint procedures served to encourage a further growth of equality rights consciousness and societal pressures for stronger legislation. By providing education about rights, and by publicizing the existence of a system of rights protection, human rights programs and institutions politicized Canadian society in the direction of making demands for wider rights. Rights consciousness and awareness of human rights commissions encouraged more and more groups to pressure for more and more rights. The result was a steady expansion of human rights protections, the entrenchment of human rights legislation, and the institutionalization of human rights commissions, embedded in an increasingly politicized society in which rights-conscious human rights interest groups demanded ever wider rights.

State forces also played a major role in policy development through the institutional rules of the state. As discussed earlier, the new constitutional system of a judicially enforced Charter of Rights had an important expansive effect on human rights legislation. Under the Charter, the courts were now mandated as guardians of constitutional rights, and this emboldened judges not only to use the Charter to strike down legislation that contradicted rights but also to provide a broad and liberal interpretation of human rights legislation. Apart from the Charter, the federal system itself played a role in expanding the legislation. Under federalism, legislative developments in one jurisdiction were able to serve as models for developments in another. Commission officials in one jurisdiction tended to use expansionary amendments in another to justify making similar amendments or revisions. And with the aid of the *Canadian Human Rights Reporter*, a legal publication established in 1980 to report on Canadian human rights law cases, and of regular meetings of the Canadian Association of Statutory Human Rights Agencies (CASHRA), commission officials were able to closely monitor developments in other jurisdictions and point to these as reasons for expansionary reforms in their own jurisdictions.[64]

By the 1980s the system of human rights legislation and commissions had become embedded in Canadian society. That it had become embedded was illustrated in the policy developments in British Columbia in the early 1980s. While a hostile Social Credit government in 1983 could dismantle the particular human rights system that had been created by the NDP in 1973, it could not eliminate the system in general. Such an act would not have been tolerated by an equality rights conscious society that had grown accustomed to and supportive of laws and agencies of human rights protection. While an attack on a particular system of human rights protection might be tolerated, a total dismantling of the system would not be. Human rights legislation had become too deeply rooted in Canadian society and the political culture. Thus the government in BC was compelled to maintain some form of system, and in 1984 established the BC Human Rights Act and Human Rights Council. While the new system was a downsized one, it continued to put into practice the basic principles of human rights legislation in Canada. This experience showed just how deeply the human rights system had become embedded in Canadian society.

2. The Public Administration of Human Rights

As human rights legislation was expanded, human rights commissions were established and developed to administer and enforce the legislation. These commissions were given a special and at times difficult mandate, in that they were expected to make administrative decisions and implement policy while at the same time embracing the rigours and protections of judicial decision-making. This called for close attention to both policy direction and procedural detail.

We will now discuss the origins and design of human rights commissions and their related adjudicative structures. We will begin by reviewing the debate over whether human rights policy and law should be entrusted to specialized administrative agencies or is best left to the common courts. We will explain why the specialized agencies prevailed but also why the demands of the 'rule of law' approach to decision-making could not be ignored in the design of human rights procedures. Following this, we will look at the leading models of human rights organization and administration as found in this country. Here we will carefully assess the Ontario model – the earliest as well as the most commonly used – and also those found in Quebec and British Columbia and at the federal level. Throughout all of this, we will highlight the often difficult relationship between rights administration and rights law and procedure.

Commission Foundations: The Institutional Perspective

The foundation and evolution of human rights commissions cannot be discussed in isolation from the activities of advocacy groups and concerned government officials in raising the profile of discrimination and promoting legal means to combat it. It is also true, however, that in resorting to the commission model as the administrative means for overseeing human rights policy, governments were acknowledging a number of legal, administrative, and political considerations. Early decisions about the organization of commissions have given these bodies some of their greatest strengths; but they have also introduced tensions into the structure of the commissions that have led to significant management problems. At issue here is the semijudicial nature of these organizations: by design, human rights commissions – in common with many other regulatory agencies – possess a dual set of key functions.

In theory, human rights commissions are administrative agencies staffed by officials who are expert in the field of human rights policy, knowledgeable in public administration, and capable of implementing human rights policy in the most economical, efficient, effective, and socially responsive manner possible. But this is only half of it. Human rights legislation establishes legal rights and obligations that may require institutional enforcement and, at times, adjudication. It follows that commissions are charged with important legal and semijudicial responsibilities and must be ready to engage in investigations, mediation, conciliation, and prosecution; and to facilitate adjudication by independent boards of inquiry or tribunals. If the commission has a strong administrative ethos and rationale, it must also embrace and reflect a strong legal sensibility and judicial demeanour with respect to its treatment of rights disputes. Clearly, commissions are designed to be multifunctional – to bring together the administrative model of policymaking and implementation with the judicial model of decision-making.

The marriage of these two approaches is ambitious in theory, and also advantageous in practice if the dual roles can be managed well. But the marriage cannot but be rocky in institutional terms, given the often competing interests and dynamics of the two approaches. Semi-judicial administrative agencies are by nature saddled with diverse and sometimes competing objectives. Their success or failure thus depends heavily on how well they are managed. They enjoy a range of options for addressing human rights issues and problems, but they also face institutional dynamics that often run counter to the values of administrative management. When the creative tension established is mismanaged, the administrative and judicial work of the agencies suffers.

Human Rights Commissions and Institutional Design: The Critique of the Courts

The 1950s and 1960s was a time of growing interest in the cause of human rights protection; it was also a time of strong growth in the public sector, and of optimism that governments would be able to solve the many problems facing society. And within governments, academia, and the mainstream political parties during this time were those who wanted to demonstrate that the state could confront and defeat discrimination by applying the resources of the government bureaucracy. Within Canada, the human rights commissions came to be the preferred means for implementing human rights policy; in effect, the ordinary courts were rejected as the best mechanism for addressing legally proscribed social behaviours. Courts were coming under increasing attack from within and without the legal community as early as the 1930s respecting their ability to address 'new' fields of law and to engage in progressive law reform.[1]

The growing criticism of the court system had several bases.[2] On one level of analysis, which resonated well with the general public, the courts were criticized for being slow, expensive, confusing, and socially hidebound. Critics argued, with much good cause, that the courts were available only to those wealthy few who had the money to pay heavy legal and court fees. While the courts adhered to the motto 'Equal Justice for All,' access to them (see Willis and Corry) required private wealth. In this era before legal aid and support groups, the vast majority of citizens simply could not afford to start litigation. And with respect to victims of racial, religious, or sex discrimination, this dynamic was even more pronounced, in that most victims belonged to economically marginalized social groups. In financial terms, as instruments to promote human rights the courts were clearly wanting.

A related criticism was often raised regarding the pace of litigation. The standard maxim is that justice delayed is justice denied. Yet seemingly from time immemorial, courts have been criticized for taking inordinate amounts of time to resolve cases. This was viewed as producing distinctly undesirable side effects. One was increased legal costs; another was the frustration experienced by many litigants. Finally, judicial delay had a sinister impact on the thinking of would-be litigants.[3] Public awareness that the court system was lengthy, slow, and expensive inhibited the use of litigation. And once again, this inhibition weighed more heavily on those fighting discrimination.

Still other criticisms were raised respecting the attractiveness of the courts as a venue for resolving disputes. The courts had honed an image and a reality that they were very special institutions, steeped in majesty and solemnity, staffed by experts skilled in the intricacies of the law, and guardians of a special wisdom leading to justice; but this highly élitist perception was criticized as a reason why many in the public felt alienated from the courts; also, it bred within the judiciary a professional sensibility far removed from that of the general public.

This issue of social alienation vis-à-vis the court system was seen as operating on a number of levels. Most generally, the courts were criticized for their complicated and intimidating procedures. The rules and regulations for launching and pursuing litigation were complex, which necessitated the involvement of legal counsel – a fact that at once brought a matter out of the realm of the ordinary and into a realm of elaborate legal behaviour. Legal counsel was expensive, and to those with 'routine' complaints of discriminatory treatment, such a procedurally legalistic approach could be intimidating. As a result, many would-be complainants simply dropped their cases. The adversarial nature of the judicial process was seen as exacerbating these problems.[4]

In common law jurisdictions, legal disputation is undertaken as a courtroom battle between contending parties, with the judge standing above and impartial to the dispute, and ultimately ruling in favour of the party with the best case according to the law. The court more or less removes itself from the presentation of evidence and argument, maintaining a studied detachment until it is time for adjudication. The litigants bear full responsibility for carrying the case forward; they present the best possible evidence and argument for their position while casting doubt on the position of their adversaries. Clearly, the litigation process is highly involved, and requires the active support of expert legal counsel as well as great perseverance from the litigants. It has never been a process to be entered into lightly.

Though the above was true for *all* would-be litigants, those alleging discrimination in the 1940s and 1950s faced the daunting task of navigating the criminal law. For most of two centuries the criminal law of Great Britain and Canada had been evolving a host of procedures and standards designed to facilitate fair and careful decision-making while granting significant protections to accused persons. The accused is presumed innocent until proven guilty beyond a reasonable doubt, and the burden of proof rests with the prosecution. Under the early antidiscrimination statutes, prosecutions for violating statutory obligations were to be carried before the criminal courts. This approach not only brought human rights matters into a highly procedurally involved decision-making framework, but also introduced a dynamic in which alleged discriminators were provided with a panoply of criminal law protections while the prosecution faced the most onerous test in law: proving guilt beyond a reasonable doubt, with guilt requiring evidence of direct action and of intent to discriminate. In the field of interpersonal relationships as regulated by antidiscrimination legislation, these were difficult thresholds to meet – so difficult, in fact, that rights advocates both within and outside of governments came to question whether the criminal process was the optimal or even a viable means of proceeding with such cases, and whether a better alternative could not be developed.[5]

Respecting the new areas of law emerging with the development of the welfare state, critics of court-centred adjudication also held an ideological reservation about the involvement of the courts in decision-making. As workers' compensation and labour relations law developed, followed by human rights law, advocates strongly questioned the involvement of the ordinary courts, to the point of seeking to have them excluded entirely from these legal developments.[6]

As Willis contended in the 1930s[7] and Nonet in the 1960s,[8] the ordinary courts and their judiciary were viewed with disdain by social progressives, law reformers, and advocates for an expansive, interventionist state. Those with a reform liberal or social democratic political orientation came to associate the courts with the political establishment and the socio-legal status quo. In short, they viewed the courts and the judiciary – with some notable exceptions – as inherently conservative: sceptical of new approaches to law; hostile to state intervention in social and economic relationships; and highly protective of social and economic *laissez-faire*. According to Willis, the courts saw themselves as defenders of individual rights and freedoms, and of contract rights and entrepreneurial competition, and also as bulwarks against creeping bureaucratization and collectivism at a time when the state apparatus was growing.[9] Lord Hewart's denunciation of the 'New Despotism,' witnessed through the development of social welfare policy in the United Kingdom in the 1920s and 1930s, was influential throughout the legal communities of the British Commonwealth for the following half-century.[10] Hewart's warning to the courts to be vigilant against the demise of individual liberty through the rise of the administrative state was as stirring to his supporters as it was detestable to those who viewed the state as a means toward social betterment.

The Canadian justice system's real and perceived hostility to law reform resulted in efforts to exclude the courts from various initiatives in administrative law. First in workers' compensation law and later in labour relations law, dispute resolution systems were established that removed adjudicative responsibility from the courts and vested it within semijudicial administrative agencies.[11] In the 1950s and 1960s, similar dynamics and debates enveloped the issue of human rights reform. Advocates of human rights legislation contended that human rights policy must inevitably involve a proactive role for the state; rights were to be not only affirmed but also advanced in society as a means of resolving particular disputes and fundamentally changing the manner by which people interacted with one another. In this light, human rights law reform required careful oversight, administration, and initial adjudication by officials specializing in and committed to the human rights project. To law reformers of the 1950s and 1960s, these officials were not generally to be found within the ordinary courts. Rather, the search for persons competent to undertake the promotion of human rights policy was to be pursued away from the courts – within the ranks of government, academia, churches, and social reform groups. As a further blow to the courts, the key institution to be vested with jurisdiction for advancing human rights policy was to be, not the courts, but rather a semijudicial administrative agency.[12]

The Administrative Rationale for Human Rights Commissions

The arguments in favour of the agency/commission model were numerous and compelling. In many respects the logic in favour of the commission model followed directly from the critique of the courts. If the courts were expensive, slow, overly formal to the point of being intimidating, and lacking sympathy for human rights reform, then specially created human rights commissions would be the opposite. Rights advocates such as Scott and Tarnopolsky argued that in establishing an administrative agency charged with promoting, administering, and implementing human rights law, governments would achieve a number of important goals. By virtue of their administrative orientation, they would be responsible for assessing and investigating cases and carrying them forward to conclusion, the commissions themselves would bear the legal costs of case management. Moreover, with adjudication in the hands of administrative boards of inquiry rather than the courts, adjudicative procedure would be faster, simpler, and far less expensive.[13]

Administrative agencies would also provide the benefits associated with specialization. Human rights commissions would be staffed with senior officials possessing a demonstrated interest and expertise in the field of human rights law and administration. And these officials and their staff would have as their sole purpose the promotion and implementation of human rights policy. This would help nurture expertise in rights policy and implementation within the commission, to the point that it – and not some department and not the courts – would be the primary body possessing intelligence and wisdom in human rights policy. This would provide for both sensitivity and critical thinking in future elaboration of human rights law, and make for the knowledgeable and efficient handling of routine cases brought before the commission. Specialization, efficiency, expertise, economy, and expeditiousness were all perceived as desirable outcomes of the agency/commission model.[14]

But all of this being said, legal considerations were not wanting. The recourse to commissions was also seen as providing important adjudicative benefits.

Advocates of the agency/commission model stressed that in contrast to courts, human rights commissions could offer an informal, practical, and sensitive approach to resolving human rights disputes. Through recourse to their staff expertise and administrative framework, commissions could engage in close mediation and conciliation between parties in an effort to reach amicable and consensual outcomes. Consensuality, with the commission offering an inquisitorial rather than an adversarial forum for dispute resolution, was viewed as a key concept in the commission approach. The 'iron hand in the velvet glove' approach, as spoken of by Tarnopolsky, was an example.[15] Within this approach there lived, and still lives, a belief that the work of the commission should not be punitive and declaratory (as with the courts) but rather educative and transformative. In dealing with rights abusers, commissions were not to punish but to reform, by bringing parties together in recognition of the importance of human rights and the need to rectify past misdeeds. The 'iron hand' of adjudication was to be used as a last resort. Much more so than the courts, the commissions were designed to change social behaviour by highlighting not only injustices but also desirable forms of human interaction.

Under this approach, the adversarial form of adjudication was considered undesirable. It was too closely associated with the values and practices of the ordinary courts, and it also established ways of thinking and behaving that rights advocates viewed as unconducive to a direct and sincere review of rights disputes. The inquisitorial model followed by commissions was much more amenable to the direct involvement of human rights administrators in the management of cases, especially at the stages of conciliation and mediation. In the inquisitorial model, which derives from the European civil law tradition, the role of the commission was to determine the truth, with the commission staff playing an active role in elucidating facts, arguments, and motivations. Through this process of 'truth finding,' commissions sought to bring the contending parties together not as adversaries but as interrelated actors who need to understand one another and to learn to live together, one with another, in accordance with the principles enshrined in human rights legislation. Ideally, no case would require formal adjudication. Rather, all cases could be resolved through fair-minded discussion by the parties involved, with commission officials educating and assisting both parties respecting their rights and responsibilities under the law. Justice would come through enlightenment and the intelligent actions of people who were sensitized to the principles and practices of human rights.

The Legal Rationale for Human Rights Commissions

Notwithstanding this idealistic vision of how human rights commissions could and would fulfil their tasks through an admixture of principles, policy sensibility, administrative wisdom, and decisional consensus-building, the creators of the commissions were acutely aware that these bodies were to bear great legal responsibilities; and with responsibilities came duties. And with these duties came the establishment of organizational systems that married administrative goals and ambitions with the legal rigour of 'due process.' Despite the call for agencies that would stand in lieu of the courts, the commissions and their systems of policy implementation would have to maintain a strong fidelity to legal procedure for no other reason than that they were to be semijudicial agencies with the power to enforce law.

By their very nature, human rights codes and acts created legal rights borne by individuals, and corresponding obligations held by other individuals to respect these human rights. The commissions, in turn, were to promote and protect these rights through their administrative and adjudicative powers. In the event that disputes arose regarding whether a right had been violated and whether some remedy was called for, commissions had the legal task of resolving such disputes. The commissions thus had to act as the law enforcement agencies of the various human rights acts, and for that reason they had to be organized so as to fulfil this legal role. This role is far more complex than it seems at first glance, given the mixed administrative and judicial functions of the commissions; yet the recognition of the legal nature of so much of the commissions' work led the designers of human rights policies and procedures to establish relatively formal legal systems for conducting commission business. Notwithstanding the scepticism with which so many rights reformers viewed the judicial process, it was generally understood that a fair system of law enforcement required a fair system of law administration. The resulting system did not need to centre on the courts, and did not need to fully conform to the procedural complexities of the courts; but there was an awareness of the need for and importance of due process that resulted in the establishment of a set of procedures clearly recognizable as 'judicial,' with a special role to be played by the courts.[16] The paradox here is apparent, and has existed within human rights policy from the very beginning.

All advocates of human rights commissions stressed that once a complaint was laid by an aggrieved party, the commission staff would attempt to resolve the dispute in the quickest and amicable manner possible. To this end, the commission staff were to interview the various parties involved, gather evidence, gain an independent perspective on the events in question, and, most important, assess whether a right under the code or act had been infringed.

Following an investigation, the investigators had the authority to render one of two decisions: they could dismiss the complaint for lack of merit, or they could accept the complaint as well founded. If the latter view prevailed, the commission then started a process of conciliation and mediation. Here, commission officers sought to communicate with the respondent whose behaviour had been found wanting, with the goal of bringing about a settlement between the respondent and the complainant. It was usually envisioned that these settlements would revolve around an admission of wrongdoing, an apology, financial compensation for the complainant, and restitutive action by the respondent so as to eliminate the initial cause of the discriminatory action.[17]

Should a dispute prove closed to conciliation and mediation, commissions then had the authority to order a full-fledged hearing into the case. It was at this stage of the proceedings that human rights law and procedures entered the realm of the semijudicial.[18] The hearing was to determine conclusively whether a discriminatory action had been performed; if it was ruled that one had been, the hearing officer was empowered to render a just settlement of the dispute, with this 'final' adjudication having the force of law.

The hearing was to be a judicial forum involving fact finding, legal analysis, and decision making. Human rights policymakers accepted from the very beginning that human rights law must adhere to certain fundamental standards of judicial organization and due process. Given that commission staff would be acting as prosecutors before the hearing, it was deemed necessary for the adjudicative officer to be organizationally independent of the commission. For this reason, most human rights acts stipulated that such hearings were to be undertaken by boards of inquiry or tribunals appointed by the responsible minister on the advice of the commission.[19] The persons sitting on these boards were not to be members of the commissions; rather, they were to be notable men and women from a variety of backgrounds, but very often law professors who shared a refined interest in human rights policy and law. Once established, these boards were to sit in adjudication of the given case, with the commission acting for the complainant and the respondent having the right to be represented by legal counsel. The commission was to bear the onus of proving discrimination, but in keeping with the desire for a simplified process, the standard of proof was to be that of the civil law – proof on a balance of probabilities.[20]

A problem with this approach related to the tension between the administrative focus on conciliation and demands by complainants that their rights be enforced. From a strong rights perspective, rights are to be taken seriously – they are not to be compromised or bargained away. Thus, a complainant whose rights have been violated may insist that the issue be decided through adjudication or the principled determination of a finding of discrimination. But according to the velvet glove approach, a dispute is to be settled through conciliation and compromise, without resort to a board of inquiry except as a last resort. Under the legislation, it is the velvet glove that prevails: possibly against the wishes of the complainant, a commission has the authority as the carrier of the complaint to insist on a settlement and to refuse a board of inquiry. Such authority can create considerable tension between the commission and the complainant, as it did in *Amber* (1970) in Ontario.[21] Denied an apartment because of her race and colour, Amber launched a complaint with the commission and wanted a hearing on her case. She found that she had no legal right to a hearing. The commission ultimately has the legal power to settle a case.

On account of the legal ramifications of board decision making, the work of the boards was cast in a judicial framework. It was accepted that legal representation was 'de rigour,' that established rules of administrative law applied such as those deriving from the concepts of natural justice and fairness, and that boards would render formal, written judgments. And it was furthermore understood by policymakers, and affirmed by the Supreme Court of Canada in *Bell* (1971),[22] that board decisions were subject to judicial review before superior courts. Through this logic of the hearing process, human rights codes and acts had highly formalized and legalized decision making built into them as an adjudicative recourse of last resort. Human rights commissions were thus designed from their very inception to be institutionally ambidextrous: in the early stages of their work they were to function as administrative bodies; later, during processes of conciliation and mediation, they were to engage in semijudicial work; and if need be, in the latter stages of case management they were to be prepared to support and engage in a legalized and judicialized form of decision making.

This desire to blend administrative and judicial functions in the working of commissions and boards directly affected the burden-of-proof standards for board decision making. In opting for the civil over the criminal standard of proof, rights advocates were supporting an adjudicative framework that was more conducive to the laying of complaints, the bringing of cases, and the resolution of disputes in favour of complainants. It is noteworthy that having so adopting the civil standard, human rights law came to be treated much like any other form of civil law, so that commissions applying the law were treated much like any other regulatory agency of the state rather than as branches of the criminal law process.

This organizing principle with respect to the assessment of cases, however, could itself be problematic. When one tips the scales of justice toward the civil side, one is consciously limiting the ability of respondents to avoid an unfavourable order. Rights advocates contend that the civil standard for finding fault in rights disputes is fully appropriate, given the noncriminal nature of the legal relationships being assessed; but an argument could be made that the civil standard unfairly limits legal rights of the respondent. It could be argued further that a finding of wrongdoing by a respondent could have a drastic impact on that person's life and career, and that for that reason the respondent's legal rights should be fully protected.

Rights advocates have never contested this basic logic, asserting that all board adjudication must be fully consonant with the broad administrative law rules of natural justice, fairness, bias, and error of law. In all matters of adjudication the rights of both parties must be protected and be seen to be protected. But in keeping with the policy goal of blending administrative and judicial functions, and of making the rights enforcement system more effective in its coverage and application, rights agencies have recourse to the civil standard of proof. The use of this standard in noncriminal adjudication has a long legacy, and is of such a nature that criticism is not warranted provided that the adjudicative hearing process fully accords with the established legal principles of administrative law.

A fine balance is thus envisaged between administrative and legal principles. The administrative goal of effective and responsible enforcement of rights protections can only be achieved through the fair and unbiased application of rights policy in conformity with the rule of law. As will be shown later, this blending of administrative and judicial roles has proven to be problematic and at times controversial. While it can be achieved by carefully balancing the competing demands of the two roles, such balance requires thoughtful, ongoing management of the work of commissions and boards. Ever since these bodies were established in the 1960s, their management has been under stress. The politics and administration of this stress will be discussed in Chapter 4.

The Organizational Design of Commissions

All human rights commissions in Canada have been established and given their mandate through legislation. Each respective code or act stipulates the organizational structure of the given commission, the broad policy mandate of the agency, and detailed procedures to be followed in executing that mandate.

The legislated mandates of all human rights commissions in Canada tend to be similar in that all are given a general two-fold task: to administer and enforce the terms of the act while promoting public awareness and respect for human rights policy through research and education programs. While the former responsibility tends to consume much the greater part of every agency's attention on a day-to-day basis, the latter responsibility should not be underestimated. All agencies stress the importance of public education as a means to creating a more just and equitable society – a society in which human rights laws should require less and less enforcing as infractions become more infrequent. Given this approach to public education, it is not surprising that virtually all commissions have been mandated to promote research, education, and consciousness-raising in human rights.[23] As will be shown later, this role has been changing in recent years as agencies have strived to maximize their public relations impact while spending less money. Historically, however – and somewhat ironically, given the importance assigned in official circles to public education programs – these initiatives have always been of secondary importance within commissions, which have always devoted most of their attention to the procedural enforcement of rights legislation. It is this enforcement module that will occupy most of the remainder of this chapter.

General Agency Structure

All commissions in Canada are organized roughly the same way. All have a number of 'commissioners' who run the agency. All agencies also have the power to establish an administrative staff to assist the commissioners in the performance of their duties and to ensure that the responsibilities of the agency are carried out in an orderly way. In all provinces except Quebec, commissioners are appointed by the Lieutenant-Governor in Council, that is, the Cabinet. In Quebec, appointment is by the National Assembly 'upon the motion of the Prime Minister,' that is, the premier. Appointment to the federal commission is subject to the authority of the Governor General in Council, in other words, the federal cabinet.[24]

Usually, human rights commissioners serve on a part-time basis. In the four Atlantic and three prairie provinces, all commissioners are part-time. In Ontario and Quebec, the chair and vice-chair are full-time while the remaining officers are part-time. At the federal level, the commission's two most senior positions are full-time, and the remaining commissioners may be appointed as either full-time or part-time officers; however, the custom is for these officials to serve part-time. The BC legislation stipulates that there be three full-time commissioners.[25]

With respect to tenure and term of office, there is significant variation across the country. Only at the federal level and in Quebec and BC do commissioners hold office with tenure, in that their positions are held 'during good behaviour' for a fixed term, with removal 'for cause' only on address of the relevant legislature. In all other jurisdictions, appointments are held 'at pleasure' of the appointing authority, meaning that provincial cabinets may remove commissioners any time they see fit.[26] While cabinets rarely use this power, they have sometimes exercised it with dramatic effect, as happened in BC in the early 1980s, when that province's system of commission appointments was operating under the 'at pleasure' form of office holding.[27] Moreover, as Tarnopolsky and Pentney argue, that such authority exists even in theory places most provincial agencies in an underprivileged position when they must confront their own governments over alleged violations of human rights law.[28]

Once senior officials have been appointed to a commission, their terms of office vary widely. Newfoundland, Nova Scotia, New Brunswick, Manitoba, and Alberta do not specify a fixed term of service. PEI and Quebec set out maximum terms of service – three and ten years respectively. Saskatchewan has fixed terms of five years, while in BC the deputy commissioner serves for three years, the commissioner of investigation and mediation serves for four, and the chief commissioner serves for five. The federal legislation fixes a maximum term of seven years for full-time officers and three years for those serving part-time.[29] With respect to numbers of officers, legislation in Newfoundland, Nova Scotia, New Brunswick, and Saskatchewan stipulates that there should be three or more members. In PEI the legislation holds that the number of commissioners should be three; in Ontario and Quebec it states that there should be no fewer than seven. In BC the legislation mandates three commissioners, while in Manitoba and Alberta it gives full discretion to the Lieutenant-Governor in Council to appoint any number of commissioners. The federal legislation holds that there should be no less than five nor no more than nine federal commissioners.[30] In current practice, PEI and Newfoundland each have three commissioners, and all other commissions have between five and eleven.

With respect to commission staff, there is once again great variety across the country. At the federal level and in Quebec and BC, the chief commissioner (or president of the commission in Quebec) acts as the chief executive officer of the commission. In all other provinces the CEO's function is carried out by a senior staff official, who is styled the director of human rights. Usually this director is not a regular member of the commission, though in Newfoundland and Nova Scotia the director acts as an *ex officio* member of the commission. It is noteworthy that between 1984 and 1996, legislation in BC made no provision for staffing what was then the BC Human Rights Council. The BC Human Rights Act, which held sway at that time, stipulated that the administrative needs of the council were to be provided by other relevant government departments, mainly the Ministry of Skills, Training and Labour.[31]

The nature of the appointment of the executive director also varies across the country. In Newfoundland, Nova Scotia, New Brunswick, and Saskatchewan this official is appointed by the Lieutenant-Governor in Council. In Quebec, as observed earlier, the president is appointed by the National Assembly, while in PEI the executive director is hired by the commission itself. In all other provinces the director is chosen through the normal hiring processes of the respective public service acts.[32] At the federal level, as noted earlier, the chief commissioner is appointed by the Governor General in Council, with removal being the prerogative of Parliament. In most agencies, commission staff are members of the general public service and are hired pursuant to and subject to the rules of provincial public service acts. Quebec and Saskatchewan are the exceptions to this: in these two jurisdictions the commissions are free to do their own hiring, subject to general labour relations law.[33]

Given how the various jurisdictions vary in size, it is no surprise that the commissions vary greatly in their organizational complexity and staff complements. As would be expected, the federal commission is the largest, with some 156 person-years allocated across a head office in Ottawa and five regional offices. The next two largest commissions, of course, are those of Quebec and Ontario, with the former being larger. The Quebec commission has a head office in Montreal and five regional offices throughout the province and a total staff of 94. The Ontario commission is headquartered in Toronto and has six branch offices with a total staff of 69.[34] The other commissions are distinctly smaller, with size being roughly commensurate to the province's population. Thus BC and Alberta have mid-sized commissions, and the smallest agencies are in Newfoundland and PEI.

Organizational Design and Procedure: The Ontario Model

As noted in Chapter 1, Ontario was the birthplace of human rights commissions in Canada. By 1977, every province as well as the federal government had followed Ontario's lead in establishing of commissions. As Ontario was the pioneer, its approach to administration naturally served as a model for other jurisdictions. While there often were variations in specific design, the general legal and administrative contours of these systems were quite similar. To provide a basic overview of human rights procedure in Canada, we will begin by analyzing the organization and workings of the 'mother of commissions' – that of Ontario. As needed, we will highlight important differences found in other jurisdictions as well as recent modifications to the Ontario system. We will then discuss separately the systems at the federal level and in Quebec and British Columbia, because of their distinct features and historical evolution. We will return to these models again in Chapter 4 when we analyse commission responses to the combined stresses of enhanced rights consciousness and financial restraint.

Commission Structure

The Ontario Human Rights Commission is established pursuant to the Ontario Human Rights Code as authorized by the Ontario Legislative Assembly.[35] Officially, the commission is an 'agency' of the Government of Ontario and is accountable to the legislature through the Ministry of Citizenship (initially it was the Ministry of Labour).

As with most rights agencies, the Ontario commission has a relatively compact organizational structure, though it should be noted that the Ontario structure is more complex than those of most other provinces because of the province's population and physical size. The Ontario commission has two executive offices and four central administrative support branches.

At the head of the commission is the Office of the Chief Commissioner. This office is mandated to support the leadership role of the chief commissioner, to liaise with and promote the work of the other commissioners, and to assist all commissioners with respect to commission management and policy development. Subordinate to this office is the Office of the Executive Director. This official is the permanent administrative head of the commission and plays a role similar to that of an assistant deputy minister. The executive director is responsible for overseeing and managing all operations of the agency. These operations, in turn, are performed through four administrative branches.

The single largest branch of the commission is the Regional Services and Systemic Investigations Branch. This branch is responsible for all of the commission's enforcement activities, including regional services, case management, and systemic investigation. The work of this branch is facilitated through activities at the head office in Toronto and fifteen district offices spread through seven regional areas. The staff of this branch are usually the public's first contact with the commission, as it is their role to deal with the intake of complaints, to undertake investigations, and to work on mediation and conciliation. This branch is also responsible for addressing instances of systemic discrimination and for promoting settlements designed to eliminate such discriminatory practices. On top of this, it manages the commission's caseload, produces key statistical indicators of the commission's work, and develops case management initiatives designed to promote more efficient, economical, and just case decision-making.[36]

In turn, this branch is assisted by the Legal Services Branch. This body provides support for the commission respecting all legal aspects of its mandate. It provides legal advice to officers and managers respecting the investigation and conciliation of cases, and offers legal opinions to the commission on all relevant case matters. Finally, the staff of this branch serve as legal counsel for the commission before boards of inquiry and courts on all matters of appeals and judicial review.[37]

A third support body is the Public Policy and Public Education Branch. This group helps plan, develop and evaluate broad commission policy and its public education initiatives. It is responsible for external communications, community liaison, and media relations. Its staff are responsible for producing guidelines and written policies relating to the interpretation and application of the code, and for interacting with all individuals, groups, firms, organizations – including schools and universities – and other government institutions interested in the work of the commission.[38]

Finally, the commission is also supported by the Corporate Services Branch. This body offers administrative support to the commission in all matters of personnel and financial management, operational planning, and management reform. It promotes the use of information technology throughout the commission and supports all its staff in matters of professional upgrading. This branch is also responsible for ensuring that the commission complies with all requirements of freedom of information and protection of privacy policy, and for helping the commission deal with inquiries from the provincial ombudsman's office.[39]

Case Procedure

All human rights cases must be initiated by a formal complaint. The Ontario code stipulates that 'anyone' – in other words, the alleged victim, a third party, or the commission itself – may launch an action. The formal complaint must be in written form and must contain certain specific allegations providing necessary background information for the commission. The complaint form must provide the following: the identity of the complainant; the place and time of the alleged rights violation; the nature of the alleged violation and the basic facts surrounding it; the provision of the code that was allegedly transgressed; and a signed affirmation attesting to the veracity of the complaint. Furthermore, the complaint form must identify the alleged perpetrator as a respondent to the action, and must provide the respondent with sufficient information to allow him or her to address the merits of the case.[40]

With regard to the launching of a complaint, the Ontario code provides that the action should be undertaken within six months of the alleged violation. The law further provides, however, that this time limitation can be extended by the commission where 'the delay was incurred in good faith and no substantial prejudice will result to any person affected by the delay.'[41] Case backlog and institutional delay has become a major concern for the Ontario commission as well as for other commissions. This saving clause has resulted in significant litigation respecting the reasonableness of delays and whether delays have, in fact, resulted in 'substantial prejudice' to any persons, particularly named respondents. These matters will be discussed in greater detail in Chapter 4.

Upon the filing of a complaint, the commission is charged with its investigation. If the complaint is found to be 'bona fide,' the agency must work to resolve the matter, ideally through conciliation and a negotiated settlement. The first step in the initial investigation, then, is the prima facie assessment of the merits of the complaint. The commission has the right to refuse to proceed with a complaint if, in the opinion of investigating officers, the complaint does not substantiate a violation of the code, or it the complaint is 'frivolous or vexatious,' or if the alleged complaint can be better dealt with by another institution working under a different legal regime. This latter option is most often followed when the dispute is between employees and employers and the commission officers conclude that it can be more appropriately addressed by agencies responsible for administering labour relations or workers' compensation law.[42]

Once a complaint has passed through this screening process and has been found to be of prima facie significance, a formal investigation is launched. Here, the commission assigns the case to a human rights officer, whose duty it is to assess the merits of the complaint, to speak to all relevant persons involved on both sides of the case, to collect all pertinent evidence respecting the case, and then to report his or her findings to the commission. At this stage the commission maintains a sharp differentiation between its investigative and conciliative roles; respondents must be guaranteed the presumption of innocence throughout the investigation. To attempt to seek a settlement through conciliation at this point would be to presume that the complaint is valid before the investigation has been completed. This in turn would be to impugn the legal integrity of the commission's work. Undoubtedly, litigation in the courts would follow, on the grounds that the commission was biased.

Following the investigation, the case officer makes a formal report to the commission that assesses whether the complaint should be upheld or dismissed for lack of cause. If the complaint is dismissed, both parties are notified of the commission's findings, with the complainant having the right to ask the commission for a formal reconsideration of this decision. If the complaint is upheld, again both parties are notified. At this point a conciliation officer meets with the complainant and respondent in an effort to broker a mediated settlement. In keeping with the initial rationale for rights commissions, the agency will stress the importance of conciliation and a mediated settlement, and that the primary goal of the commission is not to exact retribution but rather to change how people think and act toward one another. In this respect, an agreement by the respondent to desist from improper behaviour, to compensate the claimant for any financial damages incurred as well as hurt feelings, and to issue a public apology is usually the goal of the commission.

When a claim is upheld, the resulting conciliation stage is usually successful in achieving a mediated settlement that is satisfactory to all concerned. Such a settlement is, in turn, endorsed by the commission, which makes its terms and conditions legally enforceable in the courts should the respondent subsequently seek to renege on the agreement. Once the settlement is endorsed by the commission, the case is closed.[43]

Sometimes, however, mediation fails and the respondent refuses to concede that he or she has violated the human rights code. When this happens, the commission is free, upon reflection, to side with the respondent and dismiss the case or to order that the case be assessed by a board of inquiry. Should the latter route be followed, the case enters the most complex, formal, and legalistic area of human rights procedures. A hearing by a board of inquiry is designed to allow the case to be adjudicated by a semijudicial administrative tribunal that has the full legal power to resolve the matters in dispute and issue a legally binding order on the parties involved. Given the semijudicial nature of this undertaking, the nature and functioning of these boards is quite distinct from that of the commission.

Until 1995 the adjudicative process was structured around temporary, ad hoc boards of inquiry that were entirely independent of the commission. It was this dispute resolution system that characterized the Ontario model from its inception, and so it was this system that influenced the design of most other provincial commissions in Canada.

Under this 'old' system of case adjudication, when a board of inquiry was called for the commission requested the Ministry of Citizenship to establish one. The board was, and was seen to be, temporary and fully independent of the commission. This latter point was very important: given that the commission had carriage of the case, the adjudicative body had to be separate and distinct from the commission in order to ensure that no institutional bias was introduced into the proceedings. Responsibility for establishing and staffing the boards thus sat with the responsible ministry, not the commission. In making appointments to these boards, which usually comprised a single person, ministry officials would select from a roster of persons with legal training who were also expert in human rights policy, law, and procedures. Having been established, the board would hear the case, with the hearing assessing the merits of the case in light of the legal provisions of the act; the hearing would also be required to conform to the administrative law rules of natural justice, fairness, bias, error of law, and (after 1982) all relevant Charter of Rights provisions.[44]

This procedural format was heavily amended in 1995, when a standing board of inquiry was established. Now, when a board of inquiry is needed, the commission refers the disputed matter to this permanent board. This institution, also created pursuant to the Ontario code, is established by the Lieutenant-Governor in Council and comprises an indeterminate number of full-time and part-time officers, who generally serve three-year terms. The current board of inquiry, which possesses the full legal status of a statutory tribunal, comprises four full-time members and four part-time members, though these part-time numbers are expected to grow as the workload of this tribunal increases. The board is thus a permanent institution existing alongside the commission, and is designed to adjudicate disputes arising under the code.[45]

This new board is wholly independent of the commission, just like the old ones were. And the reasons for this are the same: given that the carriage of the case remains vested with the commission, the adjudicative body must be separate from the commission in order be, and to be seen to be, autonomous from the decision maker of first instance. Thus responsibility for establishing and staffing the new board and board panels still lies with the responsible ministry, not the commission. In making appointments to these adjudicative panels, which again is usually a single person (though larger panels are allowed), the chair or vice-chair of the board selects designates from among the members of the board. As under the old system, these board members tend to be people with legal training and noted expertise in human rights policy, law, and procedures. Once established, the panel hears the case, playing much the same role as did boards under the old system.[46]

Under the new system (and as with the old), hearings tend to be highly formal. The panel is mandated to review the case, to hear both sides of the matter, and to fashion a resolution that accords with law and justice. Such hearings are thus very courtlike; ordinarily, both parties are represented by legal counsel, with the commission seeking to prove its case of discrimination and counsel for the respondent challenging that case. Under the administrative law rules of natural justice, each party has the right to present all relevant evidence and witnesses and to cross-examine all evidence that their opponents' introduce. Both sides have the full right to make any arguments germane to the case, to have disclosure of all pertinent materials, and to have reasonable adjournments. While the presumption of innocence remains in favour of the respondent, the burden of proof is set to the civil standard, being a balance of probabilities. The rules of natural justice, fairness, bias, and error of law obligate the panel to protect and promote the legal rights of all parties to due process, and to ensure for those parties that the panel will render impartial justice that is free from any personal or institutional prejudice or bias. Any alleged breach of any of these legal requirements, and any alleged misinterpretation or misapplication of the substance of human rights law by the panel, will constitute grounds for judicial review of the panel's decision by the superior courts.[47]

Following the hearing, the panel must render a formal written judgment respecting the matters in dispute. This decision can uphold the position of either the respondent or the complainant. If the complaint is upheld, the panel may fashion an order stipulating how the proven discrimination is to be remedied. As outlined earlier, remedies range from formal apologies, to financial awards in favour of the complainant, to restitution on behalf of the respondent, through to compliance orders demanding that the respondent set in place procedures designed to promote human rights. These orders are legally binding as orders of the board and are enforceable through the courts. If the complaint is dismissed, the panel may award legal costs in favour of the respondent. In either circumstance, both parties are free to appeal the panel decision to the superior courts.[48]

Note here that the right of appeal is not automatic in all jurisdictions. Most jurisdictions – the federal authority, Newfoundland, Nova Scotia, New Brunswick, Quebec, Saskatchewan, and Alberta – provide for appeal rights similar to those in Ontario. However, three provinces – PEI, Manitoba, and BC – continue to follow the traditional administrative law practice of allowing tribunal decisions to be subject to court scrutiny through judicial review.[49]

Organizational Design and Procedure: The Federal Model

The Canadian Human Rights Commission was established in 1977 by virtue of the Canadian Human Rights Act.[50] The federal authority was among the last of Canadian jurisdictions to be covered by human rights legislation. The federal government came late to this field because it was recognized that the vast majority of persons needing rights protection were subject to provincial jurisdiction and to the administrative authority of provincial commissions. By the mid-1970s, however, there was growing awareness within the federal government that a substantial number of persons working in the federal jurisdiction were unprotected by provincial human rights legislation. Thus, the federal initiative of 1977.[51]

The Canadian Human Rights Commission is an independent agency of the federal government and stands at arm's length from the government. In its early days the agency possessed a reporting relationship to the Minister of Justice, in that its annual report was given to this minister; but this process was altered in 1988 so that the commission now reports directly to Parliament through the Speaker of the House of Commons. However, the Minister of Justice is still administratively responsible for the act and accountable for the policy actions of the commission. The Canadian Human Rights Act applies to the broad federal public service and to all federally regulated industries. As such, it extends human rights coverage to all members of federal government departments, agencies, boards, commissions, offices, and Crown corporations, and to the RCMP and the Canadian military. It also applies to all persons employed in national industries such as the banks, the airlines, the railways, and the interprovincial trucking industry.[52]

The legal and procedural content of the federal legislation is generally comparable to what is found in the Ontario model. As was indicated in Table 1.4 and Table 1.5, the federal legislation imposes similar prohibitions against discrimination on the standard grounds and in the standard areas of employment and the provision of goods and services. The complaint management process is also essentially the same as that found in Ontario and all other provinces; it involves investigation, mediation, and if need be formal hearings and adjudication before an independent tribunal.

With respect to tribunals, the federal framework of rights enforcement has undergone significant reform since the inception of the act. As originally constituted in 1977, the commission had full authority to refer a complaint to a tribunal, and under section 39 of the act the commission also had full authority to select the members of the tribunal. Once this tribunal was constituted by the commission, officials from the commission would in turn have carriage of the case before the tribunal.[53]

This framework for federal rights tribunals was successfully challenged in *MacBain v. Canada* (Canadian Human Rights Commission)[54] on the ground that it displayed a reasonable apprehension of bias in that the tribunal could not be reasonably perceived as an independent adjudicative actor separate and distinct from the commission. As a result of this ruling striking down the offending section of the act, the legislation was amended so that now a permanent Human Rights Tribunal exists as a free-standing institution that is organizationally separate and distinct from the commission.

This tribunal is headed by a president of the tribunal, who is appointed by the Governor in Council (i.e., the Cabinet) and holds office on good behaviour for a term of three years.[55] Other members of the tribunal are also appointed by the Governor in Council to terms not exceeding five years, with service being on good behaviour. Under this new framework, when the commission requests a tribunal hearing on a particular case, the president of the tribunal selects members of the tribunal to form a tribunal panel for the purpose of hearing and adjudicating the matter at hand. The case then proceeds on this basis, under the clear recognition that the members of the tribunal panel are in no manner beholden to any general or particular approach or position advocated by the commission. The establishment of such a tribunal as a permanent semijudicial institution responsible for adjudicating of all federal rights matters was a signal achievement in the professionalization of the rights adjudication process, and was an intiative that was to attract attention in other jurisdictions.

While the federal commission is generally similar in policy and program to the Ontario model, it also has certain features and a resulting organizational structure that make it unique. The federal agency has the routine mandate to enforce the rights protected by the act and to promote public education pertaining to the act, but it also has a number of special monitoring and reporting functions.

The commission has a duty to monitor the application of the federal Employment Equity Act through an ongoing review of the annual reports filed by all federally regulated employers covered by this legislation. The commission also has the power to take remedial action to promote employment equity within these particular places of employment. In tandem with this responsibility, the commission also has a duty to monitor all federal legislation, policies, and programs affecting specific groups – namely women, native peoples, visible minorities, and persons with disabilities. Through its annual report, the commission has the authority to assess the merits and weaknesses of such laws, policies and programs while pointing out to responsible ministries the contours of suggested reforms.[56]

The commission's structure bears the imprint of this broadened mandate. At the administrative apex of the commission stands the Office of the Secretary General, which provides executive support to the chief commissioner and other members of the commission, and also oversees the work of all commission staff at the Ottawa headquarters and all regional offices. The secretary general is a senior member of the federal public service and is appointed to the commission pursuant to the Public Service Employment Act.[57]

Reporting to the Office of the Secretary General are five line offices. The antidiscrimination programs branch is responsible for the investigation and conciliation of all complaints lodged with the commission. This branch also provides a quality control and review function for all cases to be presented to the full commission. The human rights promotion branch is responsible for promoting public education regarding the act and its provisions, and for fostering broader rights awareness. It does all this through a variety of informational programs, through media liaison, and by promoting and supporting community activities. Also, the six regional offices of the commission report to this branch. As its name suggests, the policy and liaison branch monitors all human rights issues of interest to the commission, conducts all necessary policy research for the agency, and co-ordinates international liaison activities. The employment equity branch, in keeping with its broad duties regarding equity matters, carries employment equity audits with the goal of monitoring and reporting on employers' compliance with the Employment Equity Act. The final branch within the Ottawa headquarters is the corporate and personnel services branch, which attends to financial and personnel management, telecommunications and information management, commission security, library services, and all matters of strategic planning related to these services. Finally, the commission has six regional offices located in Halifax, Montreal, Toronto, Winnipeg, Edmonton, and Vancouver.[58]

Organizational Design and Procedure: The Quebec Model

Quebec's human rights commission, *la Commission des droits de la personne et des droits de la jeunesse*, has always been quite distinct. As indicated in Table 1.4 and Table 1.5, the Quebec Charter of Rights and Freedoms is broader in scope than legislation in most other jurisdictions, with the Quebec charter making explicit provision for 'political,' 'judicial,' and 'economic and social rights,' as well as for the traditional rights to 'equal recognition and exercise of rights and freedoms.'[59]

The Quebec charter also gives the commission the authority to support the development of human rights in Quebec, to 'point out any provision in the laws of Quebec that may be contrary to the Charter and make appropriate recommendations to the Government,' and to 'receive and examine suggestions, recommendations and requests' made to it by any persons, groups, corporations, and institutions interested in rights policy. The commission also has the mandate to 'cooperate with any organization dedicated to the promotion of human rights and freedoms in and outside Quebec.'[60] As a result of this last provision, the Quebec commission has become the most activist of all Canadian commissions on the broader international stage. Since the Charter was amended in 1995, the commission has also enjoyed broad powers to promote and protect the rights of children and teenagers as codified under the Youth Protection Act and the Young Offenders Act.[60]

The commission's powers are enhanced by a supremacy clause in the act which stipulates that all substantive rights and freedoms enunciated by the charter, with the exception of economic and social rights, are supreme over all other Quebec legislation. This means that when there is a conflict between the substance of any protected element of the charter and the substance of any other Quebec law, the provisions of the charter are to prevail unless the other law is itself protected from the charter by a 'notwithstanding' clause.[62] Despite this final caveat, the legal power of the charter is indeed quite potent, far eclipsing that of most of its sister acts in the other provinces.[63] Quebec's commission is also noteworthy in being organizationally the largest in the country, with a variety of departments spanning the breadth of rights administration.

The Quebec commission is headed by a president, two vice-presidents, and 'two groups of six [commissioners] selected from the people likely to contribute in a specific way to the examination and resolution of problems relating in one case to human rights and in the other case to the protection of children's rights.'[64] All commissioners are appointed by the National Assembly. The president of the commission is unique in Canada in that he or she acts as both chief commissioner and chief executive officer, and thus presides not only over the adjudicative work of the commission but also over its routine administration. The office of the president and the assembly of commissioners are assisted in their duties by six central support departments and two sets of regional offices. At the head office in Montreal are an investigations department and a legal department. The former office is responsible for the intake, administration, and investigation of all valid complaints; the latter provides the commission with all necessary legal advice, support, and litigation services. The head office also has research, education, and communications departments, which carry out the duties normally associated with such functional specializations.

The Quebec commission also has an affirmative action programs department similar to that of the federal commission. This department provides permanent support to the commission in the development of voluntary affirmative action programs in the public sector. This department also assists the Quebec government in evaluating private sector compliance with provincial affirmative action policy as mandated through the Quebec government's contract compliance program. Through this department, Quebec has one of Canada's most well-entrenched and activist affirmative action policy and implementation systems.[65]

Since 1995 the Quebec commission has also had wide powers to promote and protect the rights of children and teenagers. The explicit coverage of this group makes the Quebec commission unique in the country. This initiative will be discussed further in Chapter 4.

Finally, the Quebec commission has five of regional support offices: one each for the Quebec City area (including the lower St Lawrence and the Gaspé), the North Shore, the Eastern Townships, Northwestern Quebec, and the Outaouais region.[66]

The most unique feature of the Quebec human rights system has to do with its enforcement and adjudication procedures. The Quebec commission follows a similar process of complaint intake, initial assessment, investigation, and conciliation as found in all other commissions; that being said, the Quebec system has always been different with respect to the treatment of disputed cases. In its earliest form, the Quebec legislation stipulated that when the commission could not negotiate a resolution to a rights dispute, the case was to be adjudicated not by an ad hoc board of inquiry but by the common courts. In this sense, a human rights dispute was to be treated like any other legal dispute in need of an adjudicated resolution. In the ensuing litigation the commission would argue the case for the complainant and the final decision would fall under the ordinary jurisdiction of the courts. In these cases, of course, hearings were conducted in accordance with strict legal procedure as set forth in the Quebec code of civil procedure.[67]

64 Restraining Equality

In 1989 this process of adjudication was substantially amended through the creation of a permanent human rights tribunal vested with responsibility for addressing all rights disputes arising from the work of the commission. After the federal reform of 1985, this tribunal became the second such permanent specialized adjudicative agency in the country. As stipulated in the charter, the tribunal will have no less than seven members, including a president and 'assessors.' The president is chosen by the government, 'after consultation with the chief judge of the Court of Quebec,' from among the judges of that court. The charter also provides for other judges from the Court of Quebec to be appointed to the tribunal for fixed periods. The assessors are selected from the ranks of public service arbitrators and are specially appointed by the government to undertake the mediative work of the commission. The term of office for the members of the tribunal is five years.[69]

Once established, the tribunal carries out the work once done by the Quebec courts. When a matter cannot be resolved through negotiation and mediation, the commission may submit the case for adjudication before the tribunal. In dealing with such a case, the president of the tribunal will assign a panel to adjudicate the matter, with the panel comprising a judge and two assessors. While all three members 'hear' the case and reflect upon it, the final decision of the panel is the prerogative of the judge. Procedures before the panel are highly legalized, as the tribunal must adhere to the rules of the Quebec code of civil procedure as well as to all established administrative law rules of natural justice, fairness, bias, and error of law. In this respect, the substantive hearing procedure followed in Quebec is essentially similar to that found in every other Canadian jurisdiction. In rendering its judgment, the panel has full authority to uphold or reject any claim of discrimination. Should a claim be upheld, the panel is free to impose any and all remedies found in the charter, including compliance orders, restitution, and the imposition of fines. Finally, a decision of the tribunal may be appealed to the Quebec court of appeal, on leave from that court.[69]

Quebec was among the first provincial jurisdictions in this country to recognize that the volume of cases coming before it justified the creation of a permanent adjudicative body. Moreover, a permanent rights adjudicative body could be staffed by officials 'having notable experience and expertise in, sensitivity to and interest for matters of human rights and freedoms.'[70] This specialization promoted effectiveness in substantive decision-making; it also enabled the tribunal to hone its knowledge of rights policy, law, and procedure, which resulted in more expeditious, efficient, and economical decision making than is routinely found in ad hoc board-of-inquiry systems. The perceived merits of a permanent tribunal have come to attract considerable attention from a number of other jurisdictions.

Organizational Design and Procedure: The British Columbia Model

As outlined in Chapter 1, British Columbia has a turbulent history with respect to its human rights policies and procedures. In 1983, in an unprecedented and controversial move, BC became the first province ever to abolish its human rights system. It was replaced in 1984 by a new Human Rights Act that dramatically reduced the scope of rights protection while establishing a very different and spartan framework for case administration. The BC Human Rights Council differed in important ways from all other systems of rights administration in Canada. The act stipulated that the council was to be led by 'members appointed by the Lieutenant-Governor in Council to hold office during pleasure.'[71] Though this form of appointment was not unique, it raised concerns in light of other administrative features of the council. One such feature was the stipulation that the council would not have a permanent staff for conducting investigations and mediation; rather, these functions were to be carried out by industrial relations officers within the employment standards branch of the Ministry of Skills, Training and Labour. (It is to be noted here that by the 1990s, due to the routine shuffling of ministerial responsibilities, this ministry was no longer officially responsible for overseeing the council, notwithstanding that it retained this responsibility for much of the work of the council.)[72]

Given this offloading of the agency's investigative and conciliative work, the work of the council members quickly became dominated by case adjudication. This had significant practical consequences. In the event that a complaint could not be resolved through investigation and conciliation, the case was forwarded to the council for determination as to whether it should proceed to a formal hearing. A governing panel of the council exercised its discretionary judgment on this matter, and if its decision was in favour of a hearing, the chair of the council designated one of the council members to conduct a hearing. In managing this adjudication process, the council had to be careful to avoid charges of institutional bias; this was accomplished by ensuring that the council member assigned to adjudicate the hearing had in no manner participated in the prior decision-making respecting the referral to a hearing. The actual hearing conducted by the council member was essentially similar in style and format to those of all other boards of inquiry or tribunals in other jurisdictions. As elsewhere, the actions of the council were governed by the common administrative law rules of natural justice, fairness, bias, and error of law. Though the legislation governing the council made no provision for a right of appeal of a council decision, all judgments were subject to judicial review as exercised by the superior courts.[73]

This special adjudicative role of the council had an important impact on the agency's operations. Through this focus on case adjudication, which came to be the primary function of the council, the agency became, in effect, a de facto permanent tribunal respecting human rights matters. This, even though the council enjoyed none of the institutional safeguards of tenure and organizational independence normally associated with permanent tribunals. Moreover, on account of this adjudicative role, the council believed itself obligated to refrain from engaging in human rights research, policy advocacy, and educational programming. By embracing these functions, it was argued, the council would be leaving itself open to criticisms of bias, in that through such other work it might have developed prejudgments on various matters that would later come before it for adjudication.[74] As William W. Black argued in a 1995 report on the BC human rights system, these limitations 'very substantially reduce the ability of the Council to suppress discrimination by any means other than the adjudication of individual complaints. If an important goal of human rights legislation is to change patterns of discrimination, the structure of the Council must be considered counter-productive.'[75]

Black's report also highlighted certain benefits arising from this structure. The most significant was that in effect, a permanent tribunal system existed. The BC model was credited with promoting a form of rights adjudication marked by the expertise, sensitivity, and consistency as well as by the economical and efficient handling of cases. Unlike ad hoc boards of inquiry (as found in most other provinces), the BC model allowed for the development of a permanent team approach to the dispute management; indeed, the council stressed that this approach maximized its judicial and administrative professionalism.[76]

Black's report endorsed this aspect of the council's operations while remaining highly critical of most of the agency's structure and functioning. In suggesting reforms, the report emphasized the benefits of having BC return to the commission model of rights enforcement as found in the rest of Canada. The report spoke of the importance of giving the commission a broad mandate to administer and promote human rights policy. It also stressed the obvious benefits of the commission being well funded and of having its own staff. In suggesting these reform options, however, the report also stressed the benefits of permanent tribunals, and recommended that such a system be part of any policy changes.[77]

All these suggestions proved to be influential when the BC NDP government revised its human rights legislation in 1996. In the new BC Human Rights Code, the government reverted to the traditional commission model of rights enforcement. The newly established human rights commission was given a much broader mandate to promote and enforce human rights than had been the case with the council. The new commission has three members – a chief commissioner, a deputy chief commissioner, and a commissioner of investigation and mediation. These members are all appointed by the Lieutenant-Governor in Council for terms of five years. These members are assisted in their work by an advisory council of at least seven but no more than eleven members, who are also appointed by the Lieutenant-Governor in Council, but to unspecified set terms. The system is designed to provide the commission with support regarding public education, public liaison, and the routine administrative work of the commission. With regard to substantive rights coverage, the new commission has explicit jurisdiction to study, identify, and challenge 'persistent patterns of inequality' and to seek remedies for such systemic discrimination through 'special programs' of affirmative action. With respect to administration, the new agency has the authority to retain and direct a permanent commission staff mandated to undertake actions ranging from investigation and conciliation through to research, public education, and community liaison.[78]

In keeping with Black's report, the legislation has also provided for a permanent adjudicative tribunal to address disputed cases. This tribunal is roughly similar to Quebec's, except that the BC tribunal is not necessarily staffed and led by members of the judiciary. The BC tribunal is to possess at least three full-time members and no more than six part-time members. Members are appointed by the Lieutenant-Governor in Council and hold office for terms of five years. These members may be taken from the ranks of the judiciary, but they can also be selected from those in government, academia, labour, social action groups, and business who display a keen knowledge and interest in the field of human rights. When hearing cases, the tribunal can sit in panels of either one or three, as designated by the chair of the tribunal. As throughout the country, the procedures of the tribunal are governed by the common rules of administrative law.

Conclusion: Administrative Options, Legal Constraints

The above review of the organization of human rights commissions illustrates both the choices and the constraints involved in establishing rights agencies. Governments enjoy a variety of options when they design commissions. At the same time, they face certain fundamental legal requirements and obligations flowing from the fact that commissions, boards, and tribunals are legal and adjudicative entities with the power to render legally binding decisions. Given these responsibilities, their actions and procedures are governed by long-established rules of administrative law that will be enforced by the courts through the processes of either appeal or judicial review. For these agencies to render sound, viable, and enforceable decisions, their decision-making processes must be legally and procedurally impeccable. It is generally recognized that all decision making of rights agencies must conform to the rules of natural justice and procedural fairness. The effect of this is that despite the range of administrative options open to the different governments in fashioning rights regimes, the basic procedural structures for handling human rights cases are strikingly similar across this country.

This highlights the strictures placed on anyone seeking to reconfigure how rights policy works. The rules of administrative law and due process must be seen as constituting a vital part of rights administration. Given the nature of this policy field, the courts will not countenance any form of rights administration or process that does not conform to established administrative law principles. And in a deeper sense, rights observers and analysts, interested parties, the media, and governments themselves would reject any system of rights administration that contradicts the principles and practices of the established 'rule of law' tradition. This tradition is very truly 'embedded' within the field of rights policy in Canada. The 'rule of law' tradition has resulted in commission activities becoming highly legalistic and procedurally complicated, as the requirements of due process not only must be met but manifestly must be seen to be met. A decision-making system initially designed to be simple, inexpensive, efficient, and easily comprehensible has come to be anything but all of this. This same tradition also imposes significant restrictions on the theory and practice of rights reform. This topic will be the focus of attention in Chapter 4, where we address reform initiatives, their strengths and weaknesses, and the relationship between commission models and the reform process.

In the 1980s and 1990s, in the climate of strong public and governmental concern about the need for governments to trim their operational costs, human rights commissions have been confronted with major problems. These problems are the focus of the next chapter.

3. Fiscal Restraint

The evolution of human rights legislation was double-edged. On the one hand, the development was expansionary, which had operational implications for the commissions. As human rights protections were broadened across the country, so were the mandates and functions of commissions, and this increased their workloads significantly. On the other hand, because of government policies of fiscal restraint during the 1980s and 1990s, the commissions found it much more difficult to handle their increased workloads. The commissions needed more funding to carry out their expanded mandates, and they were not getting it. This need was related not only to the growing number of cases but also to the increased legal complexity of procedures. However, at the same time as the need for budgetary resources was increasing, fiscal restraints were placing limits on the growth of human rights budgets. This was to present a major challenge for the commissions in fulfilling their mandate to enforce human rights legislation.

We now examine this double-edged development. We begin by reviewing the expanding workloads of the commissions. We will focus on growing caseloads, but will give attention to the widening responsibilities of the commissions, such as in public education and affirmative action. We will then examine government policies of fiscal restraint and their impact on the commissions. Finally, in seeking reasons why fiscal restraint was applied to the commissions, we will analyze patterns of human rights funding across the provinces and over time. Although we will pay some attention to the federal commission, we will focus on the provinces for purposes of comparative analysis. Our chief finding will be that there has been considerable provincial variation in funding and that funding levels are related to ideology. We will conclude that while all governing parties apply programs of fiscal restraint to commissions, parties of the left are relatively more willing to provide greater resources to human rights commissions.

Expanding Commission Workloads

The enlargement of human rights protections through legislation, the broad judicial interpretations of the law, and the expansion of commission responsibilities all had a strong effect on human rights enforcement. The most obvious effect was to expand the workloads and responsibilities of the commissions and tribunals. When commissions were first established in the 1960s, their caseloads were relatively small, although certainly much greater than under the old system of fair practices legislation.[1] For example, in the Ontario commission's first year of operations (1962–63), the total number of formal cases was only 45.[2] Most were race-related and dealt with discrimination in employment. But by the late 1970s, total annual cases in the province exceeded 1,000, and by the mid-1990s, exceeded 2,500.[3]

This pattern of growth was found in other jurisdictions. As indicated in Table 3.1, the trend across jurisdictions was generally upward, with caseloads more than doubling between 1980 and the mid-1990s. The jurisdictions with the largest and fastest growing caseloads were Ontario, British Columbia, and the federal level. Quebec also had a large caseload though it did not show the same upward growth as other large jurisdictions. The provinces with the smallest caseloads were Prince Edward Island, New Brunswick, and Newfoundland. The trend in Newfoundland was upward, in PEI was mixed, and in New Brunswick was generally downward. The pattern in BC is worth noting: caseloads decreased significantly after the old human rights system was dismantled in 1983, then climbed again in the 1990s under a new NDP government and the subsequent planning for new legislation (which eventually resulted in the 1996 BC Human Rights Code). Overall, caseloads increased across Canada.

Besides growing caseloads, commissions encountered a fundamental shift in the *types* of cases brought to them. In the 1960s, most cases involved race or ethnicity. By the 1980s, most dealt with sex (gender) discrimination. In the 1990s, most cases still dealt with sex discrimination, but complaints involving disability were in strong second place. Table 3.2 shows the distribution of complaints in the mid-1990s. In most jurisdictions, complaints of gender discrimination (which includes sex-

TABLE 3.1
Human rights caseloads, 1980–97

Year	BC	AB	SK	MB	ON	PQ	NB	NS	PE	NF	FED
1980–81	828	281	201	457	994	2,002	147	102	20	—	432
1981–82	881	253	176	503	689	1,563	138	102	26	—	379
1982–83	1,065	370	287	641	759	1,343	135	104	31	—	447
1983–84	1,008	328	216	813	780	1,355	160	130	38	—	237
1984–85	490	315	224	803	1,509	1,272	139	145	42	—	318
1985–86	406	240	263	804	1,736	1,144	168	135	43	28	410
1986–87	391	287	198	590	1,816	1,610	142	148	167	53	494
1987–88	501	235	239	604	1,838	1,450	116	196	179	87	366
1988–89	536	290	229	628	2,229	1,334	103	158	87	78	419
1989–90	424	433	245	607	2,635	1,380	100	188	210	109	592
1990–91	576	539	265	664	2,851	1,735	101	253	—	113	1,997
1991–92	878	509	246	649	2,535	1,676	98	285	—	128	1,972
1992–93	1,127	620	309	588	2,317	1,508	112	237	—	167	2,389
1993–94	1,560	610	356	428	2,286	1,515	105	243	24	180	2,511
1994–95	2,382	528	259	368	2,452	1,374	101	255	33	140	1,998
1995–96	2,181	676	428	416	2,560	1,273	122	264	700	72	2,111
1996–97	1,439	825	386	440	2,775	1,409	189	403	150	164	2,025

Source: Commission annual reports and official statistics.
Notes: Cases refer to both new and carry-over cases from previous year. Data not recorded in Newfoundland 1980–85 and PEI 1990–93. Most commissions use fiscal years except for Manitoba, PEI, Quebec, and the federal commission, where figures above refer to the second year. Federal cases above are based on complaint outcome statistics.

TABLE 3.2
Percentage of distribution of complaints, 1995–96

Grounds	BC	SK	MB	ON	NB	FED
Race-related	16	19	15	23	9	21
Gender	37	38	38	27	39	23
Disability	24	28	23	26	13	33

Source: Commission annual reports.
Notes: The jurisdictions above use fiscal years in their statistics, except for Manitoba and the federal jurisdiction, which use calendar years. For these two jurisdictions, the calendar year 1996 applies here. Gender includes sexual harassment and pregnancy.

ual harassment) predominate. In some jurisdictions (e.g., the federal jurisdiction in Table 3.2), the leading category of complaints is disability. But in virtually all jurisdictions, sex, disability, and race are the main grounds for complaints, in that order.

As a result of legislative amendments and judicial interpretations, the complaint of sex discrimination has evolved considerably in the past few decades. In the early 1980s in most jurisdictions, complaints of this type were usually related to claims of unequal treatment in employment. But by the 1990s, complaints of sex discrimination covered not only unequal treatment in the workplace but also pregnancy as a barrier to employment and sexual harrassment in the workplace.

Complaints based on sexual orientation were among the last to be accepted by human rights commissions. Legislatures were very hesitant to pass legislation protecting gay and lesbian rights, and adjudicators were reluctant to accept sexual orientation as a basis for sex discrimination. As discussed in Chapter 1, the first jurisdictions to accept such complaints were Quebec in 1975 (under Quebec's Charter of Human Rights) and British Columbia, also in 1975 (as the result of liberal judicial interpretation in the *Gay Alliance* case).[4] In BC, coverage for gays and lesbians was reversed temporarily under the 1984 Human Rights Act, but then included under an amendment in 1992. This legislative coverage was provided for in Ontario in 1986 and in Manitoba and the Yukon in 1987. By 1998, as the result of legislative amendment and – in Alberta, PEI, and the Northwest Territories – of the *Vriend* decision by the Supreme Court of Canada,[5] all jurisdictions included sexual orientation as a prohibited ground of discrimination. Newfoundland had accepted complaints based only on commission policy, but in 1977 passed a legislative amendment to include sexual orientation.

As a result of all of this legislative change and judicial interpretation, complaints based on sexual orientation gradually began to come forward. However, in most jurisdictions they continue to be a relatively small percent of complaints. For example, in 1996 these complaints represented 2 per cent of total complaints in Manitoba and 5 per cent in the federal jurisdiction; and in 1995–96 they represented 1 per cent in Saskatchewan, 2 per cent in Ontario, 4 per cent in BC, and 20 per cent in New Brunswick.[6]

Increased caseloads were but one indicator of expanding commission workloads. Another indicator was the growth in the number of inquiries, referrals, and informal complaints (ones received but determined to be outside the commission's authority). This area of activity was not part of commissions' core mandates; even so, it diverted considerable resources and time away from actual cases. To illustrate the growth in this area, in 1980–81 there were 19,637 inquiries in Ontario, 2,183 in Manitoba, and 7,000 in BC; by 1990–91, these numbers had risen respectively to 56,448, 4,252, and 8,980.[7] Commission annual reports were indicating a general increase across the country. This growth is attributable to a number of factors, including the public education component of commission mandates, expanding equality-rights consciousness, and the ever-widening range, complexity, and diversity of human rights issues.

Workloads also increased in the areas of public education, affirmative action, and systemic discrimination. For example, with respect to public education initiatives, in 1985–86 the number of initiatives totalled 52 in BC, 349 in Saskatchewan, and 233 in Manitoba; by 1992–93 the numbers had increased respectively to 200, 529, and 247.[8] There were exceptions to this trend. In Ontario, for instance, educational activities that totalled 1,725 in 1980–81 had declined to only 332 by 1990–91.[9] Still, the general trend was upward. The trend also was upward with respect to affirmative action initiatives. For example, in 1982–83 Saskatchewan's commission initiated only 1 affirmative action program, Manitoba's 5, and Ontario's 57. However, by 1987–89 the number of programs in Manitoba had increased to 33 and in Ontario to 128; and by 1989–90 in Saskatchewan they had increased to 18, rising again by 1996–96 to 57.[10] Again, there were exceptions to the trend. In Ontario, for instance, the number of such programs had declined to 51 by 1989–90. However, overall activity across the country showed a general increase. Finally, for commissions with the mandate to investigate systemic discrimination (e.g., in Ontario, British Columbia, and Nova Scotia), activity increased.

Workloads also increased not only for commissions but also for tribunals and boards of inquiry, and for courts dealing with human rights cases. Reliance on tribunals, boards, and the courts as a means of dealing with difficult cases grew considerably with the increasing complexity of human rights issues. For example, in the six years between 1974 and 1979, there were 134 human rights cases reported across the country.[11] In contrast, between 1980 and 1985, as recorded by the *Canadian Human Rights Reporter*, there were 487 cases – 81 cases per average year.[12] And between 1992 and 1997, again as indicated in the *Reporter*, there were 1,189 cases across Canada – 198 cases per average year. Between 1980 and 1995, Ontario and the federal jurisdiction had the highest number of cases, followed by BC, Quebec (which did not use boards until 1990), and Saskatchewan. It is interesting to note that in an environment of fiscal restraint during the 1990s, while commissions and governments have been quite concerned about the considerable costs of tribunals and boards of inquiry, the numbers of boards and tribunals have not decreased. It also is interesting to note the growth of cases in BC under the downsized system established in 1984: cases more than tripled from 1982–83 to 1994–95.[13] The reason was that while the new system did not emphasize conciliation, it did emphasize adjudication. It is further interesting to note that BC had not only a relatively higher number of board cases but also a quite liberal record in the judicial interpretation of human rights law.

Accompanying the growth of workloads and commission responsibilities was the general enlargement of staff and the establishment of regional offices to deal with complaints in outlying areas. In the 1970s and 1980s, provincial commissions opened new offices in northern and outlying areas, especially in BC, the prairie provinces, Ontario, and Quebec. The Canadian Human Rights Commission also opened new regional offices during that period, and expanded its staff accordingly. In addition, the larger commissions such as those in Ontario and Quebec and at the federal level established specialized internal units to deal with legal issues, public relations, and policy and planning. This expansion in commissions' structures as well as in workloads brought about a need for increased resources.

The Contraction of Resources

As the scope of human rights protections was expanding and as commission workloads were increasing, human rights officials began to express concern about the availability of resources to meet their increased workload. To match their growing workloads, commissions obviously needed more higher budgets for staff, legal work, and offices. Otherwise, the system would experience strain and problems in effectiveness and credibility.

This concern was expressed as early as 1977 by the Ontario Human Rights Commission in its *Life Together* report.[14] The commission was explicit in its concerns about the future public funding of human rights administration in the province, given the plans to expand the legislation. If human rights coverage was going to be extended, as recommended by the commission in the report (and as acted upon by the government in 1981), commission funding and staffing was going to have to keep pace. According to the commission, its caseload had doubled in the 1970s and its community relations initiatives had tripled, and it had not been allotted adequate resources to cope with this increased workload.[15] Its budget and staff had been increased slightly, but this increase was not sufficient to deal with its expanded responsibilities. The problem, said the commission, was not simply one of quantity: cases were becoming more complex and discrimination more difficult to detect, which meant higher costs per case in terms of legal work and investigation. The overall result was a serious imbalance between public demands on the commission and its ability to meet those demands. The commission concluded that since it was official policy in Ontario to give priority to human rights protection, it was imperative that the commission's resources match its workload. Otherwise, the community would come to feel that human rights protection was symbolic rather than genuine public policy.

Human rights officials and advocates in other jurisdictions began to express similar concerns. However, because of the more sluggish economy during the 1980s and 1990s, declining government revenues, and growing deficit and debt problems, government expenditures generally did not match the budgetary needs of the commissions. Like many other government agencies, human rights commissions did not escape the effects of fiscal restraint. The massive restraint program launched by the Social Credit government in BC in 1983, which resulted in a sharp downsizing of that province's human rights system, was a harbinger of the restraint that human rights programs would soon be facing across the country. Later programs of fiscal restraint between the mid-1980s and mid-1990s, ranging from the Klein Conservatives in Alberta to the Romanow NDP in Saskatchewan to the Chrétien Liberals in Ottawa, all left their mark on human rights programs. When budgets were drawn up, human rights funding was generally allowed to increase, but not in proportion to the increased workloads and responsibilities of the commissions.

Whether measured on a per capita basis or as a percentage of overall expenditures, human rights funding has not grown in pace with the volume and complexity of commission workloads. As indicated in Table 3.3, between 1980 and 1996, while provincial human rights funding per capita increased in real dollars, its rate of growth was relatively modest. In 1980–81, for example, average provincial funding per capita was $0.76; in 1996–97, it was $0.98. This was a 29 per cent increase, but far short of the growth in caseloads during the same period, which increased at twice that rate (see Table 3.1). This analysis does not factor in the increased costs per case over time, nor does it consider the increased demands on commission resources as a result of additional inquiries and referrals and as a result of activities in public education and affirmative action. Between 1980 and 1997, the largest funding increases overall were in Ontario, Quebec, PEI and Newfoundland. Funding was relatively stable in Nova Scotia, New Brunswick, and Manitoba. In Saskatchewan and Alberta (more slightly), funding actually declined. In BC there was a substantial decrease after 1982–83 – reflecting the downsizing by the Social Credit government – followed by an upward trend in the mid-1990s.

Federal funding for the Canadian Human Rights Commission is not comparable to the funding for the provincial commissions. This is because of the broad mandate of the federal commission, which covers pay equity and employment equity as well as antidiscrimination complaints, and because of the broad geographic territory it covers. Table 3.4 shows the pattern of federal funding between 1981 and 1997, including the cutbacks after 1992. Between 1980 and 1992, funding for the federal commission increased erratically from year to year; however, only in 1986 was there an actual decrease in funding relative to the previous year. Although funding increases were erratic during this period, the percentage of total federal expenditures was fairly consistent: as seen in Table 3.4, it was 0.005 per cent in 1981, and increased slightly each year until it peaked at 0.012 per cent in 1992. Beginning in 1993, however, both the levels of funding provided to the federal commission and the percentage of total federal expenditures began to decline. In 1993, funding fell by 8 per cent, and it continued to decrease through the 1990s.

Provincial funding for human rights commissions also can be mea-

78 Restraining Equality

TABLE 3.3
Provincial spending on human rights per capita (real 1991 dollars)

Years	BC	AB	SK	MB	ON	PQ	NB	NS	PE	NF
1980–81	0.64	0.73	1.33	0.92	0.57	0.62	0.66	1.35	0.59	0.19
1981–82	0.67	0.62	1.37	0.92	0.68	0.64	0.70	1.45	0.59	0.16
1982–83	0.68	0.62	1.47	1.09	0.82	0.65	0.75	1.49	0.66	0.25
1983–84	0.46	0.61	1.53	1.07	0.71	0.60	0.74	1.26	0.66	0.25
1984–85	0.17	0.88	1.50	1.17	0.74	0.79	0.78	1.10	0.61	0.23
1985–86	0.38	0.54	1.40	1.22	0.79	1.10	0.77	1.17	0.76	0.15
1986–87	0.39	0.55	1.27	1.04	0.96	1.12	0.84	1.22	0.96	0.27
1987–88	0.44	0.64	1.06	1.04	0.98	1.21	0.87	1.37	0.77	0.38
1988–89	0.43	0.57	1.08	1.14	1.05	1.25	0.83	1.37	0.91	0.43
1989–90	0.51	0.58	1.09	1.18	1.22	1.19	0.78	1.66	1.08	0.42
1990–91	0.53	0.63	1.00	1.19	1.31	1.21	0.86	1.58	1.90	0.45
1991–92	0.49	0.64	1.03	1.12	1.43	1.18	1.05	1.50	1.96	0.45
1992–93	0.70	0.64	1.15	1.19	1.41	1.21	0.77	1.43	2.67	0.50
1993–94	0.64	0.57	1.07	1.19	1.18	1.07	0.70	1.58	1.25	0.49
1994–95	0.72	0.51	1.12	1.27	1.22	1.06	0.80	1.37	0.90	0.53
1995–96	0.77	0.51	1.07	1.24	1.07	0.95	0.79	1.33	0.85	0.50
1996–97	1.30	0.72	0.88	1.15	1.02	1.38	0.79	1.28	0.80	0.48

Source: Based on provincial public accounts, commission financial statements, and census data.

sured as a proportion of overall government expenditures. When provincial human rights spending is calculated over time as a percentage of provincial expenditures, a similar pattern of underfunding emerges.[16] Between 1980 and 1996, expenditures on human rights programs declined on this basis in BC, Alberta, Saskatchewan, New Brunswick, and Nova Scotia. Proportional spending remained relatively constant in Manitoba and Newfoundland. In Ontario, Quebec, and PEI, the proportional spending increased during the middle period but then declined again between the early and middle 1990s. What this pattern shows is the general unwillingness of governments of the time to give human rights commissions a higher fiscal priority, even in the face of their growing caseloads and program responsibilities. A revealing comparison can be made between provincial spending on tourism development and spending on rights protection between 1980 and 1985. In all provinces – even in provinces where the proportion spent on rights protection was the highest (Ontario, Nova Scotia, and PEI) – funding for the promotion of tourism and recreation was always greater.[17]

TABLE 3.4
Federal human rights spending, 1981–97

Year	Commission funding (millions $)	Change (%)	Total federal spending
1981	5.4	–	0.005
1982	5.9	+10	0.005
1983	6.5	+9	0.005
1984	8.5	+31	0.006
1985	9.3	+10	0.006
1986	8.9	–5	0.006
1987	10.3	+16	0.007
1988	11.3	+10	0.008
1989	11.8	+4	0.008
1990	14.0	+19	0.009
1991	17.8	+27	0.011
1992	19.2	+8	0.012
1993	17.7	–8	0.011
1994	17.2	–3	0.011
1995	16.6	–3	0.010
1996	16.3	–2	0.010
1997	15.4	–9	0.010

Source: Based on financial statements of the Canadian Human Rights Commission and on Public Accounts Canada.
Note: Percentage of total spending is calculated in real 1991 dollars for fiscal years in which the indicated calendar year is the last year.

The Impact of Restraint

The immediate result of the restricted funding was that commissions had difficulty coping with growing caseloads and workloads and with meeting public expectations in an era of expanding equality rights conciousness. Common problems were these: inadequate commission staff due to hiring freezes or lay-offs; increased delays in responding to formal complaints; case backlogs; and difficulty carrying out new responsibilities in areas such as affirmative action, race relations, and systemic discrimination. These problems led to sluggish human rights operations and to the symbolic (rather than substantive) treatment of rights. They also led to rising criticism by human rights advocates, minority groups, and even the officials of the underfunded commissions. These criticisms were reported periodically in the media, in the academic literature, and in Auditor General reports, interest group briefs, and legal cases.

For example, the issue of underfunding and backlogs was referred to numerous times in newspaper articles during the 1980s and 1990s. In some articles the problem was presented as a general one being faced by virtually all commissions across the country.[18] Other stories focused on particular provincial commissions, especially the ones in Ontario, Alberta, Saskatchewan, Manitoba, and Nova Scotia.[19] Articles also appeared about the underfunding of the Canadian Human Rights Commission.[20] The issue also surfaced a number of times on television public affairs programs. In 1987 and 1994, for example, CTV ran stories on *W5* about problems in human rights enforcement, including the problem of inadequate funding. As well, reference was made to the problem in academic literature.[21] Authors such as Day, Norman, and Howe and Andrade presented commissions as having developed reputations for being lethargic, slow-moving, and underfinanced. Finally, this subject was a common theme of editorials and articles in the *Canadian Human Rights Advocate*, an advocacy journal of the 1980s and early 1990s that specialized in equality rights issues. Again, the picture drawn by that journal was one of sluggish, underfunded, and understaffed commissions.

The problem occasionally was addressed by provincial auditor's and ombudsman's reports. For example, in his annual report for 1986, the Auditor General of Ontario criticized that province's commission for its long procedural delays. He noted, among other things, that 'it took more than one year for the commission to discover that a hospital was not discriminating against a blind man by refusing to allow his guide dog into a sterilized unit.'[22] Similarly, in a 1993 *Special Report on the Ontario Human Rights Commission*, Ontario's Ombudsman found that the problem of delays in case investigations was both systemic and endemic, and recommended that 'the Commission take immediate action to erradicate its backlog and rectify the inadequacies of its case handling procedures.'[23] Alberta's Ombudsman expressed similar concerns in his 1994 *Report*, in which he recommended an in-depth review of investigative procedures, especially as these related to backlogs, delays, and communications with complainants.[24]

Concerns about inadequate resources also were expressed by human rights interest groups, minority organizations, and women's groups. For example, in Ontario in 1994 the problem of delays and inadequate resources was a recurring theme in interest group briefs presented to the Cornish Task Force, which was reviewing that province's code.[25] Similar sentiments were expressed during reviews of human rights legislation in Manitoba in 1987, Newfoundland and PEI in 1988, Nova Scotia in 1991, New Brunswick in 1992, Saskatchewan in 1993, and BC in 1995. The sentiment also was expressed in a cross-provincial study of the views held by advocacy groups regarding the effectiveness of commissions.[26] A common message was that the calibre of commissions was far from satisfactory and that a large part of the problem related to inadequate budgets and staffing.

Finally, the issue arose in a number of legal cases during the late 1980s and 1990s. A leading one was *Kodellas v. Saskatchewan Human Rights Commission* (1989).[27] Gus Kodellas charged the Saskatchewan commission with unreasonable delay in dealing with human rights complaints made against him. Complaints of sexual harassment had been filed against him in 1982, yet a board of inquiry was not scheduled until 1986. Kodellas successfully obtained a court order staying board proceedings on the grounds that his right to security of person under section 7 of the Charter of Rights was being violated by unreasonable delay. A delay of 48 months was held by the court to be unreasonable. The commission then appealed to the Saskatchewan Court of Appeal. The court ruled in Kodellas's favour, with the following reasoning given: Under the Charter, everyone has a constitutional right to security of person. This right may be violated in unreasonably long legal proceedings, which commonly involve stress and anxiety, high legal costs, disruption of family life and work, and stigmatization of the respondent. As this right must be provided for in the courts, so too must it be provided for in human rights proceedings. In the case at hand, unreasonable delay did occur, and Kodellas's right to security of person was violated, so the complaints against Kodellas could not be heard. Commissions have a duty to proceed expeditiously, and legislatures have a duty to provide the necessary resources.

A similar conclusion was reached the same year in *Douglas v. Saskatchewan Human Rights Commission*.[28] John Douglas, the respondent in a complaint of sexual harassment made 48 months before a board of inquiry hearing, successfully sought a court order preventing the hearing. His argument was the same as that of Kodellas – that there had been unreasonable delay, which violated his constitutional right to security of person. The commission appealed to the Court of Queen's Bench, and the court gave a similar ruling to that in *Kodellas*. But in other cases, decided by the Manitoba Court of Appeal and the Federal Court of Appeal in the 1990s, the argument of delay accepted in *Kodellas* has been rejected.[29] It is thus unclear whether section 7 of

82   Restraining Equality

the Charter provides a remedy for undue delay. What the cases do highlight is the reality of delays in human rights cases, the common lack of resources for commissions to proceed expeditiously, and the problem of procedural justice this poses for both complainants and respondents.

The issue of delay also has been raised in cases on the basis of another section of the Charter – the section 11 right to be tried within a reasonable time. In a series of Ontario cases, delay was held not to be a justification for dismissing complaints. *Gohm v. Domtar* (1988),[30] and in *Dennis* (1990),[31] against the claim that long human rights proceeedings violate section 11 of the Charter, boards of inquiry ruled that legal rights under section 11 do not apply to commission delays in dealing with complaints at any stage. Thus, in reference to section 11 as well as to section 7, there does not appear to be any clear constitutional right against unreasonable delay. Neither do there appear to be any overriding legislative rights against delay. In *Tabar v. Scott* (1989),[32] the board ruled that neither the Code nor other Ontario legislation dealing with procedural rights provides a limitation period for the Commission proceeding to a board hearing. However, this did not mean there were absolutely no time limits. In *Lutz v. Gray's Lakehouse Restaurant* (1990),[33] the board ruled that motions by respondents to dismiss complaints might succeed on the basis of unreasonable delay if the respondent could show it was impossible in the circumstances to make a proper defence. For example, key witnesses or certain kinds of proof might no longer be available. But the onus was on respondents to demonstrate clearly that they could not fully defend themselves because of long delay.

Thus, in legal cases as well as in the media and in official government reports, the issue of delay and inadequate commission resources has periodically arisen. But while the problem has been recognized, rulings have been mixed as to whether cases can be dismissed because of unreasonable delay. On balance, there does not seem to be a clear legal or constitutional requirement that commissions be given adequate resources to handle cases expeditiously. This issue must be dealt with in the political and legislative arenas.

Variations in Restraint

It would be misleading to say that the contraction of budgetary resources was uniform. There were variations from province to province and across time (see Table 3.3). Overall, commissions in Nova

Scotia, Saskatchewan, Manitoba, and Ontario were funded at relatively higher levels than those in Newfoundland, Alberta, British Columbia, and New Brunswick. Commissions in Prince Edward Island and Quebec experienced a considerable degree of fluctuation in funding over time.

In this section we analyse the following factors responsible for the differential patterns of funding: (1) provincial revenues, (2) the relative size of minorities, (3) interest group pressures, (4) the administrative structure of commissions, (5) women in cabinet, and (6) the political party in power. Our attention is restricted to the provincial jurisdiction for comparative purposes. As territorial human rights programs are relatively new, they do not provide a sufficient time frame for comparisons. And as the federal commission mandate and territorial coverage is quite broad, it would be difficult to compare federal funding with provincial. Thus the provincial jurisdiction provides the best basis for comparison. We examine provincial human rights funding among the ten provinces over a seventeen-year period, from 1980–81 to 1996–97.[34] We analyse the factors involved and tie our findings into theories of public policy development. Society-centred theory would predict the importance to funding of societal factors such as interest groups and minority pressures. State-centred theory would predict the importance of factors such as the beliefs and values of policymakers. In our concluding section, we will connect our findings to these theories and attempt to account for government restraint in human rights programs and for variations in that restraint.

We measured provincial funding for human rights administration on a per capita basis. First we gathered funding data from provincial public accounts for the period 1980–81 to 1996–97. This gave us comprehensive data for each province on administrative costs, costs of regular commission or council staff (we did not include the costs of part-time officials borrowed from other government departments), legal costs, and board of inquiry or tribunal costs. Boards of inquiry usually are funded by regular human rights budgets, but where they are not, as in Saskatchewan, we have added these costs. Legal costs are quite significant items in budgets. The manner in which legal costs are met varies from commission to commission. The larger commissions, such as Ontario's, use staff lawyers, and the smaller ones use legal services from a government department or private legal counsel on a case-by-case basis. But such variation was covered in the figures from public accounts. We then had the figures reviewed and verified by the commissions.

84 Restraining Equality

We converted the nominal dollar figures into real 1991 dollars to account for inflation, and then divided the amounts by the provincial population to derive a per capita measure. These figures are summarized in Table 3.3. As indicated in Table 3.3, in recent years the higher-funding provinces have been Ontario, Nova Scotia, Quebec, Manitoba, and (very recently) BC. The lower-funding ones have been Alberta, New Brunswick, and Newfoundland. What accounts for this variation? Possibilities include provincial revenues, the relative size of minority populations, pressure group activity by human rights interest groups, the administrative structure of commissions, the background of decision makers, and the political party in office. One variable we did not examine was differences in public opinion on equality rights. Presumably, these differences could result in different pressures on politicians and different levels of human rights spending. But surveys on attitudes toward equality rights in Canada suggest that provincial variation is not significant.[35] Broad public support for the value of equality has been established across the country.

Revenue Availability

Does the relative fiscal capacity of provinces to spend money in the human rights area make a difference? Revenue availability theories of government expenditure would predict that human rights spending varies with government revenues rather than with factors such as the political party in power.[36] Assuming a relatively even distribution of public and political support for human rights legislation across the country, governments with more revenues would tend to outspend governments with less revenues.

For evidence of this, we compared the per capita human rights spending over time of provinces that have more fiscal capacity, with those that have less. We measured fiscal capacity on the basis of federal calculations for equalization payments, dividing provinces into the 'haves' (Ontario, Alberta, and BC) and the 'have-nots.' As indicated in Table 3.5, revenue status is not a determining factor. Indeed, when spending is averaged out, the have-not provinces spend more than the have provinces on human rights enforcement.

The Size of Minorities

Does the relative size of minority populations in the different prov-

TABLE 3.5
Human rights spending by provincial financial status

Province type	Average spending per capita
Have provinces	$0.74
Have-not provinces	1.14

Source: Based on provincial public accounts.
Note: Have provinces refer to Ontario, Alberta, and BC; have-not provinces refer to the remaining provinces.

inces make a difference for funding? Society-centred theories – and in particular the pluralist theory of policy development – would predict that human rights spending will vary with direct and indirect societal pressures on policymakers. The prevalence of ethnocultural minorities in a given province would be a form of indirect societal pressure. Assuming that minorities are concerned about discrimination relatively evenly across the country, and that they want the legislation strongly enforced through a proper level of funding, politicians in office would find it important as a vote-earning measure to respond in proportion to the size of minorities.[37]

To assess this prediction, first we calculated the percentage of ethnocultural minorities in each province's population. We assumed that these percentages would vary, whereas the percentages for other minorities (e.g., the disabled) and for women would be relatively constant. We looked at ethnocultural minority status in terms of the proportion of the population in different provinces reporting origins other than British or French – the so-called Third Force in Canadian politics.[38] From census data for 1986, 1991, and 1996, we calculated the percentage of persons of European (non-British) origins, native origins, and visible minorities. From the percentages of these three groups, we calculated the percentage of total minorities for each census year and for each province. These data are summarized in Table 3.6.

We then compared the human rights spending records of provinces with relatively higher percentages of ethnocultural minorities and relatively lower percentages. As can be seen in Table 3.6, there is a clear division between Ontario and the Western provinces on the one hand, and Quebec and the Atlantic provinces on the other: the percentage of total minorities is higher in the former and lower in the latter. For each

86 Restraining Equality

TABLE 3.6
Percentage ethnocultural minority population by province

Province	European			Aboriginal			Visible Minority			Total Minority		
	86	91	96	86	91	96	86	91	96	86	91	96
BC	17.4	16.6	13.1	2.1	2.3	2.1	4.7	12.0	17.9	24.2	30.9	33.1
AB	22.0	20.9	16.2	2.2	2.7	7.6	5.8	7.6	10.0	30.0	31.2	28.6
SK	27.0	25.9	19.7	5.6	6.8	7.4	1.8	2.0	2.8	34.4	34.7	29.9
MB	27.8	26.1	20.8	5.3	6.9	7.3	4.2	5.6	7.0	37.3	38.6	35.1
ON	20.3	19.9	17.8	0.6	0.7	0.7	6.7	10.5	15.8	27.6	31.1	34.3
PQ	6.9	7.2	6.4	0.8	1.0	0.8	2.7	4.4	6.2	10.4	12.6	13.4
NB	1.7	1.9	1.5	0.8	0.6	0.9	0.6	0.7	1.1	3.1	3.2	3.5
NS	5.0	5.4	4.0	0.7	0.8	0.9	1.8	2.3	1.8	7.5	8.5	8.4
PE	2.0	2.1	1.8	0.3	0.3	0.3	0.6	0.7	1.1	2.9	3.1	3.2
NF	0.6	0.7	0.6	0.7	0.9	1.4	0.4	0.5	0.7	1.7	2.1	2.7

Source: Calculated from Statistics Canada, Census Nation tables, 1986, 1991, and 1996.
Notes: 'European' origins refers to Western European origins, Eastern European origins, Southern European origins, and other (non-British) origins. 'Aboriginal' includes the single response of Inuit, Métis, and North American Indian. Table does not include the multiple origins category or Canadian origins.

province type (higher minority and lower minority), we compared human rights spending records over time. As the data from the 1981 Census were not as directly comparable for ethnic origins, we limited our study to data from the 1986, 1991, and 1996 censuses. We matched spending data, beginning in 1984, to each census year and to the two years immediately preceding and following each census year.

As indicated in Table 3.7, the size of ethnocultural minority populations does not make a difference. When funding is averaged out, provinces with lower percentages of ethnocultural minorities outspend (by a small margin) those with higher numbers. When minorities are calculated in terms of nonwhite minorities (the total of visible minorities and native groups), the result is the same. Ontario and the Western provinces have a relatively higher proportion of nonwhite minorities, and Quebec and the Atlantic provinces have a smaller proportion.

Interest Group Pressures

Do the activities of human rights interest groups in the different provinces make a difference for funding? According to society-centred and

TABLE 3.7
Human rights spending by ethnocultural minority, population size

Province type	Average spending per capita
Larger minority size	$0.92
Smaller minority size	0.98

Source: Based on Statistics Canada, Census Nation tables, 1986, 1991, and 1996, and provincial public accounts.
Notes: Human rights spending per capita calculated from 1984–85 through 1996–97. Larger minority provinces are Ontario and the western provinces; smaller minority provinces are Quebec and the Atlantic provinces.

pluralist theories of public policy, we would expect human rights spending to vary with direct societal pressures in the form of pressures from human rights interest groups.[39] These interest groups would include women's organizations, ethnocultural groups, organizations advocating for the disabled, native groups, civil liberties associations, and labour organizations. For it is these groups that historically have been associated with pressure group activities and with the enacting and expanding of human rights legislation. In all provinces, they have long lobbied for extensions to antidiscrimination coverage, for a more proactive commission role, and for greater human rights funding and enforcement.

To test for this effect, we included in a survey of human rights interest groups across the country a question about activity levels of the groups.[40] The names of the leading groups in the categories mentioned earlier were gathered from national organizations (e.g., the National Action Committee on the Status of Women, the Canadian Jewish Congress, the Canadian Labour Congress) and from human rights commissions. We asked for the number of contacts made over a five-year period (1988–93) with relevant commission or government officials (contacts were defined as briefs, letters, and participation in public hearings). In all, 182 surveys were returned, in rough correspondence with provincial populations. We calculated interest group activity levels on the basis of average number of contacts made per group, adding up the number of contacts and dividing by the number

TABLE 3.8
Human rights spending by interest group activity

Province Type	Average spending per capita
High group activity	$0.92
Medium group activity	1.09
Low group activity	0.65

Source: Based on survey results and provincial public accounts.
Note: Commissions with high group activity were Ontario, Alberta, and Manitoba; with medium group activity, Nova Scotia, New Brunswick, Saskatchewan, and Quebec; with low group activity, Newfoundland, BC, and PEI.

of groups. We confirmed the results through follow-up interviews with interest group leaders and human rights commission officials. Based on the degree of contact, we then divided provinces into high-activity (Ontario, Alberta, Manitoba), medium-activity (Nova Scotia, New Brunswick, Saskatchewan, and Quebec), and low-activity (Newfoundland, BC, and PEI). If activity levels did made a difference, there would be a correspondence between activity levels and funding. But our findings (see Table 3.8) indicate that there is no correspondence. Funding is greater in higher-activity provinces than in lower-activity provinces; but funding in medium-activity provinces is greater than in higher-activity provinces. Activity in a province like Alberta is relatively high, but funding is low; whereas activity in PEI is low, but funding is relatively high.

It is interesting to note how the groups themselves perceive their own influence. We sent a follow-up questionnaire to groups in the three highest-funding and the three lowest-funding provinces.[41] We asked how effective they thought their interest group activities had been in the past five years: very effective, moderately effective, or ineffective. Most (70 per cent) believed they had little effect (or did not know). Most noteworthy here is that the groups in the highest-funded provinces expressed the least belief in their own effectiveness (77 per cent thought they were ineffective). Groups in the lowest-funded provinces were less likely to express that they were ineffective (63 per cent).

Administrative Structure

Do variations in administrative structures and procedures make a difference in funding? As a practical consideration, we might expect different structures to involve different costs and thus to require different levels of funding. There are similarities and differences in the procedures and administrations of provincial commissions. They are all similar, in that they must establish an administrative framework for receiving, investigating, and resolving complaints. And all commissions also share a common legal environment, in that they are all subject to a common process of judicial review with respect to the rules of natural justice and the application of the Charter. But there are also interesting administrative and procedural distinctions across jurisdictions. For example, Ontario, Quebec, Manitoba, Saskatchewan, and Alberta are noteworthy in that they tend to have more complex provisions respecting complaint procedures, time limits, conciliation procedures, parties to proceedings, conflicts with other statutes, and remedies. Also, the sheer size of the target populations in Ontario and Quebec has resulted in commissions that are quite organizationally complex, replete with various offices and sub-units. In contrast, other commissions have relatively simple procedural frameworks and organizations. In Newfoundland, PEI, New Brunswick, and Nova Scotia, for example, procedures respecting complaint filings, time limits, conciliation, right of appeal, parties to proceedings, and remedies are more basic. Administrative offices are fewer and bureaucracies are smaller. British Columbia is a special case in that its system underwent radical change in 1984 and again in 1996 and that for most of the years between 1984 and 1995 it did not include the important conciliation function that other systems possessed. Thus, as BC's structure has been unique, it is not included here for comparison.

To test for an administrative structure effect, we grouped human rights administrations into three types: high-complexity, medium-complexity, and low-complexity (or simple). We then averaged human rights spending per capita for each type over time. We would expect spending to increase with complexity. But as seen in Table 3.9, this expectation is not met. While there is more spending in high-complexity than in medium-complexity administrations, spending is as high in the simple as in the high-complexity ones. Indeed, spending is higher in Nova Scotia, which has a relatively simple administrative system, than in Ontario, which has a more complex one. The evidence suggests

90 Restraining Equality

TABLE 3.9
Human rights spending by administrative structure

Degree of complexity	Average spending per capita
High complexity	$1.09
Medium complexity	0.49
Low complexity	1.08

Source: Based on commission annual reports and provincial public accounts.
Notes: BC is not included here due to the uniqueness of its system between 1984 and 1995. Commission structures with high complexity were Ontario and Quebec; medium complexity, Manitoba, Saskatchewan, and Alberta; and low complexity, Newfoundland, PEI, New Brunswick, and Nova Scotia.

that administrative structure is not a major influence on rights spending by governments.

Women in Power

The central policymaking body is Cabinet, which ultimately makes the key decisions about allocating budgetary resources. Does the social composition of Cabinet make a difference in human rights funding? We might anticipate, for example, that where there are relatively more women in key policymaking positions, resources allocated for the enforcement of equality rights will be greater. We might expect that women on balance will be more sensitive to discrimination and thus more likely in Cabinet to push for more resources for human rights programs.

To test for this effect, we calculated the percentages of women cabinet ministers in provincial cabinets from 1989–90 to 1996–97 (we begin in the late 1980s, when the numbers of women in office appreciably rise). We might have also calculated the percentages of ethnocultural minority ministers and those with disabilities, but we did not have the data. We divided the provinces into higher and lower women-minister provinces on the basis of a median split. Higher women minister provinces over the time period were Ontario (32.3 per cent average), BC (26.1 per cent), PEI (20.1 per cent), Quebec (19.8 per cent), and Saskat-

TABLE 3.10
Human rights spending by percentage of women in cabinet

Province type	Average spending per capita
Higher percentage of women in Cabinet	$1.11
Lower percentage of women in Cabinet	0.91

Source: Based on data from the *Canadian Parliamentary Guide* (1989–96) and provincial public accounts.
Notes: The division between province types was calculated on the basis of a median split. Provinces with the highest percentage of women, in order, were Ontario, BC, PEI, Quebec, and Saskatchewan. Provinces with the lowest percentage of women, in order, were Newfoundland, Nova Scotia, Alberta, Manitoba, and New Brunswick.

chewan (17.8 per cent). Lower women minister provinces were Newfoundland (6.6 per cent), Nova Scotia (6.7 per cent), Alberta (15.3 per cent), Manitoba (15.4 per cent), and New Brunswick (16.8 per cent).

As seen in Table 3.10, gender seems to make some difference. Funding is somewhat higher overall in provinces with more women ministers. However, the relationship is not significant statistically. A correlational analysis of spending patterns and percentage of women in Cabinet indicated that there is no relationship between the number of women in Cabinet and the amount of spending on human rights ($r(N = 80) = .1275$). Indeed, comparisons between particular provinces suggest that gender is not a factor. In Nova Scotia, where human rights funding is higher, there are few women in Cabinet. In BC (after 1991), where funding was relatively low until 1996, the percentage of women in Cabinet is high. While it may be difficult to generalize from this short time period, the results suggest that what is important may not be the gender of policymakers but rather their beliefs and commitments. However, this question requires more research on other social characteristics of cabinet ministers, such as ethnicity.

Political Party in Office

Does the political party in office make a significant difference in funding patterns? Ideological theories of parties, as presented by William Christian and Colin Campbell, would predict human rights funding to

TABLE 3.11
Human rights spending by governing political party

Governing party	Average spending per capita
New Democratic Party	$1.05
Liberal Party	1.01
Conservative Party	0.89
Parti Québécois	0.80
Social Credit	0.48

Source: Based on data from the *Canadian Parliamentary Guide* and provincial public accounts.

vary with party.[42] One would expect leftist parties (NDP, PQ), which place greater emphasis on social equality and state intervention, to outspend rightist parties (Social Credit, Conservative Party), which emphasize free markets and smaller government. And one would expect centrist parties (such as the Liberal Party) to be in the middle of the spending pattern. It are be anticipated that differences in political philosophy or party ideology are reflected in differences in commitment to the enforcement of equality rights.

To test for this possibility, we averaged human rights spending for the different parties across provinces and over time. As shown in Table 3.11, political party indeed does appear to make a difference. The left-to-right ideological spectrum generally was related to differential levels of human rights spending. The highest spenders were governments of the most left-of-centre party, the NDP. The lowest spenders were governments of the most right-of-centre party, Social Credit. And as predicted, the Liberals followed the NDP in spending, while the Conservatives followed the Liberals. Somewhat outside the expected pattern was the PQ, which was second only to Social Credit in low spending. Part of the reason for this anomaly perhaps was that the PQ was in office for only seven years, at the beginning and very end of the under consideration. Meanwhile, across the time frame, the NDP was in office for 24 years, the Liberal Party for 46 years, the Conservative Party for 80 years, and Social Credit for 11 years. Overall, the ideology-based theory seems to hold. That the NDP has demonstrated the greatest support for human rights spending is consistent with survey research showing that NDP leaders and their supporters believe more strongly in equality rights than their counterparts in other political parties.[43]

It is interesting to note variations in human rights spending in terms of individual premiers. In the top five are Donald Cameron (PC, Nova Scotia, $1.50), Catherine Callbeck (Liberal, PEI, $1.42), Allan Blakeney (NDP, Saskatchewan, $1.35), John Buchanan (PC, Nova Scotia, $1.34), and Bob Rae (NDP, Ontario $1.33).[44] In the bottom five are Brian Peckford (PC, Newfoundland, $0.26), William Van Der Zalm (Social Credit, BC, $0.46), Clyde Wells (Liberal, Newfoundland, $0.46), William Bennett (Social Credit, BC, $0.50), and Donald Getty (PC, Alberta, $0.60). What is striking is that while party ideology, generally, is associated with human rights spending, the commitment of particular premiers and their cabinets seems to be important also. For example, while Conservative Donald Cameron was the highest spender, Conservative Brian Peckford was the lowest. Liberal Catherine Callbeck was in the top five, yet Liberal Clyde Wells was in the bottom five. NDP premiers Blakeney of Saskatchewan and Rae of Ontario ranked third and fifth respectively, yet Michael Harcourt of BC ranked eighth from the bottom. Thus, apart from general party philosophy, the value that particular premiers place on human rights enforcement seems to be a major factor.

It is also interesting to note the linkage between political leadership and human rights spending in the federal arena. We cannot compare federal with provincial spending, given that the Canadian Human Rights Commission differs from its provincial counterparts in its much wider mandate and territory. Even so, it is interesting to see what our prime ministers have done over the same time period (1980–96) to fund the federal human rights commission. For this analysis we have studied only those prime ministers who were in office long enough to oversee budget preparations (thus, John Turner and Kim Campbell are excluded). Again we examine human rights spending per capita, using the overall Canadian population and public accounts as the basis for analysis. Somewhat surprisingly, despite the recent climate of social spending restraint, Prime Minister Jean Chrétien has been the most generous human rights spender per capita over the report period ($0.57). He is followed by Brian Mulroney ($0.54) and Pierre Trudeau ($0.40). Combined, the Liberals average $0.49 compared to the Conservatives' $0.54. Clearly, this finding does not conform to the left-to-right pattern found at the provincial level. It may be that individual leaders and cabinets make more of a difference than party ideology.

In reference to theories of public policy development, the state-centred theory seems better able to account for variations in government support for human rights legislation; social and economic pressures seem to have a more limited impact. The evidence further indicates that societal forces in the form of interest group pressures and the prevalence of minorities do not exercise direct influence over human rights policymaking. Policymakers do not make their funding decisions on the basis of interest group demands or electoral calculations. The evidence also suggests that economic factors, such as the availability of revenue, are not decisive. Nor is the distribution of provincial revenues a factor, as indicated by the fact that Alberta and BC are outspent by their poorer cousins, Nova Scotia and PEI.

The evidence does suggest, however, that the ideological or philosophical preferences of premiers, their cabinets, and their policy advisers do make a significant difference. While in office, politicians from left-of-centre parties as a rule outspend politicians from the right. This appears to reflect historical ideological differences over the issues of social equality and the proper role of the state. Historically, those from the left have been more committed to policies of state intervention on behalf of equality and social reform. Those from the right have been more hesitant, for a variety of reasons: greater distrust of government bureaucracy; greater concern about the costs of social spending and the deficit; and a general preference for relying on market forces, and on private solutions to the problem of discrimination (e.g., through education), rather than on legal and administrative remedies. This philosophical difference partly explains variations in human rights funding.

This interpretation also highlights the leading role that premiers and their cabinets can play in the determining human rights priorities and policies. The evidence supports the arguments made by Perlin, Wearing, and Whitaker[45] that parties in power become highly élitist bodies, even by cadre party standards, as premiers and cabinets vest themselves with the authority to set the political and administrative direction of their governments. Once parties become governing parties, the influence of the caucus and of the extra-parliamentary party wanes substantially. While one can still observe ideological differences between parties, the ideological vision of the governing party is very much conditioned by the perspective of the party's leadership. This dynamic lends credence to the state-centred approach to policymaking. In the policymaking process one must distinguish between the influences held by the extra-parliamentary wing of the governing party, by its caucus, and by the ruling élite in Cabinet. The evidence suggests that it is Cabinet which plays the pivotal role of setting the ideological tone and practical direction of the government and the governing party.

As has been noted often in Canada, however, differences between left and right and among parties are not as simple as first appear.[46] Those with a 'conservative' ideology may be far to the right, as in 'neoconservative,' but they also may be somewhat to the left in many respects, as in 'red tory.' A red tory Conservative would support human rights legislation not in terms of social rights philosophy but in terms of a paternalistic duty to take care of the disadvantaged. Thus, some Conservative leaders and Conservative Parties may be to the right, not too distant from Social Credit (or the Reform Party), but others may be left-leaning on the issue of social equality, closer to the Liberals and NDP. This may explain Conservative variations in human rights spending. Those premiers more influenced by red tory thinking, such as Cameron and Buchanan of Nova Scotia, spend more on human rights; while those influenced by neoconservative perspectives, such as Peckford of Newfoundland and Getty and Loughheed of Alberta, spend less. Thus the role of ideology comes into play with respect not only to party label but also to particular party leaders.

This ideological explanation of human rights policy highlights the importance of a state-centred approach to understanding policy development in the human rights field. The key actors seem to be governmental leaders and their senior policy advisers, not individual citizens, human rights interest groups, or even rank-and-file members of parties. This is not to imply that these societal forces have no impact on the development of rights policy. It *is* to imply that their impact is only indirect, and arises from their ability to contribute to the development of the political cultures in which particular leaderships, parties, and governments exist.

Why Human Rights Restraint?

All governments in Canada placed their human rights systems under fiscal restraint during the 1980s and 1990s. What accounts for this? On the one hand, there was a strong official commitment to human rights legislation across Canada. The legislation had acquired the status of primary law, and in many of the codes and acts it had primacy over all other legislation. As well, human rights legislation was declared by the Supreme Court of Canada to contain 'fundamental' and 'quasi-constitutional' law. While it did not have the status of the Charter, the Court declared it to be of special constitutional importance. Yet in actually administering and enforcing the legislation, governments subjected human rights budgets to substantial fiscal restraint. Funding was not increased to match the expanded workloads of commissions. This requires some explaining.

We begin our analysis by returning to the point made in Chapter 1: that by the 1980s the human rights system in Canada had become part of the 'embedded state' – that is, deeply established in Canadian society and in the policy process. Commissions had become embedded agencies of human rights protection and promotion, symbolic of Canada's concern with equality rights and with society's commitment to fight discrimination. A hostile government such as the Social Credit government in BC might revamp an existing human rights system, but it did not dare eliminate the system completely: human rights legislation simply had become too deeply entrenched in Canadian society and political consciousness. Even the partial revamping carried out by the Social Credit government in 1983 and 1984 aroused widespread public condemnation. More serious change, in the form of eliminating the system, would not have been tolerated.

That human rights commissions had become embedded in Canadian society did not mean they were immune from fiscal restraint. The severe fiscal restraint imposed by the Social Credit government in BC in 1983 was a signal of developments about to occur across the country in the 1980s and 1990s. Governing parties of all ideological stripes came to believe in the need for major fiscal restraint as a means for reducing deficits and for dealing with the forces of globalization. For the Social Credit in BC, this belief came early. For the NDP in Ontario, governing the early 1990s, it came later; for the federal Liberal Party, governing in the mid-1990s, it came later still. In facing the economic recession of the early 1990s, the Ontario NDP initially pursued a Keynesian spending policy, but then turned to fiscal restraint. At the federal level, fiscal restraint came in stages: under the Mulroney Conservatives it was moderate; and under the Chrétien Liberals, especially with the 1995 budget, it was more severe.[47] But despite the timing, virtually all governing parties and policymakers came to believe (some more reluctantly than others) in the need for serious fiscal restraint in dealing with problems of deficits and debts.

The underlying logic of this belief is as follows.[48] Governments in Canada face a new reality: the growing forces of globalization and international competitiveness. With globalization, countries are becoming more and more interdependent, so Canada must develop policies that enhance its economic and industrial competitiveness. More than ever before, the Canadian economy, Canadian corporations, Canadian workers, Canadian provinces, and indeed Canadian society are in global competition with other economies, corporations, workers, provinces, and societies. International competition for investment, sales, jobs, and economic activity is becoming increasing intense. While this new reality must be faced by all countries, it is especially important for trading nations such as Canada to do so. With growing international competitiveness comes the need to expand support for business, to deregulate business activity, to reduce corporate taxation, and to decrease government spending and intervention. In this new world dominated by the mobility of capital, governments are unwise to set policies that encourage corporations and investors to transfer their investments and holdings to other countries or other provinces. Because international corporations can now move their business operations to other jurisdictions, they have greater leverage over governments. Policymakers must therefore minimize the chances of losing investment, jobs, and their tax base. Hemmed in as they are by globalization and international competition, their policy options are limited.

According to analysts such as those connected with the Fraser Institute and the C.D. Howe Institute, in dealing with globalization the problem of deficits must be addressed. Their reasoning is based on the premise that deficits force governments to borrow money on international money markets in order to finance their shortfalls. It follows that governments must repay those loans, with interest. One problem with large deficits is that a large share of government revenues must go to interest payments and debt service charges, rather than to expenditure items. This problem is compounded when interest rates are high and when government revenues flatten out. Because a large part of the money that federal and provincial governments borrow is raised outside the country, another problem is foreign indebtedness. Countries that finance their deficits in foreign financial markets increase their dependence on those markets. Canadian governments thus become vulnerable to high interest rates and to the credit ratings of international investment houses. Finally, because governments absorb a considerable portion of private sector investment, another problem is that the private sector is crowded out. Government borrowing displaces other, more productive uses for the money of investors.[49]

According to the same analysts, it follows from all of this that governments have little choice but to give top priority to reducing and eliminating the deficit (and perhaps later the debt). And to this end, they have little choice but to cut or restrict government and social spending. The alternative is to increase taxes, but this would lead to political opposition (middle and upper class resistance to more taxation), to a dampening of investment, and to capital flight. Thus, the only viable alternative is fiscal restraint and spending cuts. Fiscal restraint is necessary in order to balance the budget and sharpen the competitive edge of the country or province.[50]

Such has been the general logic of fiscal restraint – logic that has become conventional wisdom among policy advisors and policymakers. But why was this thinking applied to human rights commissions in particular? Why was it applied despite official recognition that human rights legislation is fundamental law in Canada? While the evidence does not allow for conclusive answers to these questions, a number of administrative and political factors seem to have been in play. An administrative factor was that across-the-board budgetary cuts or restrictions generally are much easier to implement than selective cuts or restrictions. Given the opposition that inevitably arises to cuts, governments generally are reluctant to reduce expenditures. But if they cannot avoid it, it is much easier for them to distribute the burden relatively evenly across programs, agencies, and departments rather than on a selective basis.[51] Those affected may not be happy, but they also realize that no special preferences have been given to particular programs or groups. Although particular agencies and groups that believe themselves special may be resentful, administrative bodies as a whole accept across-the-board reductions more easily than other kinds of cuts. Governments are aware of this, and it encourages them to apply across-the-board cuts, which apply to human rights commissions just as to other government agencies. Thus one factor in human rights restraint has been the general use of a managerial approach to implementing fiscal restraint – an approach in which exceptions are anathema.

An important political factor was the lack of strong public pressure for human rights funding. In considering targets for fiscal restraint, governments usually are more hesitant to target programs for which public commitment is very strong: the political cost is too great. When public commitment wavers or weakens, governments find it easier to apply restraint to those same programs. This is what generally happened with human rights programs during the 1980s and 1990s. On the one hand, as indicated by public opinion polls and by the continued legislative expansion of protections, public support for equality rights remained high across the country.[52] For example, a substantial majority of Canadians expressed support for the equality rights for women, the disabled, ethnocultural minorities, and other minorities. This support encouraged governments to continue expanding human rights legislation: wider legal protection may mean political gains without substantial financial costs. On the other hand, as was also indicated by the polls and by government action, there was a wavering of public commitment to government spending in aid of minorities and women.[53] In an environment of economic insecurity and uncertainty, the public was more critical of the size of government and more willing to allow social program cuts, including cuts to programs for minorities and women. While certainly not enthusiastic about all areas of spending cuts, especially in the health care system, the public came to accept the general need for spending cuts and for the scaling back of social program spending. By the mid-1990s, this acceptance was substantial, as indicated in the year-end 1996 *Maclean's*/CBC poll.[54] This growing acceptance gave governments the opportunity to apply restraint to human rights spending and to other program spending.

It is important to note that support for a value in the abstract is not the same thing as commitment to that value in concrete situations. Public support for equality rights is not the same thing as commitment to human rights funding and enforcement in times of economic insecurity. This difference can be explained in reference to the classic work of Abraham Maslow.[55] According to Maslow, there is a hierarchical order to human needs. Individuals first seek to fulfil basic subsistence needs such as for food and shelter. When these needs have been met, says Maslow, they continue their search until they have accumulated enough material needs to achieve a reasonable margin of economic security. Priority is given to materialist and security-related values such as a growing and stable economy and law and order. Security having been attained, individuals turn to higher-order needs such for belonging, dignity, and the fulfilment of intellectual or artistic potential. Priority is given less to security and materialism and more to broader values such as community well-being, environmental protection, and social equality. Expanding rights consciousness flourishes under such conditions, as does support for the principle of equality rights.

However, upon a return to an environment of insecurity and scarce resources, such as in Canada during the 1980s and 1990s, individuals become more obsessed with their own well-being and less concerned with broader social values. In this environment, abstract support may be given to equality rights, but commitment to their enforcement is likely to weaken. Human rights interest groups and particular individuals who are victims of discrimination may be very concerned about human rights funding and enforcement. But citizens whose lives are remote from the operations of human rights commissions will be generally much less concerned. They will be more preoccupied with issues that affect them more directly, and with immediate and pressing economic concerns. This perspective makes it much easier for political decision-makers to subject human rights systems to fiscal restraint: they are not under public pressure to do otherwise.

Another possible reason for the lack of strong public pressure for human rights funding was the public's ambivalence toward the affirmative action component of human rights legislation. On the one hand, there was wide support among the Canadian public for the principle of equality rights. This principle was understood in the traditional sense of equal treatment and equal opportunity without discrimination. On the other hand, as indicated in survey research, many Canadians also were ambivalent or plainly opposed to affirmative action, which is understood as preferential treatment to historically disadvantaged groups.[56] Exceptions were citizens in Quebec and partisans of the NDP and PQ, who expressed majority support for the principle. This general public ambivalence toward (or opposition to) affirmative action suggests that as commissions became involved in recommending or ordering affirmative action programs during the 1980s and 1990s, support weakened for the overall enforcement of human rights legislation.

Given the above attitudes, governments were not encouraged by the force of public opinion to maintain human rights spending at the old levels. The embeddedness of human rights commissions in Canadian society did not allow for their elimination. But changing economic conditions and shifts in public values did allow for funding cuts. As we observed, these cuts varied in depth across the country. Governing parties of the left, with their deeper ideological commitment to social equality, resisted the slippage more strongly than parties of the right. But in the absence of strong public pressure and in the context of the forces of globalization and deficit reduction, all governing parties were encouraged to restrain human rights spending as well as other public spending.

4. Coping with Restraint

As we saw in Chapter 3, today's human rights commissions face an administrative environment marked by underfunding and fiscal restraint. At the same time, most commissions have seen their legislative mandates remain stable, when they have not increased in breadth and complexity. As a result, commissions are facing increasing criticism from rights advocates, and are seeking ways to improve their 'service delivery.'

In this chapter we will consider how financial restraint has affected human rights commissions and how these agencies are coping with this reality. We will start with a theoretical debate regarding the best means for government bodies to deal with restraint, providing an overview of the reinvention/reform discourse as found in the current literature on public administration. The bulk of the chapter will then be given over to an empirical assessment of how commissions across this country are actually dealing with their straitened circumstances. We will assess matters ranging from the reconfiguration of case management techniques through to issues of organizational design and educational programming. We will highlight that the changes underway in commissions reflect more the reform than the reinvention of human rights policy and administration in this country.

The Context of Contemporary Rights Administration

Commissions have been mandated the task of promoting equality rights, and this requires them to perform a broad array of administrative, adjudicative, and educational activities, and many rights advocates are calling upon commissions to adopt even more activist and interventionist roles in the interest of rights promotion. At the same time, commissions across the country are confronting the grim reality of funding restraint. Commissions have been witnessing their operational workloads increase; most have also seen their funding decline in relative terms. All commissions are being required to maintain if not improve their service delivery while consuming fewer financial resources. In the 'new governmental reality,' they are being called upon to do more with less.

Human rights agencies, of course, are not alone in confronting fiscal restraint. Many other types of agencies are also undergoing the wrenching process of organizational redesign in order to become more economical, efficient, and effective. According to some, the broader organizational dynamics at work here constitute the 'reinvention' of government. According to authors such as Osborne and Gaebler, Borins, and Purchase and Hirshhorn,[1] governments throughout the Western world are confronting great financial and popular pressures to fundamentally reconfigure the ways in which they operate and the scope and nature of the services they provide. And in various instances, governmental bodies are said to be 'reinventing' themselves as they establish new approaches to public administration.

In contrast to this position, authors such as Savoie, Trebilcock, and Thomas,[2] recognize the need for administrative change to accommodate financial pressures, but are sceptical that these changes can or should lead to a 'reinvention' of government. These authors suggest that incremental reform, rather than rationalistic reinvention, will be and should be the appropriate governmental response to demands for greater economy, efficiency, and effectiveness in program administration.

This chapter will consider carefully these broad debates respecting current and future trends in public administration; the focus will be on how federal and provincial human rights agencies are coping with the pressures of restraint.[3] In implementing expanding mandates with relatively or absolutely diminished institutional resources, these agencies have been forced to reconceptualize and reconfigure how they perform their roles. Concomitant with this process we are currently witnessing certain intriguing experiments in institutional redesign and renewal. All human rights agencies, to a greater or lesser extent, are reassessing their institutional mandates, their exercise of discretion, and the procedures they follow for implementing their duties.[4]

The Reconfiguration of Public Administration: Reinvention or Reform?

In recent years there has been a growing theoretical and practical debate about how to improve governmental organizations and services. Governments throughout the Western world are seeking ways to balance budgetary restraint with service delivery, and there has been an explosion of interest in methods for achieving this. By far the most celebrated work on the future of public administration is that of two American analysts, David Osborne and Ted Gaebler. In their treatise on 'reinventing government,' which borrows heavily from the private-sector management reform movement of the 1980s, these authors stress that governments must reorganize themselves to be less bureaucratic and more catalytic. Rather than being institutions providing traditional public goods and services to their societies by traditional means, governments need to become institutions that provide strategic leadership to their communities, and create socio-economic and administrative environments for the public and private generation and supply of needed goods and services. In the words of Osborne and Gaebler, governments need to be concerned more with 'steering rather than rowing.'[5]

The argument is made that as part of this redesign of government, governing institutions must become much more market-oriented: they should be transformed from 'rule-driven' organizations that focus on administrative 'inputs,' into 'mission-driven,' 'results-oriented' bodies concerned with the policy and service 'outputs' of government work. They should be geared to 'customer service'; they should be community-centred and as decentralized as possible; and they should be competitive. According to the reinvention thesis, governing institutions need to be entrepreneurial in their thinking about the services they provide; they need to anticipate developing trends in the service 'demands' of their 'customers'; and they need to be able to respond to these demands through a variety of means, from traditional service methods through to market-oriented approaches such as contracting out, public/private partnerships, and fee for service. According to Osborne and Gaebler, the result will be a system of governance that is more responsive to public needs and at the same time financially viable and politically more accountable.[6]

The idea that contemporary government can and should be 'reinvented' along market lines is not foreign to this country. In Canada the reinvention thesis is supported by various analysts, including Borins, and Purchase and Hirshhorn. In defending the 'new public management,' Borins is quick to stress that the concept of reinventing government is not a 'simplistic Big Answer,' a panacea to current fiscal problems, but rather a theoretically and practically viable reconfiguration of public administration. In keeping with the general position of Osborne and Gaebler, Borins contends that a growing body of empirical evidence from Canada and abroad confirms that through major innovations in service delivery, managerial autonomy, and the use of performance indicators geared to competitive, entrepreneurial models, the nature and quality of government services can be dramatically improved.[7] The new dynamics of innovation, spurred both by the public's demand for greater services and by government's need to restrain costs, are now, according to Borins, a fundamental part of the organizational environment facing all governments in the Western world. According to this approach, which is endorsed in the work of Purchase and Hirshhorn, reinvention is the shape of things to come.

According to these authors, reinvention is part of the 'post-bureaucratic paradigm' in public administration, in which the core concepts of the old 'bureaucratic paradigm' – namely, the 'public interest,' 'efficiency,' 'administration,' 'functions, authority, and structure,' and 'cost justification' – are to be transcended by other, stronger principles. In this new mode of thinking, public administration will be centred on considerations such as these: 'results citizens value,' 'quality and value,' 'production,' the identification of 'missions, services, customers, and outcomes,' and the delivery of 'value.'[8] The means to these ends range from the consolidation and streamlining of bureaucratic organizations, through to the development and use of new information technologies, and the inauguration of entrepreneurial, market-oriented ways for public sector managers and staff to perceive and undertake their work in society.[9]

The proponents of 'reinvention' and the 'new public management' have been quite effective in publicizing their views, to the point that many Western governments, to various degrees, have seized upon this approach. But the reinvention thesis has not gone unchallenged. The concept has faced criticism within the United States;[10] and in Canada, Savoie has been among its most eloquent detractors. Influenced by the work of James Q. Wilson, Savoie contends that the 'new public administration' is 'basically flawed' in that it purports to offer a highly rationalist, drastically different approach to public administration. Its prescriptions, however, are predisposed to fail because they do not recognize that government policies and programs exist in a world of political and legal constraints ranging from public expectations of service standards, to established practices and professional understandings of bureaucratic actors, to judicially recognized rights to given administrative procedures. In a world in which policies and programs develop in a climate of practical wisdom, diplomacy, and respect for political/legal trade-offs, administrative decision making is inherently incremental and restrained. This 'slow and steady' approach to public administration not only accords with empirical realities but, according to Savoie, is theoretically desirable. This is because cautious, gradual reform, rather than rationalist reinvention, allows for accumulated wisdom to develop that is sensitive to specific political, legal, and administrative factors. This, in turn, provides ongoing intelligence to decision makers regarding whether any given procedural or substantive change to existing policy and administration is valuable and viable, and capable of being implemented successfully in any given policy and program field, given existing constraints and limitations peculiar to the given situation.[11]

This defence of reform over reinvention is also reflected in the work of Trebilcock and Thomas. The former, in keeping with Savoie, supports the need for governments to carry out their duties more economically and efficiently; but he also contends that 'institutional evolution, rather than revolution in the way governments do their work is all that we can reasonably aspire to.'[12] Besides the constraints of the law, and of accepted policy and program understandings, Trebilcock also stresses the importance of established administrative cultures within bureaucracies and the interrelationship between those bureaucracies and the broader political environment within which any institution exists. Given that both are 'embedded' in one another, in Cairns's terminology,[13] a radical alteration of one is unlikely unless it is supported by, and influenced by a like change in, the other. And as Trebilcock suggests, a fundamental reinvention of democratic politics and public expectations respecting public service and the role of the state is not to be observed in this society. The public is concerned about greater efficiency and economy in the public bureaucracy, but there is no broad public consensus favouring a radically altered, commercialized, and downsized public sector.[14]

Thomas echoes these concerns, stressing that change within any organization, public or private, is contingent on a host of factors, including 'size, structure, process, leadership and culture.'[15] The ability to adapt is important for any organization, as Thomas stresses, but one should beware the allure of a fundamentalist, holistic prescription – the 'Big Answer' spoken of by Savoie. In Thomas's analysis, substantial organizational change 'tends to be disorderly, disjointed and problematic. There is no magic recipe for success.'[16] Within the public sector, then, bureaucratic reconfiguration emerges incrementally, in an environment in which managers respond to pressures for reform and to the political and institutional expectations, rules, and conventional understandings that constrain their behaviour. As does Trebilcock, Thomas affirms the importance of administrative culture as crucial to the process of change: 'Culture has replaced structure as the most popular variable in the organizational change process.'[17] Significant change in government organizations is thus contingent on that change being in accordance with, and supportive of, established and respected values, attitudes, and beliefs regarding the appropriate role of government institutions and of the state generally. Given the incremental nature of attitudinal and philosophic change, the pace of this change will be slow and measured rather than quick and radical; change in government organizations thus involves reform, not reinvention.[18]

Human Rights Commissions and Reinvention

What would a reinvented human rights agency look like? If the federal and provincial governments were to address the operational and fiscal tensions confronting rights agencies through a major reconfiguration of these bodies, in keeping with the theoretical vision of Osborne and Gaebler, what would be the practical result? In this section we will consider the reinvention/reform dynamic by establishing a reinventionist archetype as a basis for comparing theory with practice.

If we applied Osborne and Gaebler's elements of reinvention to a rights agency in a rough way, the following organizational design would likely be encountered. The agency would be 'catalytic.' It would 'steer' rights policy and enforcement through a variety of public/private partnerships, through rewards and incentives for those complying with rights policy, and through the innovative use of new information technologies, communication services, and even volunteer labour. The agency would be 'community owned.' It would be closely tied to community groups, with group members and leaders sharing fully in the management and administration of the agency. The agency would promote strong 'client' access to its operations.

The agency would also stress 'competitive' government. It would promote the privatization of a number of its functions, with any necessary adjudicative services to be provided by private firms competing for this work. Similarly, other agency functions such as public education, research, and document production would be contracted out to service providers on the basis of cost-effectiveness. In this manner, the agency would be 'mission-driven.' Its management would focus more on policy 'results' than on 'rules and regulations.' Desired ends would be promoted in a variety of innovative ways such as providing financial rewards to agency officials and contractees for efficient and effective work. Likewise, regulated firms might receive financial and tax rewards and other incentives for complying with rights policy and law. In all instances, cases would be screened rigorously to ensure that only those problems truly in need of agency services would be addressed. Cases that could be dealt with through less intrusive and expensive forms of conciliation and mediation, would be. Also, cases that could be transferred to other forums, or dismissed entirely as peripheral to the agency's concerns, would be.

Taken together, these initiatives would establish an 'enterprising' and 'anticipatory' agency: one that sought to blend rights services with an entrepreneurial mentality. Thus, user fees for various services and goods would be commonplace, as would be the dynamic use of agency funds in various private investments designed to generate capital for agency initiatives. In this manner, the agency would be promoting its own financial well-being while anticipating and responding to changing circumstances in its policy environment. Ultimately, all these initiatives would make the agency 'market-driven.' It would be protecting and promoting human rights through a series of actions and approaches designed to marry service effectiveness with organizational efficiency and financial stability and profitability.

Human Rights Commissions: Coping with Restraint

Throughout the 1980s and 1990s, most human rights commissions have had to reconfigure themselves in the face of increased workloads and depleted resources. A number of governments have reviewed their human rights policies and procedures with the goal of improving them.

By far the most radical of these reviews was Ontario's. The Cornish Report of 1992 offered a burning indictment of that province's system of rights enforcement, stressing that its system was so outmoded that changes were needed urgently. The report commented that the 'current model was developed when discrimination was understood more as an individual problem. This view is outdated and wrong.'[19] In assessing the commission's current operations, the report was equally blunt, stressing that the commission was plagued with 'excessive delays,' and was placing a misguided emphasis on individual rights claims, 'with the result the Commission has not challenged systemic discrimination in a strategic and proactive way.'[20] Furthermore, while some commission officials were credited as being 'sometimes helpful and dedicated,' others were 'sometimes uninformed, insensitive and biased.'[21]

The report asserted that the existing rights enforcement system was inadequate: 'The Task Force was told many times that the present system is seen as so ineffective that there is no point in making a claim. Those the Code is meant to serve said they have no confidence in the human rights system.'[22] In seeking to remedy this sorry state of affairs, the Cornish Report called for a major reorientation of rights protection. It argued that the system should move away from its focus on individual rights protection and show deeper concern for systemic discrimination. As it boldly proclaimed, 'discrimination is entrenched in Ontario society,' and this required a major proactive response.[23] This response would centre on the commission being more an advocate for human rights promotion and protection, as opposed to a concerned third party. The commission was to support the 'empowerment' of those experiencing discrimination; it was to promote a 'compliance culture' through 'proactive measures' and 'serious sanctions'; it was to focus on issues of systemic discrimination and was to actively promote rights education and discrimination awareness. As further reform, a new, independent human rights tribunal was to replace the existing system of boards of inquiry. Underlying all of this was the demand that the commission's financial resources be significantly increased.[24]

The Cornish Report was scathing in its criticisms of the Ontario system and far-reaching in its recommendations. Other provinces have also subjected their human rights systems to meticulous review. Over the past decade, major reviews have been undertaken in New Brunswick, Saskatchewan, Alberta, and BC.[25] These reports have steered clear of the vociferous condemnations that characterized the Cornish

Report; even so, they have directed attention to a number of perceived problem areas. Common to all these reports have been recommendations that rights policy be taken more seriously by governments; that public education programs be expanded; that the scope of rights protections be enlarged; that commissions be given stable and enhanced funding; that problems of case delay be addressed through improved managerial techniques; and that permanent adjudicative tribunals be created based on the federal and Quebec models.

In response to these pressures across the country demanding that commissions do more – often much more – with respect to rights protection and promotion, observers, advocates, and officials in the human rights community have expressed concern about the levels of government funding for commissions and about the effect on their work of fiscal restraint. While senior commission officials have been understandably reluctant to publicly criticize the funding they receive, it is nevertheless noteworthy that a substantial majority of these officials have commented on the problems their agencies face because of underfunding. All these officials contend that despite the 'fiscal crunch,' their agencies have been able to maintain high-quality service and to fulfil their legal and administrative obligations; that being said, certain tensions can be discerned as well as certain intriguing initiatives.[26] Given the 'new fiscal realities,' rights agencies across the country have been engaging in a significant re-evaluation and redesign respecting how they manage cases that come to them, and how they carry out their other responsibilities. This redesign, however, bears more resemblance to organizational reform than to reinvention.

Rethinking Case Management

As there can be no right without a remedy, remedial functions are integral to rights commissions. It is with respect to the management of cases, however, that many commissions encounter their greatest problems. And it is with respect to the handling of cases – their investigation and disposition – that commissions are most likely to confront vociferous criticism from interest groups. Because of expanding grounds for rights protection in the 1970s and 1980s, coupled with increasing rights consciousness among the general public over this time period, most commissions have experienced significant increases in their caseloads. As these caseload increases have generally not been matched by funding increases, the administrative result has usually been case delays or backlogs. The following concern, voiced by the Saskatchewan Commission, is representative of a dynamic encountered nationwide: 'At the end of March 1996 ... the commission's core funding was cut by 9.2 percent. This reduction required the commission to reduce the number of permanent investigators to below 1986 levels. As a result, the backlog of unassigned cases can be expected to grow every year. By the end of March 1997, some people may be facing a wait of well over a year for an investigation of their case to begin.'[27] In similar vein, in the summer of 1995 senior officials of the commissions in Nova Scotia, New Brunswick, Ontario, and Alberta, for example, were reporting routine delays of three to six months between the filing of a complaint and the initiation of case investigation by a human rights officer.[28]

Once a case is under investigation, its duration can vary greatly depending on a host of factors, ranging from the perceived validity of the complaint in the eyes of commission officers, to the case's complexity, to the willingness of the affected parties to conciliate. Though the vast majority of cases are either dismissed or resolved within three weeks of investigation, complex cases have been known to consume six to eight months of investigation, conciliation, and negotiation.[29] If a negotiated settlement cannot be reached and the case goes to a board of inquiry, there will be delays while a hearing is scheduled and (at least) two sets of legal counsel are formed, in addition to the time required for the hearing itself. While most boards of inquiry seldom require more than two days of hearing time, some have been known to last for weeks. When board decisions are appealed or judicial reviewed, particular cases can drag on for three to four years.[30]

It is delays and backlogs such as these that embitter the opinion of rights advocacy groups. Their criticisms are now a common refrain.[31] The same criticisms have also been made by various rights policy review panels. In 1994, Alberta's review panel had this to say: 'The serious problem facing the Commission is that there are too many cases, too few staff and an increasingly unwieldy backlog. Time and again during the public hearings we were reminded that "Justice delayed is Justice denied."'[32] These criticisms have even been made by some ombudsman's offices. The Manitoba Ombudsman's Office, for example, has roundly criticized the Manitoba commission for failing to implement procedures to expedite the flow of cases through the organization. Similar complaints about awkward administrative practices have been levelled by ombudsman's offices in Nova Scotia and Ontario.[33] As noted in the previous chapter, delays can also result in significant litigation, with respondents challenging commission procedures and behaviour as constituting a violation of the right to be 'tried' in a reasonable time. This type of litigation not only is costly and time-consuming for all involved but also directs public attention to the procedural weaknesses of commissions rather than to their policy strengths.

The need to expedite case flows and greatly reduce if not eliminate backlogs is recognized by senior officials in all commissions as a lead priority. This point has also been addressed by Charles Ferris in his review of rights policy in New Brunswick: 'Throughout the course of this work, the refrain has echoed that some means must be found to obtain a speedier resolution of complaints. The perception shared by practitioners and other experts is that it is easiest to resolve a human rights complaint at the time the allegation of discrimination arises. The passage of time, it is argued, results in a hardening of positions followed by resort to more formal legal procedures.'[34]

Yet effective caseflow management is no easy thing to establish, in that legal rights and duties are at stake, as are the procedural entitlements associated with natural justice. While there is a common desire among senior officials to expedite decision making, there is also an awareness that rushed justice is often justice denied. These officials accept the responsibility that commissions bear for procedural integrity – a responsibility that is also stressed repeatedly by those who represent respondents and business groups. Commissions have often been criticized by such parties for using intrusive and meddlesome tactics in their pursuit of less than reasonable allegations of wrongdoing.[35] Though these criticisms often have been unfair and do not take common case procedure into account, they have done much to impress on commissions that they must be highly sensitive to the fact that they are law enforcement agencies, and bear all the responsibilities for fairness and due process that such a designation carries. When commissions move to promote more efficient and effective case management practices, they must do so fully aware that they need to be, and to be seen to be, impartial and judicious regulators.[36] Clearly, the balancing act they face is fraught with difficulties.

In seeking to address the problem of case backlogs and delays, commissions have either adopted or are in the process of adopting a number of administrative reforms. Given these organizations have similar mandates and confront similar administrative strains, it is not surprising that their major reform initiatives have much in common.

Case Screening

First, all commissions have sought to improve their intake procedures by developing more rigorous approaches to case screening. At the time of initial contact, commission officers have always exercised significant discretion as to whether to accept or reject or refer complaints. All commissions have the authority, formally or informally, to reject complaints as frivolous or vexatious, or as falling outside their jurisdiction. All commissions also have the discretionary power to advise a complainant that there may be a more suitable venue for pursuing a complaint – for example, a labour relations or workers' compensation board.[37] While commissions have long exercised discretion in this way, the need to expedite cases, and to manage cases with fewer resources, has led them to exercise this discretion in certain new ways.

Many commissions have introduced screening procedures whereby incoming complaints are assessed not only for their conformity to the agency's mandate but also in light of the commission's given policy priorities. In Nova Scotia, for example, the commission gives priority to those valid complaints in which the complainant is an AIDS sufferer or is currently employed in a workplace that is the site of alleged harassment related to occupation. All other valid complaints are placed in queue for an available rights officer.[38] Saskatchewan has a similar but more striking policy of giving priority to cases that raise interesting and important questions of human rights law as perceived by the commission. Thus, complaints respecting sexual orientation and same-sex benefits are likely to receive preferential consideration over 'routine' cases of discrimination based on race or religion.[39] Yet another approach is found in Manitoba. There, the agency divides complaints into 'A' and 'B' cases, with the former referring to obvious violations of the act, and the latter referring to cases in which the spirit but not the letter of the law seems to have been violated. In drawing this distinction, officials exercise substantial discretionary judgment, and they admit that in the 1990s, because of the need to reduce caseloads and commission expenses, they have become much more strict in establishing this threshold. They also admit that this increased strictness has led to growing frustration among many complainants, who are told that their complaints are grade 'B' and not worthy of investigation.[40] All screening initiatives are designed to highlight and promote the claims of persons who are particularly vulnerable or needy, or claims that are exceptionally notable. But this process involves tradeoffs, as well as the 'ranking' of complaints. This prioritization does not reflect misplaced values within commissions so much as the constraints that commissions face as a result of diminished funding.

Screening is also conducted by certain commissions in the area of systemic discrimination. Agencies such as those in Quebec, Ontario, Nova Scotia, Saskatchewan, and PEI have long recognized that this form of discrimination is most pervasive and serious, especially with respect to women and visible minorities; but other commissions either discount the issue or claim that their resources are inadequate to address it. Officials in Quebec and Saskatchewan were adamant in stressing the importance of focusing on claims of systemic discrimination, their reasoning being that such an approach is best able to attack discrimination at its roots, and that remedial action against systemic discrimination, such as employment equity plans, is an efficient and cost-effective way to benefit large numbers of people in affected groups.[41] In these provinces, cases involving systemic bias are thus given priority. This approach, however, is downplayed in practice in such provinces as Alberta and Newfoundland. These commissions take a more traditional and restrained approach to case management, in the belief that discriminatory treatment is best addressed on an individual case basis, and that by resolving particular cases and eliminating discriminatory treatment in particular cases, future discriminatory treatment will decline overall. One possible advantage to this approach is that offensive behaviour can be addressed without the need for elaborate and expensive investigations into cases of systemic discrimination.[42]

Investigation and Conciliation

Commissions have also been working to develop more expeditious ways to resolve cases accepted for review. All commissions are placing more emphasis on resolving cases through speedy conciliation. Senior human rights officials in Canada almost universally emphasize that in situations where code provisions have clearly been breached, the most desirable outcome is a speedy settlement overseen by a human rights officer and endorsed by the parties involved and by the commission.[43] This interest in negotiation, conciliation, and settlement is by no means new: mediation and conciliation have been at the heart of commissions' work since their inception. As Tarnopolsky has long stressed, the key role of commissions is to attack discriminatory behaviour, not to engage in lengthy legal battles – hence his contention that commissions should always emphasize fast conflict resolution.[44]

This emphasis is found in all provinces. In fact, many commissions are developing formal or quasi-formal initiatives to promote early-settlements. The commission in Ontario has an early-settlement initiative designed to identify cases in which mediation has a likely chance of success and to encourage the parties to reach a compromise settlement.[45] Commissions throughout Atlantic Canada have adopted less formal means to the same end. In Newfoundland, Nova Scotia, and New Brunswick, commissions instruct rights officers to push for mediated resolutions wherever possible.[46] In New Brunswick, rights officers are encouraged to engage in informal mediation within the first forty-eight hours of a case being launched. If, over the phone, a human rights problem arising out of a misunderstanding or lack of knowledge and sensitivity can be resolved to the satisfaction of all parties, then this sort of informal action is desirable, both to the parties involved and to the agency. Of course, this approach only works if the commission can successfully avoid backlogs, and if rights officers have the time to engage in such work. Other commissions in Western Canada have mandated similar initiatives.[47]

However, this greater emphasis on conciliation and compromise-making can create subtle problems relating to the commission's priorities and to the consistency of its case dispositions. Conciliation has always been one of the basic tools used by commissions in their pursuit of justice; but in certain circumstances, conciliation can inhibit the achievement of justice. As Ronald Dworkin has long argued, compromises in the interpretation and application of rights in society should never result in compromised rights.[48] All commission officials were united on this point. Commissions clearly recognize that when they bring parties together in an effort to resolve their differences, they must balance the desire for a negotiated settlement with the need to adhere to the principles enshrined in legislation and recognized in jurisprudence. However conciliatory or adversarial the given parties, similar fact situations must reach similar ends. In the same vein, the presence or absence of private legal counsel at the conciliation stage should not be allowed to affect the substantive outcome of any case. An emphasis on conciliation cannot be allowed to inject variability into any commission's application of the law.

Commission staff are well aware of this tension between conciliation and consistency. Most commissions require their rights officers to submit their negotiated settlements to senior staff and commission members for approval.[49] This way, senior staff can make certain that the negotiated settlements are faithful to the law and to jurisprudence. Note, however, that this oversight procedure is only a standard operating procedure, and is not mandated by law. Potentially, this weakens its value as a safeguard.

Moreover, within some commissions there are concerns about how funding patterns may affect settlement practices. A number of officials are worried that increased workloads, static or diminished levels of staffing, and increasing case backlogs are encouraging commissions to adopt overly flexible standards of discretionary decision making. The concern is that rights officers will be given greater flexibility in negotiating settlements so as to bring them about more quickly. This will expand the number of cases that any one officer can handle, by reducing their complexity; it will also reduces the number of cases requiring full board investigation, and thereby reduce the work (and costs) to be borne by commissions at this stage of final adjudication. This concern that pressures for greater efficiency may threaten the effectiveness of commission decision making is still theoretical; even so, there are growing and disquieting indications that funding constraints are affecting the discretionary judgment of certain commissions.

The increasing scepticism directed toward claims of systemic discrimination in Nova Scotia, New Brunswick, and Alberta suggests to certain rights advocates that the commissions of these provinces are becoming less rigorous in enforcing racial and gender discrimination. Similarly, the growing case backlogs and delays in Ontario, coupled with a growing conservative counterreaction there to expansive rights policy – as evidenced through critical commentary in the media and business community, and in the election of the Mike Harris government – suggests to many rights advocates that the Ontario commission is beginning to change its discretionary approach in the direction of becoming much more restrictive in interpretating its legislation.[50] These are matters for future research into whether, and to what degree, financial and administrative pressures, as well as broader social and political pressures, have resulted in a mandate shift respecting the discretionary judgment of commissions. But clearly, the pressure is there, is being felt, and is a concern to commission officials.

Caseflow and Management Information Systems

As commissions throughout Canada struggle to develop new, more efficient, and more economical ways to manage cases, it is not surprising that they are adopting information management systems. Most commissions have fully computerized their case records or are in the process of doing so. This makes rights officers more efficient in their paperwork and enables senior officials to closely monitor the processing of cases. The experience of the Saskatchewan commission is quite representative: 'Over the past three years, the commission has addressed investigative delays through procedural change and policy development. For example, it developed the early resolution process and completely computerized all investigative records. In 1993 and 1994, it adopted policies setting investigation priorities and establishing a one-year limit on the right to file a complaint.'[51] If there is a surprise in this development, it is the length of time it has taken most human rights agencies to appreciate the importance of systematically overviewing and analyzing case management trends, and of developing rigorous standards of caseflow management. The courts have been developing and using caseflow management systems for well over a decade; only recently have most commissions embraced these systems as a priority.[52] Some officials suggest that this use of caseflow management techniques heralds a more rigorous and systematic handling of cases.[53]

Indeed, all the reforms we noted earlier – modified intake procedures, case screening, enhanced conciliation initiatives – can be explained in terms of commissions assessing their case flows more rigorously. Such assessments help determine points at which procedures can be modified. As Solomon and Somerlot argue in their analysis of court administration, enhanced knowledge gained from the close observation of caseflow patterns allows performance measures to be established that can become benchmarks for operational and managerial accountability.[54] Quebec, for example, has developed time guidelines for the disposition of cases.[55] Similarly, the New Brunswick commission has declared that within forty-eight hours of contact an initial response will be rendered to the complainant.[56] Ontario has a highly developed case-tracking system that tells its officials at which stages proceedings are most commonly delayed, and that measures productivity at particular stages of the process and for particular officers.[57]

Boards of Inquiry and Adjudication

Reform initiatives have also been directed at the board of inquiry or tribunal stage of complaints. Note that while the work of boards, and increasingly tribunals, tends to be the most newsworthy activity in human rights administration, only a small proportion of complaints proceed to this stage: only 3 to 5 per cent of cases require that an adjudicative hearing be established.[58] According to the Cornish Report, in 1991 in Ontario only some 2 per cent of cases were referred to a board of inquiry. Likewise, the 1996–97 annual report of the BC commission noted that only 3.3 per cent of that province's cases proceeded to board adjudication.[59] As noted earlier, most complaints are either screened out at the outset or resolved through conciliation. The remainder however, become important not only on account of their legal and moral complexities but also on account of their costs. Many officials were quick to assert that boards pose the single greatest financial management problem for commissions, since boards entail costs, such as legal fees for adjudicators and counsel, and often rental costs for hearing facilities, and since the required number and duration of boards in any given year cannot be predicted.[60] This problem is felt most acutely in the smaller provinces, where an abnormally high number of lengthy board hearings can drastically affect a commission's budget. In PEI, for example, the great increase in funding for human rights administration in the late 1980s and early 1990s was solely attributable to the significant number of political discrimination cases flowing through the board process.[61] Commissions in Atlantic Canada have come to struggle with this issue, and have recently been joined by those of Saskatchewan and Manitoba.[62]

A number of initiatives in this area have been undertaken or are being considered across the country. Some commissions are moving to control costs by controlling the fees paid to board participants. In many jurisdictions, especially in Atlantic Canada and Manitoba, board members are remunerated by a set per diem fee, and these fees are being scrutinized more and more closely. In those provinces where commissions retain private legal counsel to carry their litigation, the fees for these services are likewise coming under restraint. For example, the Newfoundland commission imposes a flat $75 per day fee for counsel services.[63] Officials from other commissions have remarked that a fee this low inspires expeditiousness, whereas the much higher fees in the larger provinces tend to result in prolonged legal argument.[64]

With a similar concern for expediting hearings, and thereby reducing overall costs, commission officials across the country are emphasizing the importance of rigorous caseflow management and case investigation as means for speeding up the presentation of cases before board hearing officers. Well-researched, well-organized, and well-documented cases generally result in faster case resolutions, because they make it easier to arrive at reasoned decisions.

Many commissions (or their responsible ministries) have established rosters of persons qualified to act as board officers. These persons – usually lawyers or legal academics – are thoroughly familiar with human rights law and procedures, and form a nucleus of talent and knowledge that can be routinely called upon to serve on boards as the need arises. The benefit of this 'pool approach' is that such members generally do not need to be 'educated' by legal counsel regarding the details and nuances of rights law and jurisprudence. Conversely, these board members are able to hold counsel to high standards of case presentation and analysis.[65]

As outlined in Chapter 2, the logic of this approach – valuing established wisdom and knowledge, expertise, consistency, and relative permanence and order – has informed substantial reconfigurations of the human rights adjudication process in Quebec and BC end at the federal level. And as a result of these initiatives, other jurisdictions – notably Ontario, Alberta, and Saskatchewan – have gained models to emulate. The first move in Canada toward establishing a permanent rights tribunal was in 1985, when the federal government created a rights tribunal comprising a pool of officials who could be drawn upon, on an ad hoc basis, to hear contested cases. This agency has been highly praised as an expert, independent, and expeditious, yet sensitive, force for resolving disputed rights cases. However, given its nature as a quasi–ad hoc body with a relatively large membership, not all of whom contribute equal amounts of time and effort to the tribunal, this body's influence on other jurisdictions has been only partial. The idea of a permanent tribunal has been increasingly accepted by human rights administrations in this country and, in this regard the development of the federal tribunal has been significant; some jurisdictions, however, have experimented with this organizational design.

In 1990 Quebec became the first province to establish a tribunal staffed with permanent rights officers. This body was given the task of hearing and deciding all human rights complaints requiring a 'board' resolution.[66] Quebec's tribunal has been praised for bringing high standards of knowledge and expertise to case adjudication, for its sensitivity to rights policy, and for its concern for the speedy administration of justice. It has been commended by the province's rights advocacy groups and business associations. Officials with the Quebec commission respect the tribunal's legal work, and point out that it is a leader in rights jurisprudence not only in Canada but also internationally. That English-Canadian rights advocates know little about this tribunal is explained, with sadness, as being a result of the language divide that separates the Quebec tribunal from the rest of the country. Because the vast majority of its decision making and jurisprudence is produced in French, the vast majority of English Canadians are unaware of its work.[67] This is not to suggest that human rights officials in the other provinces are unaware of the work of this tribunal; quite the contrary.

This tribunal model is now beginning to attract the attention of senior rights officials in a number of other commissions. As noted in Chapter 2, when the BC government amended its human rights legislation in 1996, it established a permanent tribunal for hearing disputed cases. In Ontario, the Cornish Report advocated that a permanent rights tribunal be established along the lines of the Quebec model;[68] but in the fall of 1995, Ontario's Progressive Conservative government opted instead to establish an adjudicative format that was much more permanent than the previous system of ad hoc boards yet still fell short of the Quebec model.[69] The Ontario system now provides for a 'standing board of inquiry,' comprising both full- and part-time members, that possesses the legal powers of a statutory tribunal. These officials are fully empowered to hear and resolve all disputed cases arising under the legislation, to interpret the Ontario legislation as they deem appropriate, and thus to develop a consistent jurisprudence that is consonant with the principles of administrative law as subject to judicial review. This Ontario system is still in a state of flux, and some senior officials with the board fully expect their organization to evolve toward the Quebec model, with a large institution staffed completely by full-time, permanent officials.[70]

In Alberta and Saskatchewan, human rights policy reviews have called for the establishing of permanent rights tribunals. In Alberta, the provincial government accepted this recommendation in 1995, and in 1996 amended the Human Rights, Citizenship and Multiculturalism Act to establish a 'Standing Human Rights Panel.'[71] In defending this change in the adjudicative process, the Department of Community Development stressed how such a panel 'would develop expertise in the adjudication of human rights matters,' and how the permanent panel 'would be cost effective and assist in cutting back significantly on the time a complaint takes to go through the system.'[72] Of course, these arguments echo those previously advanced in Quebec and at the federal level. Alberta's tribunal system is unique, however, in that the legislation stipulates that members of the panel will be chosen from the members of the commission itself; thus, members of the commission will be called on to act both as commission officers and as tribunal adjudicators. Whether this blending of responsibilities will rise above allegations of institutional bias remains to be seen; this arrangement will surely be subjected to judicial review. In contrast, Saskatchewan's proposal for a permanent tribunal is much more consistent with the Quebec model; the Saskatchewan government is leaning toward establishing a tribunal that will be completely independent of the commission.[73]

Officials in Atlantic Canada recognize the organizational and jurisprudential benefits to be gained from permanent tribunals, and the financial savings to be generated thereby, and are now reviewing the tribunal model as a reform option. In New Brunswick, the Ferris Report has advised that province to establish a 'panel of adjudicators' and a 'chief adjudicator,' all of whom will provide expertise for resolving disputed cases.[74] In the other Atlantic provinces, commissions are small, as are their workloads, and some officials suggest that the best approach would probably be to expand the mandate of existing provincial labour relations boards to include jurisdiction for rights disputes. In Newfoundland, for example, the labour relations system already uses ad hoc adjudicative panels for resolving disputes, and the same people often adjudicate both labour relations panels and human rights boards. Advocates of amalgamation stress that the formal union of the two roles would provide the benefits witnessed within Quebec, and would do so without raising serious administrative difficulties.[75]

Everywhere in the country, the pressures of fiscal restraint are leading officials to re-evaluate how they administer rights policy and to consider creating new institutional forms for implementing such policy.

Public Education

The realities of fiscal restraint have been leading many commissions to reform their case management practices. Commissions have also been reassessing how they carry out their public education responsibilities. Officials from all commissions continue to stress that public education programs are central to the work of their agencies; and that this work, while it accounts for only a small part of commission time and funding, is integral to the promotion of rights awareness within society. The reasoning here is that as public awareness of rights issues increases, the incidence of discrimination will decrease. Thus, education remains a central feature of commission responsibilities.

This priority, however, is under financial constraint across the country. Educational practices are being carefully reviewed, certain educational activities are being cut back, and innovative methods are being developed to provide educational services in effective and economical ways. Officials of every commission except Quebec's admit reluctantly that financial restraint is compelling their agencies to reduce the number of educational events and information sessions that commission staff may attend. Officials are accepting fewer public speaking engagements at schools, universities, and service clubs because their growing case loads and administrative responsibilities are placing too great a premium on their time.

Notwithstanding these assertions that public education is important, in most rights agencies, again except Quebec's, public education initiatives do not have quite as high a priority as commission officials would have citizens believe. This secondary status for education policy in practice reflects the primary function of human rights legislation, which across the country is to establish an administrative and legal framework for receiving, investigating, conciliating, and if necessary adjudicating rights complaints. Thus, in times of financial restraint, most commissions look for savings in nonprimary areas of their mandate. This accounts for the streamlining of activities relating to educational policy and administration.

Because of this enforced rationalization and priorization of educational activities many senior commission staffs are establishing interesting alliances with various rights advocacy groups. For example, the commissions in Newfoundland and Nova Scotia generously provide womens' and minority rights groups with agency pamphlets, flyers, and reports, and encourage these groups to disseminate this material through their own educational activities.[76] Similarly, the agencies in New Brunswick, Ontario, Manitoba, and British Columbia are providing educational materials to school, college, and university instructors interested in teaching rights-related modules or courses.[77] A senior official in New Brunswick emphasized that the priority was to publicize the material, not the people disseminating it. Commissions view this informal delegation of educational activities as an economical way to reach their audience, and as far more efficient than in-house programs.

In keeping with this approach, many commissions – in Alberta, Saskatchewan, Manitoba, New Brunswick, and Nova Scotia – are seeking to establish human rights education as a part of the social studies curriculum in high schools.[78] Commissions provide the schools with teaching materials – documents, videos, projects – while leaving the actual teaching to the schools' professional staff. This approach gets a commission's message out in a way that reaches thousands of formative minds.

In the matter of alternative program delivery systems, New Brunswick's commission leads the country in developing the Internet as an educational resource. The New Brunswick commission is 'wired,' with a web page that provides information on the commission, the act, and complaint procedures as well as highlights of particular procedures, such as for sexual harassment and racial discrimination.[79] Other commissions, such as Quebec's, have followed suit in developing Internet resources; still others, such as Ontario's, Nova Scotia's and those of the Western provinces, are preparing to use this technology.[80] New Brunswick officials contend that in the future, people will be able to use the Internet to file complaints, which will be entered immediately into the commission's database and information management system.[81] As computer technology spreads through society, initiatives such as these will expedite the flow of cases into case management systems, though the main challenge will be the same: to screen complaints quickly and manage cases expeditiously.

In creating innovative educational programming, the Quebec commission is quite progressive. Over the past decade this commission has repeatedly demonstrated the practical value of agency-sponsored public conferences on particular issues of interest to the commission, interested groups, the media, and the general public. Conferences about race relations in the Montreal taxi industry and with respect to the Montreal police, and most recently about gay rights, have provided forums where serious matters of rights policy can be explored and assessed. And, as officials from the commission are quick to note, these conferences are highly cost effective. The commission acts as organizer and host and provides a venue for presentations, debates, and colloquia over a number of days. Representatives of rights advocacy groups, other governmental bodies, business, and universities are invited to participate. These people provide the conference with its essential substance; commission officials act as *rapporteurs* for the agency. The commission benefits from the exchange of ideas and from the criticisms and suggestions generated; it also benefits from the media exposure that such conferences generate. As a return for its investment of some thousands of dollars in organization and rental costs, the commission receives a bonanza of free media publicity that reaches the entire province and that highlights the importance of the issue being discussed and the commission's leading role in addressing it. Officials with the Quebec agency emphasize that their conferences are among their most important educational initiatives, as well as an imminently pragmatic use of scarce resources.[82]

Traditional educational programming is contracting in most provinces, yet it continues to grow in Quebec. The most recent impetus for this growth has been the recent enhancement of the Quebec commission's role with respect to children's rights (see Chapter 2). The commission has been mandated a special role in promoting children's rights, and a significant aspect of this role involves the promotion of public education about these rights. To this end, the Quebec commission has undertaken a variety of research projects relating to children and teenagers. One has focused on child labour, especially among children under fourteen. Another has dealt with the right to daycare services for children afflicted with HIV/AIDS. Still another study was devoted to the issue of sexual discrimination in education and to the problem of girls receiving differential treatment in teaching, with the result that educational and career paths for girls and boys become quite distinct.[83] The commission disseminates its research findings in a number of ways: reports, media releases, community meetings, and educational events in the schools themselves. By means of this latter mechanism, the commission brings its own research and public education teams together with the institutional and personnel resources of Quebec's school systems. In this manner the commission obtains additional support for its educational initiatives, while remaining the driving force behind these undertakings.[84]

The interaction between commissions and the business community is fertile ground for innovation. Officials with all commissions were unanimous in expressing support for cordial relations with business. Many human rights disputes arise in the workplace, and commission officials recognize that the best way to reduce discrimination and create a positive work environment is to promote rights awareness among business owners, managers, supervisors, and employees. Employers' groups have often been critical of rights policy, seeing it as an intrusion on the private sector; commissions realize this and understand that a sound rapport with business is vital to the work of commissions.[85] This is why we see commissions developing communication links with businesses, and generally being far more proactive than is traditional. Rather than simply enforcing the law, commissions now are much more likely to seek out businesses – large and small – and provide them with seminars and workshops on the nature of the law and on how to develop personnel policies and practices that conform with the law. As commission officials stress, early compliance is far cheaper and more efficient than complaint investigation and litigation.

All commissions report using special, business-oriented seminars to disseminate rights information. Officials in a number of provinces, including Nova Scotia, Quebec, Ontario, and Alberta, also note the encouraging phenomenon that large businesses and business umbrella groups are beginning to contact their commissions for information and advice respecting compliance with human rights legislation. This has been most observed in reference to race relations, gender relations, and employment equity; commissions are able to provide legal advice to firms with respect to establishing personnel policies that will accord with human rights policies.[86] Senior officials with these agencies are encouraged by this phenomenon, as it suggests to them that they are developing a relationship with business in which firms view them as legal advisers as well as law enforcers. This emerging relationship has led officials in some commissions to consider initiating user fees for the legal advice they give businesses. These fees would be very competitive with private legal fees, but the returns could still be significant for institutions facing straitened financial circumstances.[87] Commissions are being compelled to be more 'businesslike,' and as a result the business community itself may end up footing the bill for their activities.

Systemic Discrimination

Fiscal restraint has also had a strong effect on commission responsibilities in the area of systemic discrimination. In the 1980s, most commissions moved away from their traditional focus on individual cases in favour of the more elaborate and proactive systemic approach. This change came about for a number of resons. Rights advocacy groups lobbied strongly for this new approach; at the time, in the political arena they were developing and legitimizing the concept of systemic discrimination, their argument being that it was the most effective means of attacking discrimination and that special programs of affirmative action and employment equity were justified. This pressure from without was coupled with support for systemic approaches within many commissions. Most senior officials in rights agencies came to support the systemic approach. In Ontario in 1992, the Cornish Report came down in favour of this new approach, and was favourably received by the Ontario commission. As this report stressed: 'A frequent recommendation was to focus much more attention on overcoming systemic discrimination. Significant progress toward equality has not been, and will not be, made through taking the same kinds of individual claims over and over again.'[88] This boded well for a move toward systemic approaches across the country. Support for investigating systemic discrimination was endorsed, in turn, by British Columbia, Saskatchewan, Manitoba, Quebec, New Brunswick, Nova Scotia, and Prince Edward Island.[89] The Saskatchewan commission has defended its move toward systemic approaches thusly: 'The complaint system is an inadequate method of transforming the working environment. Complaints have very limited impact. They usually address only a single issue in a single workplace, only after discrimination has occurred, and only of a complaint is filed ... In contrast, employment equity programs focus on positive results. They seek to hire and promote members of groups which have traditionally been excluded from employment opportunities for reasons unrelated to ability. They provide comprehensive coverage and protect employers from complaints of discrimination.'[90]

Initiatives with respect to systemic discrimination and employment equity have also been significant at the federal level. In 1996 the Employment Equity Act was amended to strengthen protections for women, visible minorities, native people, and the disabled, and to extend the ambit of the legislation so that it also applied to companies and Crown corporations subject to federal regulation. The new law requires all 'federal employers to submit annual reports on the representation in their ranks of people from the four designated groups. They also retain the obligation to conduct analyses of their workforce and employment systems in order to develop appropriate action plans.'[91] The legislation also assigns important duties to the federal human rights commission. This agency is now mandated to audit the employment equity reports of all federal employers subject to the act and to advise employers on how best to 'systematically achieve the sort of diversity that exists in Canadian society and in the labour force at large.'[92] The commission's compliance officers now have the authority to seek, through 'persuasion and negotiation,' specific undertakings by employers for improvements in employee situations where quantitative data suggest that the organization may not be meeting its employment equity objectives. The commission is also empowered to issue legal directives to an employer should this process of informal mediation fail, and such an order can be appealed to a tribunal panel. Officials of the federal agency hope that these substantial new powers will help advance employment equity policy objectives. Yet even the commission recognizes that the impact of the new act will take years to assess and that its importance will be tied to the strength of its enforcement.[93] This latter point is of great concern among the provincial commissions.

Financial constraints are compelling some provincial commissions to re-evaluate their support of systemic initiatives. In New Brunswick, for example, senior commission officials are worried that because of increasing demands for service, coupled with restricted funding, systemic investigations may have to be de-emphasized or foregone. The critical factor here is held to be the amount of time, effort, and funding required to assess and demonstrate systemic discrimination. Such investigations are far more complicated than 'routine' cases of individual discrimination, in that systemic investigations require time-based longitudinal studies of employment or service practices affecting entire classes of people. Studies must document patterns of employment or service delivery in a way that distinguishes nondiscriminatory from discriminatory patterns. From a collective perspective, systemic policies focus on addressing discriminatory practices at their roots. However, this approach to rights policy enforcement is double-edged. While many rights advocates stress that it is the most logical approach to addressing discriminatory behaviour, the very logic of the collective approach demands that collective behaviour be studied in depth over time. Studies of this kind are costly, time consuming, and often highly controversial, in that they seek to describe the social patterns of entire groups rather than the explicit behaviour of particular individuals.

These concerns are more than theoretical; they are highly practical, and are being voiced, albeit in muted tones, within many of Canada's commissions. Within the New Brunswick commission it is being discussed whether scarce agency resources might be better invested in traditional, individual investigations rather than elaborate systemic studies.[94] The same issue is being raised within commissions in Nova Scotia, Prince Edward Island, Manitoba, and even Ontario. These discussions are often tinged with regret, in that senior officials in these bodies remain convinced of the value of systemic investigations.[95] This is more evidence that fiscal restraint is beginning to influence commission priorities and objectives.

The Ontario commission has reported on how difficult it is becoming to carry out systemic investigations in a climate of financial restraint while continuing to address individual complaints. As Rosemary Brown, the province's chief commissioner at the time, stated in 1996: 'While the focus on enforcement and the processing of approximately 2,000 individual complaints filed annually has often meant that the proactive work has suffered, the Commission has continued in its attempt to address issues of systemic discrimination and to carry out public education.'[96] The implicit message here is quite clear: the commission is being forced, because of funding restraints, to concentrate its resources on core activities – namely, the management of individual complaints. This has limited its ability to undertake the more expansive policy goal that it set for itself in the late 1980s and early 1990s. The commission is striving to achieve its goals respecting the investigation of systemic discrimination, but these goals are being rendered more and more peripheral relative to its core responsibilities: the investigation and resolution of individual cases.

This dynamic is not coincidental, an unintended byproduct of fiscal restraint. Quite the contrary. In 1995 in Ontario the Progressive Conservatives under Mike Harris campaigned on a platform that called for an end to systemic discrimination programs, in particular the Employment Equity Act, which the previous NDP government had passed. The PCs defended this approach to rights policy by stressing that they, like many in society, believed that systemic approaches to combatting discrimination were themselves discriminatory, and resulted in reverse discrimination, and corroded good race, ethnic, religious, and gender relations. They did not reject the principle of rights protection; rather, they stressed that the appropriate mechanisms for dealing with violations of human rights were to be found in the procedures for individual complaints outlined in Ontario's human rights code. The PCs stressed that the commission would continue to play a vital role in administering human rights policy, but insinuated that this role would be attenuated to embrace the new government's more traditional values.

Restraint and Reform

As the foregoing illustrates, in recent years human rights agencies across this country have been involved in a process of reconfiguration. In an effort to address broad governmental demands for fiscal restraint while improving their efficiency and effectiveness, agencies have launched a host of new initiatives ranging from the mundane to the substantial. They have adjusted their staffing and their training procedures; they have reset their policy priorities respecting systemic discrimination; they have revamped their educational programming; and they have reformed their procedures for case adjudication.

All of these changes are best understood in terms of organizational reform, not reinvention. The initiatives witnessed are tied much more closely to the theories of Savoie, Trebilcock, and Thomas than to those of Osborne and Gaebler, Borins, and Purchase and Hirshhorn. Notwithstanding the broad, sweeping claims of the latter authors that Western governments are undergoing a process of reinvention, developments in Canadian human rights policy fall squarely within the bounds of reform. The changes observed in rights policy and administration simply are not as broad and rationalistic as those envisioned by the proponents of reinvention. While they are making changes, human rights agencies are not radically reinventing themselves. They are not becoming catalytic, market-driven, entrepreneurial bodies seeking new, private-sector models for delivering public services; as a result of their changes, the implementation of human rights policy will not be substantially different from before. On the contrary, the established entitlements are still in place, as are the procedures that flow from them. The changes being made amount to administrative fine-tuning. Similarly, although various agencies are experimenting with educational partnering, resetting their priorities, and contemplating user fees, these initiatives hardly amount to the 'reinvention' as envisioned by Osborne and Gaebler. For all the changes underway within Canada's human rights commissions, these agencies haven't changed their identities much. There are a number of broad reasons why.

First, all human rights agencies are constrained by their legislative mandates and legal obligations as to how and to what degree they can change their organizations and procedures. Agency jurisdiction, the scope of rights protection, complaints procedures, and the composition and functions of boards and tribunals are all established by law and cannot be easily altered. In Quebec, British Columbia, Ontario, Alberta, and Saskatchewan, substantial changes in adjudicative processes were achieved only by legislative amendment and after years of study and planning. The reforms to the federal commission were made somewhat more quickly, because of the need to respond to a Supreme Court judgment, but even these required a legislative enactment. Furthermore, all agencies are bound by administrative law jurisprudence as established by the courts; this means that the rules of natural justice and fairness must be adhered to no matter how organizational procedures are redesigned. In the same way, any operational reforms must be consistent with a commission's legal obligations as they relate to such matters as bias, error of law, and jurisdictional competency. These legal obligations, which are external to the discretionary authority of agency management, significantly constrain management's ability to reinvent procedures. So in a very real sense, agencies and their responsible governments are limited in the changes they can make to human rights procedures.

Second, the broad legal frameworks that have been established reflect approaches to human rights that have been developed and accepted by various provincial governments over the past three decades. Generally speaking, these approaches have gained and kept at least some political support from interest groups – support that ranges from grudging (from business interests) to enthusiastic (from rights advocacy groups).

Any fundamental change in human rights policy would attract the close attention of various influential groups. A fundamental reconfiguration of rights policy would have to either involve close consultation with these interests, or be achieved over their opposition. Any attempt to 'dictate' a reinvented rights policy would probably elicit widespread criticism from such groups. It would also generate criticism in the media, the opposition parties, and the public at large. Most governments would dread this prospect. Yet, reinventing human rights policy by a process of widespread consultation with the major interests in play would be a daunting task, and unlikely to succeed. Any attempt to fundamentally transform human rights policy would confront the antagonistic positions of the right and the left; of the business community seeking a more market-oriented approach to rights policy, and of rights advocacy groups critical of the free-market perspective and seeking an expansion of rights coverage and enforcement. Given the oppositional positions long encountered in the rights policy environment, it is not surprising that governments have been reluctant to open this policy field to rationalistic discussion and planning. Instead, they have proceeded incrementally, reforming and adjusting human rights policy as problems arise, and doing so as quietly and simply as possible.

This cautious approach very much reflects a fundamental tension embedded in the reinventionist logic. Advocates of reinvention stress the need for government agencies to be more 'market-driven,' 'entrepreneurial,' and responsive to their 'customers,' but this perception of public administration downplays the reality that the 'customers' of a rights agency are citizens, and possess fundamental human rights that have been bestowed on them by legislative enactment. As citizens, these people have a legal claim to commission services when they believe that their rights have been infringed, and they will expect commissions to take their rights claims seriously. From a slightly different perspective, it must also be recognized that fully half of the 'customers' of commissions are, in fact, respondents and have no choice but to use the 'services' of the commission. The 'customer' analogy thus seems quite ill-suited to describing the relationship of respondents to the commission, though just like complainants, respondents possess the rights of citizens and will demand that commissions treat those rights with the greatest respect. We have seen this dynamic time and time again. In the past decade in Canada the frustration of citizens, both as complainants and as respondents, in their dealings with commission bureaucracies has become one of the great problems confronting rights agencies. The point here is that from a legal and administrative perspective, people who approach to commissions do so not as customers but as citizens who possess certain rights of citizenship. The duty of all rights agencies is then to assess, review, and manage these rights claims as carefully and professionally as possible. In this process, agencies can be and have been influenced by the logic of the new public administration; but this influence has always been constricted by the fact that these agencies are dealing with citizens and rights in the public sphere, not with customers and interests in the private sphere.

The third constraint on reinvention arises from the first two: the administrative culture of rights agencies does not lend itself to any fundamental transformation of human rights policy and practice. Senior officials simply don't support the concept of reinvention. They well realize the administrative difficulties inherent in developing equity investment financing with public funds, and contracting out work, and employing volunteer labour over the opposition of public service unions. Likewise, the development of compliance incentives, 'community ownership' councils, and public–private partnering initiatives would pose significant administrative challenges to agencies.

Such a radical transformation of already beleaguered and overstretched institutions is hardly a priority for senior agency managers.[97] The administrative culture within rights agencies much prefers reform to reinvention.

To recognize that human rights agencies are more amenable to reform than to reinvention is not to suggest that reform is simple and problem-free. Some reform initiatives are highly controversial in that they represent significant changes to established practices. This is most obvious in relation to case-screening practices and the setting of commission priorities that may result in the downgrading of certain types of cases, such as 'routine' cases in Saskatchewan, and 'systemic' cases in provinces like New Brunswick, Manitoba, and Ontario. These reforms attract public attention and draw criticism from those interests that are harmed or offended as a result of changes in priorities. Likewise, the diminishment of the commissions' traditional role in public education may attract critical commentary as rights advocacy groups perceive that commissions are disengaging themselves from this area of their mandate. As result of these reforms, commissions and their responsible ministries will eventually be criticized for sacrificing effective and responsive human rights policy on the alter of fiscal expediency. The difficult challenge facing all human rights agencies, then, is to implement rights policy in an effective manner while realizing gains in economy and efficiency as demanded by governments. This is, of course, no easy task, and the assessment of whether agencies have successfully accomplished this feat will rest not only with agencies and their ministries, but with those who act as agency watchdogs, be they interest groups, businesses, parties, ombudsmen, auditors, media and academic analysts, or members of the general public. These reform initiatives will thus be subject to heated debate in which consensus unlikely. For reforms to be viable, they will have to maintain political and administrative support within agencies and governments, and be broadly accepted by concerned groups and the wider public.

We are not suggesting that the reinvention thesis in itself is suspect. We are simply pointing out that for the various reasons elucidated above, reform initiatives have been far more common in rights agencies than any type of reinventionist activity. The reinventionist approach may be more applicable to other policy fields, and to those other governmental entities which are more compatible with a market-oriented, entrepreneurial ethos.

Commissions and Organizational Models

With respect to structural reform in the field of human rights, one final point is worthy of mention. Jurisdictions in Canada have used a variety of organizational models to administer human rights policy. The Ontario model has been most influential, but other provinces, such as Quebec and BC, have developed their own unique approaches. Similarly, the federal model provides a good example of how a complex human rights regulatory process can be established. Do any of these various models offer a better organizational framework for commissions and their responsible governments to confront the conflicting pressures of rights consciousness and fiscal restraint?

Canadian human rights commissions are coping with these pressures in remarkably similar ways, regardless of their organizational structure. All commissions share a concern for developing new and modern approaches to case management, for reformulating their case screening systems, for streamlining their investigation and conciliation practices, and for reappraising and redesigning their public education programs. The similarities in commission thought and action are striking; but they should not be too surprising, given that all these institutions have similar mandates and face similar tensions – particularly fiscal ones. Remember also that the commissions share a common legal framework and swap information with one another. Viable reforms in one jurisdiction quickly become known in other jurisdictions half a continent away. These general administrative convergences are found regardless of what organizational model commissions use.

Beyond this general point, however, organizational models do matter, with certain aspects of some models rising in influence while others fade. BC's human rights council never captured the imagination of human rights advocates and administrators in other parts of the country; indeed, this model ultimately failed to win hearts and minds in BC itself. As a consequence, it died in 1996 and was replaced by a 'new' human rights commission based on the 'old' Ontario model.

The Ontario model has been dominant across this country for three decades, but even it has been touched by reformist ideas. In the past ten years the most significant change in Canada's human rights system has been the rise in popularity of permanent human rights adjudicative tribunals, or standing boards of inquiry, at the expense of the temporary, ad hoc adjudicative boards that were a hallmark of the 'old'

Ontario model. In this respect one can observe the growing influence of the federal model and, even more importantly, of the Quebec model. In both models, but especially Quebec's, the need for a permanent, standing tribunal to address the adjudicative needs of the human rights system has been clearly recognized. Such a tribunal offers expertise, consistency, economy and efficiency in caseflow management, and jurisprudential effectiveness, as well as stature and prestige among the broader society in general, and within the human rights and legal communities in particular. In this sense the influence of Quebec's tribunal system is being felt across the country, from BC to Alberta and Saskatchewan and even in Ontario itself. Clearly, the various models noted in Chapter 2 are important, require study, and can influence human rights systems in other jurisdictions. Organizational design is never static, nor is the administrative thinking that lies behind it.

Conclusion

An important irony is to be observed. Human rights agencies are engaging in significant reform, yet this reform is being pursued through a highly state-driven, top-down, élitist form of managerial decision making that is consistent with state-centred theory. The major reforms currently under way or being contemplated – reforms unprecedented since agencies were first established in the 1960s and 1970s – have generally not been the product of broad public participation, debate, and analysis. Notwithstanding such societal initiatives as the Cornish Task Force and the various Quebec symposia, rights interest groups, business interests, political parties, the media, and the general public have been generally disengaged from the reform process. While one cannot forget that social forces occasionally play a major role in the development of rights consciousness and rights policy development, our research confirms a key proposition of state-centred theory: over time, the dominant force for change in bureaucracies is the state actors themselves.

As agencies have been compelled to reform themselves – as exemplified by the New Brunswick commission in the late 1980s and the Saskatchewan, Alberta, and BC commissions in the mid-1990s – they have tended to adopt the decision-making model that is most compatible with and amenable to the needs and interests of senior commission managers and their political supervisors – namely, centralized executive judgment and action. Senior commission managers identify problems and search for viable organizational and policy initiatives in light of the fiscal restraints established by their responsible ministries, and the institutional and political constraints perceived by senior management in consultation with their political masters. The result is that significant reforms are undertaken and contemplated with minimal public involvement and consultation. For human rights agencies, in which so many individuals and groups feel a proprietary stake, this is indeed ironic; but to date, this seems to be the price that must be paid if those agencies are to address the 'new fiscal realities' with dispatch while striving to achieve greater service delivery. Whether this 'democratic deficit' in human rights administration will continue is something worth watching.

5. The Paradox of Human Rights Policy

Developments in human rights legislation have led to a paradox. We live in a society that is highly rights-conscious, that values human freedom and equality and is dedicated to the proposition that discrimination on the basis of immutable personal characteristics is morally wrong. From these beliefs has emerged a body of public policy and law designed to entrench and promote human rights policies and to attack, and hopefully lessen, the incidence of social discrimination. Yet despite this demonstrable political interest in advancing equality rights, the policies guiding the legislation seem not to be working.

Despite the reforms discussed in Chapter 4, members of the human rights policy community remain highly dissatisfied with human rights commissions, procedures, and programs. From the perspectives of equality-seeking groups, business and employer organizations, and even human rights officials, the system is in deep crisis. In the view of rights advocates, the system has failed to protect the weakest and most vulnerable members of society, to punish wrongdoers, and to increase social awareness of human equality and dignity. They see the rights system as plagued with case delays and backlogs, shoddy administration, and slack enforcement. More conservative individuals and groups, including many businesses that become respondents in human rights cases, view the system as one that can easily run amok, fuelled by naïve idealism and a predilection for labelling and punishing discriminators. These critics of the system fear that the legal right to due process is all too often disregarded in a rush to politically correct judgments and social expiations.

Meanwhile, those who work within the system as members and officers of human rights commissions often wonder whether governments value their work. On the one hand, governments tell them they support the broad policy objectives of human rights legislation, and often extend rights coverage to cover more groups in society. On the other hand, these same governments over the past decade have subjected human rights commissions to rigorous policies of financial restraint, thereby inhibiting their ability to meet all the increasing responsibilities being placed on them.

Regardless of the source of the criticism, certain concerns have become a common refrain: Human rights policies are not working. The ideals of the system are not being met. The commissions are burdened with case delays and unfulfilled programs and are performing sluggishly. Yet at another level, beyond the criticism and the dissatisfaction, this cloud of dissatisfaction and resentment is not as dark as first appears. Despite disagreements over policy direction, and regardless of disputes over the roles of commissions, and notwithstanding the drastic impact of financial restraint policies, the human rights system is achieving its key policy goals: complaints are being taken, heard, and resolved; gross violations of rights legislation are being acted on and remedied; unsubstantiated complaints are being dismissed; the public is being educated through a variety of means; the legislation and regulations are being routinely revised; the commissions are being managed; and the law is being enforced.

Indeed, it is possible to suggest that concern for procedural entitlements, coupled with fiscal restraint, has helped make rights policy more effective. The incorporating of procedural rigour and legal entitlements into the system has helped legitimize human rights commissions. These features may have added to the costs of case processing and to caseflow bottlenecks, but they have also made the system more acceptable to the broader legal and political community. In this age of the Charter of Rights, this is very important. Even fiscal restraint has an upside: it is forcing administrative innovation and is thwarting or delaying controversial programs. At a time when affirmative action and related programs are generating controversy, fiscal restraint has done much to maintain the legitimacy of the human rights system. Thus the paradox in human rights policy: the system is in disarray yet is working.

We now examine this paradox. We begin by assessing the performance of human rights commissions. We find that equality-seeking groups, business and employer organizations, and even human rights staff and officials rate the performance of the commissions relatively poorly. For various reasons, they generally give commissions low grades for promptness, objectivity, and accessibility. We then analyse overall human rights policy in light of the criticisms so often heard. We argue that the criticisms do not indicate that the policy is failing.

Great Expectations

Before we examine how the human rights policy community assesses the performance of commissions, it may be helpful to review the general expectations placed on those commissions. Given the expansion of equality rights consciousness and the growth of rights consciousness in general, expectations are very great. In this time of reduced resources, commissions are expected to handle cases quickly, efficiently, and fairly. That complaints are to be responded to promptly was a major reason why cases were first assigned to commissions. Commissions are expected not only to be prompt but also to be accessible to the public and to victims of discrimination. Accessibility was another reason why commissions were established. Commissions are expected to make themselves known to the public, through educational programs and through publicity from cases, in order that victims of discrimination can make complaints and that the affected public can gain information.

Commissions also are expected to administer efficient complaint procedures. They are expected to fully investigate the facts of each case and to make every effort to achieve a satisfactory settlement, before recourse to a board of inquiry or tribunal is considered. At the same time, commissions are also expected to be fair. They are expected to be objective and unbiased in discrimination disputes, and to favour neither the complainant nor the respondent. They are expected to ensure fair procedures and to make fair decisions based on facts and on law. In addition to all this, commissions are expected to deliver special programs and initiatives – to meet the objectives spelled out in their mandates in the areas of race relations, public education, affirmative action, and the investigation of systemic discrimination.

Various groups in the policy community have somewhat different expectations. Equality-seeking and advocacy groups strongly emphasize speedy justice, accessibility, and results that help achieve social equality.[1] They often see commissions as part of an ideological movement for equality rights. For this reason, they attach great importance to prompt and efficient complaint procedures and to affirmative action initiatives and investigations of systemic discrimination. In contrast, business and employer groups stress the importance of fairness in complaint procedures and of objectivity among investigating officers and officials.[2] They also stress the importance of fair procedures whereby commissions screen out trivial or vexatious complaints. Because they are sensitive to charges of discrimination and to unwanted publicity, they are troubled by the abundance of complaints. They would prefer that relatively few cases come forward, and that these cases address demonstrably serious problems and be settled quickly and fairly. In summary, equality-seeking groups emphasize the advocacy role of commissions, while business groups emphasize the dispute-settlement role and the importance of fairness and impartiality. Thus, a problem for commissions is that they are expected to be both advocates and objective dispensers of justice.

A Human Rights Report Card

To determine how members of the policy community (or stakeholders) rated the performance of human rights commissions and systems across Canada, we designed a report card (see Table 5.1). Our goal was to see how stakeholders evaluated the performance of the commissions, given the changes and reforms undertaken by them to cope with the restraints of the 1980s and 1990s. Our focus was on complaint handling, since this is the main responsibility of commissions. Respondents were asked to grade the human rights system with which they were most familiar on the basis of accessibility, promptness, adequacy of investigation, adequacy of conciliation, objectivity, fair procedures, fair decisions, and adequacy of compensation.

The report card was distributed in the summer of 1997 to three key stakeholder groups in the policy community: (1) equality-seeking groups and advocacy organizations (including women's groups, ethnocultural organizations, groups representing persons with disabilities, native groups, gay and lesbian organizations, civil liberties associations, and labour unions); (2) employer organizations and business groups; and (3) human rights officials and commission staff. Equality-seeking groups were included as stakeholders because of their support of complainants and their advocacy role in the development of human rights legislation. Since they monitor issues and cases and receive feedback from complainants as to the effectiveness and fairness of the complaint process, they are well positioned to assess

The Paradox of Human Rights Policy 139

TABLE 5.1
Human rights report card survey: 'What grade would you give your human rights system in the following areas?'

A	B	C	D	F
Excellent	Good	Fair	Poor	Fail

Area	Definition	Grade
Accessibility	The staff of the commission are accessible to members of the public, always available to take complaints and answer inquiries.	____
Promptness	The commission is prompt in dealing with complaints of discrimination, able to settle cases quickly without long delays.	____
Investigation	The commission conducts thorough investigations of the facts of cases, taking no shortcuts.	____
Conciliation	The commission makes every effort at conciliation, attempting to bring parties together to settle a case.	____
Objectivity	The officers of the commission are objective in their investigation of complaints, without bias to either side.	____
Fair procedures	The commission's procedures in dealing with complaints are fair to both sides, giving each party in a case a fair opportunity to make a case.	____
Fair Decisions	The final decision reached in a case is a fair one, based on an impartial assessment of the facts and the law.	____
Compensation	The human rights system ensures proper compensation to those found to be victims of unjustified discrimination.	____

commission performance from the perspective of complainants. Employer and business groups were included as stakeholders because business practices are greatly affected by human rights policies and because their members are most likely to be the respondents in complaints of discrimination. Business organizations are also familiar with many of the legal and administrative issues and with the views of many of their members as to the effectiveness and fairness of human rights procedures. They are thus in a good position to make assessments from the business and respondent perspectives. Finally, human rights officials (commissioners, directors, managers, staff) were included because they at the very centre of the system, and well positioned to observe and assess commission performance.

Report cards were distributed to 150 leading advocacy organizations, 150 leading business and employer groups, and 75 human rights staff and officials of the provincial and federal commissions – a total of 375.[3] The report cards were sent to parties in all jurisdictions in proportion to population size and commission caseloads. Thus more report cards were sent to Ontario and the federal jurisdiction and fewer to Prince Edward Island and Newfoundland. All human rights staff, as identified through government telephone books and commission annual reports, were sent report cards. Advocacy groups were selected randomly from the membership lists of national organizations (e.g., the National Action Committee on the Status of Women, the National Association of Native Friendship Centres) and from the *Canadian Almanac*. Business and employer groups were also selected randomly, in this case from the membership lists of national organizations (e.g., the Canadian Chamber of Commerce) and from the *Canadian Almanac*. In the cases of both advocacy and business groups, executive directors (or their designates) were asked to complete and return the report card, with both business groups and human rights staff, confidentiality was emphasized. Bilingual forms were sent to parties in Quebec and New Brunswick. Of the 375 report cards sent out, 177 were returned – a 47 per cent rate of return. Returns were in proportion to jurisdictional differences in population and commission caseloads.

As indicated in Table 5.1, the report card contained eight areas for evaluation. A definition or statement was provided for each area. Respondents were asked to grade each area A, B, C, D, or F. They were also asked to assess the human rights system from a historical perspective. In response to the statement, 'In recent years, the system of protecting people from discrimination has been getting ...,' they were asked to indicate 'better,' 'worse,' 'remained the same,' or 'don't know.' Finally, in the report cards and in subsequent interviews (with those willing to be interviewed), respondents were given the opportunity to provide comments. Fifty-four respondents (40 per cent) included comments in their returned report cards. Most of these were advocacy groups (30), followed by human rights staff (18) and business groups (6). A further 40 respondents provided comments in interviews. Again, most were from advocacy groups (32), followed by business groups (8). The distribution of comments from both report cards and interviews was fairly even across jurisdictions. Our intention was to use the comments as the basis for describing the advocacy, business, and commission perspectives on the functioning of the human rights system.

TABLE 5.2
Overall report card results

Jurisdiction	Percentage (grade)
Ontario	52 (D)
Federal	52 (D)
Manitoba	58 (D)
British Columbia	60 (C)
Newfoundland	60 (C)
Nova Scotia	61 (C)
Alberta	62 (C)
Prince Edward Island	62 (C)
Quebec	65 (C)
Saskatchewan	65 (C)
New Brunswick	69 (C)
Overall Average	61 (C)

The Overall Results

Before offering an analytical review of the survey results by stakeholder groups, we will look at overall responses. The data were summarized according to the following scale: an 'A' response earned a score of 5, 'B,' 4, 'C,' 3, 'D,' 2, and 'F,' 1. We then totalled scores for each report card, the maximum score being 40. Next, we grouped the report cards by jurisdiction, regardless of stakeholder group, and calculated the total score and average for each jurisdiction. Finally, we converted scores into percentages and grades. As in a school report card, a grade of A was 80 per cent and above, B was 70 to 80 per cent, C was 60 to 70 per cent, D was 50 to 60 per cent, and F was below 50 per cent.

The results provide a snapshot of how members of the human rights policy community assessed the performance of commissions and systems by jurisdiction (see Table 5.2). The overall grade was a very low C, or 61 per cent. This was not a failing grade, but it certainly was not complimentary either. Variations across jurisdictions were not substantial, but there were some differences. New Brunswick, followed by Saskatchewan and Quebec, earned the highest grades (though still Cs), while Ontario and the federal jurisdiction earned the lowest (low Ds). It is noteworthy that there was no relationship between the level of human rights funding and the performance rating.[4] The New Brunswick system is among the lowest funded (see chapter 3), yet it earned

TABLE 5.3
Advocacy report card results (percentages)

Criterion	Excellent	Good	Fair	Poor	Fail
Accessibility	11	36	33	14	6
Promptness	0	9	29	36	26
Investigation	3	28	34	19	16
Conciliation	5	42	34	12	7
Objectivity	8	34	36	10	12
Fair procedures	11	29	37	13	10
Fair decisions	5	31	37	12	15
Compensation	0	15	32	28	25
Average	5	28	34	18	15

the highest overall rating. Meanwhile, the relatively higher-funded Ontario and Manitoba systems scored the lowest.

The Perspective of Advocacy Groups

The results from advocacy and equality-seeking groups are summarized in Table 5.3. These results apply to commissions in general, as the number of returns did not justify a jurisdictional breakdown. Advocacy groups did not give commissions high ratings. A substantial majority (67 per cent) gave grades of C and under. The grade of C accounted for the greatest percentage of responses (34 per cent). As many respondents assigned grades of poor and fail (33 per cent) as excellent and good (33 per cent). The lowest ratings were for promptness in dealing with complaints, followed by level of compensation. The highest scores given were for accessibility and attempts at conciliation. But even in these categories, most respondents gave grades of fair, poor, or fail.

In comment sections of the report cards and in the interviews, the most frequent comments made by advocates were as follows: Despite recent efforts at reform, human rights systems remain plagued by delays and backlogs. Much of this is the result of understaffing and underfunding of commissions. As well, commission staff are highly complacent, a result of decreased morale, which in turn is the result of inadequate funding. Commissions spend too much time and energy on high-profile cases at the expense of more ordinary complaints. Human rights staff are too willing to screen out 'trivial' cases, and when they do accept complaints, they too often give them inadequate attention and investigation. Human rights officers try too hard to discourage complainants from initiating complaints and, once initiated, from continuing on with them.

Advocacy groups also commented on the symbolic nature of human rights policy: In attempting to gain the support of minorities and women's groups, governments tend to stress rhetoric over substance. Governments are reluctant to back up their official support for equality rights with vigorous policies of enforcement. Not only do they underfund commissions, but they also tend to appoint 'like-thinking' people as commissioners in an effort to facilitate the mild and symbolic policy approach they desire. In the words of one advocacy group representative, 'neither the provincial nor federal government has ever valued human rights activity as having any value other than as a political sop to minorities.' Another commented that the Ontario Commission 'has become a body which the government would like to disappear.' This sentiment was also reflected in a comment from Ontario regarding a perceived lack of enforcement capability: 'Human rights need the back-up of enforceable remedies for violations. Section 15 of the Charter should force governments to provide meaningful protection from discrimination.'

Advocacy groups commonly criticized commissions for failing to take a strong proactive approach to discrimination – that is, for not placing sufficient emphasis on investigations of systemic discrimination and on affirmative action as a remedy. The traditional, reactive, case-by-case approach, even if it was carried out well, makes only a small dent on the problem of inequality. With respect to public education, advocacy groups noted initiatives in Ontario and Nova Scotia to incorporate human rights education into the school curriculum, but stated further that publicity and educational measures were generally inadequate. They also expressed dissatisfaction with compensation levels. Respondents from Nova Scotia and British Columbia indicated that decisions and compensation awards were sometimes made in a 'quick and dirty' fashion for the sake of speed. This did not solve the problem of discrimination; it merely glossed it over. Inadequate compensation sends the message that discrimination is not such a serious problem.

Finally, a significant number of advocacy group respondents (47 per cent) believed that systems of human rights protection were getting worse at providing protection against discrimination (see Table 5.4). Only about half as many (24 per cent) believed the systems were get-

TABLE 5.4
Has human rights protection been getting better or worse in recent years?

Respondent type	Better	Worse	The same	Don't know
Advocacy	24%	47%	25%	4%
Business/employer	28	24	24	24
Rights officials	47	24	26	3
Average	33	32	25	10

ting better, while slightly more (25 per cent) felt they were remaining the same. This indicates that from the perspective of equality-seeking groups, recent reforms in human rights administration have not improved systems of human rights delivery. In summary, human rights commissions were depicted in general terms as slow-moving and timid vehicles for equality rights, and as incapable of making significant progress.

This criticism from advocacy groups is quite in line with commentary during the 1990s in the media and in the human rights advocacy literature, and even with statements by government officials. For example, Kathleen Ruff, former editor of the *Canadian Human Rights Advocate*, has asserted: 'The small number of staff results in unacceptable delays in handling complaints. In the best of circumstances obtaining evidence to prove discrimination is not easy; long delay before an investigation is started can make it virtually impossible.'[5]

Shelagh Day, editor of the *Canadian Human Rights Reporter*, has made a related criticism: 'Currently, Commissions appear to be bogged down in individual complaints. There are long delays in the resolution of these complaints, and apparently few resources for anything else. Some Commissions have established systemic discrimination units, but there are no real results to be seen yet from this reallocation of resources.'[6]

There have been stories in the media critical of the sluggish performance of human rights commissions. For example, in a long *Globe and Mail* story in 1997, Canada's entire human rights system was described as 'overwhelmed by its caseload of complaints' and human rights commissions as 'swamped by backlogs of cases, [having] become more intent on closing files than tackling [new] complaints.'[7]

Similar criticisms have been made by government officials. In 1994 a special report by the Ontario Ombudsman identified delays and inefficiencies as a major problem and called for the province to 'get cracking

TABLE 5.5
Business report card results

Criterion	Excellent	Good	Fair	Poor	Fail
Accessibility	5%	58%	16%	21%	0%
Promptness	0	9	29	38	24
Investigation	0	14	62	24	0
Conciliation	5	24	33	38	0
Objectivity	0	29	9	43	19
Fair procedures	0	43	24	24	9
Fair decisions	0	19	43	29	9
Compensation	10	14	52	24	0
Average	3%	26%	33%	30%	8%

on a broad overhaul of its Human Rights Commission to carry it into the next century.'[8] Similarly, in 1998 at the federal level, Canada's Auditor General strongly criticized the Canadian Human Rights Commission for doing too many things and taking too long to do them.[9] The Auditor General complained that even while the commission was continuing to expand interpretation of the legislation through tribunal and court cases, there were major delays in the processing of complaints and the commission was unable to eliminate its backlog. Similar commentary came even from the United States. In 1997 the U.S. Department of State assessed the quality of human rights protections throughout the world, and found that while Canadian human rights programs and processes overall were doing a fair job of rights protection, procedural delays in many provinces, especially Ontario, were a clear source of concern.[10] It noted in its analysis that cases were sometimes dismissed as a result of delays caused by the commission itself. Also, rules of evidence were not always followed, and the investigative process was neither open nor accountable.

The Perspective of Employers and Business Groups

The report card results for the employer and business groups are summarized in Table 5.5. These groups also did not give commissions good grades overall. As with the advocacy groups, only a minority gave average grades of excellent (3 per cent) or good (26 per cent). Most gave grades of fair, poor, or fail. What is particularly interesting here is the target of criticism: advocacy groups awarded relatively high scores for objectivity and for conciliation efforts; business and employer groups awarded the lowest marks to these categories. This reflects the general view in the business community that commissions are too often biased in favour of complainants and equality groups. Also, advocacy groups were quite critical of the level of compensation awarded to successful complainants; employer and business groups were relatively satisfied with the current level. In the area of promptness, business groups were as critical of commissions as advocacy groups.

Recurring comments by employers and business groups were as follows: Commissions have an institutional bias in favour of complainants. In the criminal law and civil law systems, attempts are made to strike a proper balance between individual rights and the interests of society; human rights systems go in the opposite direction. Commission staff tend to assume from the outset that employers (respondents) are guilty. They are less concerned with fairness and objectivity than with achieving outcomes favourable to the complainants. In the words of one business group representative in British Columbia, 'I have experienced many situations where the facts presented by an employer have not been taken into consideration at all.' Commissions are too willing to pursue trivial or unreasonable complaints and are much too insensitive to the growing legal costs faced by respondents.

Also criticized by employer and business groups was the training provided to human rights staff and the quality of their work. Human rights officers, it was suggested, lacked skill in dispute resolution. Commission staffs should be required to take courses in dispute resolution as a means of addressing the ongoing problem of bias toward employers. A representative of an employer organization working with the federal commission stated that that commission was contracting out part of its investigative work to the private sector rather than doing it all in-house. He was quite concerned that this practice might adversely affect program efficacy and consistency. Other business groups stated that because of reductions in human rights staff and increased workloads, commissions were unable to do proper public education and training for employers on human rights issues. Finally, the view was expressed that an excessive amount of time was spent by commissions in investigation and by tribunals in adjudication. The system had become overly bureaucratic and legalistic.

Many of these comments are in line with views expressed in pro-business publications. For example, in an article in *Canadian Lawyer,*

Michael Crawford suggested that the current trend toward 'political correctness' has created a situation where employers fear that any hiring practice whatever could subject them to a human rights investigation: 'Some lawyers think so, particularly those who represent the business community, which is finding itself under increasing attack from human rights commissions. Owners and managers of many companies view human rights investigations and laws as intrusions into their private business affairs.'[11]

Accusations of bias against business have also been made in response to court cases and new government initiatives. For example, in Ontario in 1994, *The Financial Post* noted that as the result of lower court rulings allowing civil actions, employers would have to defend 'both the human rights claim and a civil action for constructive dismissal simultaneously, while the suing employee is still working in the business.'[12] In 1995 the *Post* was similarly critical of an initiative by BC's NDP goverment to revise the province's human rights legislation. In its views, the plan would strenghten the powers of government investigators to the point where they could 'intrude upon any company where there had been no whisper of complaint from the employees and impose equity quotas, requiring the company to hire as many women, handicapped, native or other minority groups as the inspectors demanded.'[13] From the business community's perspective, the new directions in human rights policy and procedures reflected a general bias against business, and so did the general outlook and approach of commissions.

In percentage terms, more business groups than advocacy groups believed that human rights systems were improving (see Table 5.4). However, many business groups (24 per cent) believed that the systems were getting worse. The same percentage (24 per cent) noted no change. The results suggest that from the business community's perspective, recent administrative reforms have been somewhat successful.

The Perspective of Human Rights Staff and Officials

The report card results for human rights officials (intake officers, investigating officers, managers, commissioners) are summarized in Table 5.6. As indicated, and not unexpectedly, the views expressed here are relatively more favourable to the commissions. A majority (63 per cent) gave average grades of A or B. What is quite striking is that a large minority (37 per cent) gave grades of C or D or F: over one-third of

TABLE 5.6
Commission officials report card results

Criterion	Excellent	Good	Fair	Poor	Fail
Accessibility	35%	32%	18%	12%	3%
Promptness	0	15	39	27	19
Investigation	18	50	26	6	0
Conciliation	24	44	29	3	0
Objectivity	47	32	21	0	0
Fair procedures	53	32	15	0	0
Fair decisions	44	38	9	9	0
Compensation	9	27	45	19	0
Average	29%	34%	25%	9%	3%

respondents rated the performance of commissions as fair (25 per cent) or poor (9 per cent) or as a failure (3 per cent). As with advocacy groups, officials were most critical of commissions' promptness in handling complaints, followed by inadequate compensation to successful complainants. Only 15 per cent of respondents gave commissions a grade of good for promptness; not one assigned a score of excellent. Respondents gave the highest ratings for commissions' objectivity, followed by fair procedures and attempts at conciliation. Overall, their report cards resembled those of advocacy groups more than those of employers.

The most critical members of the commissions were human rights officers and front-line staff rather than the higher-level managers and commissioners. Their comments were the most plentiful and were as follows: Commission delay and slowness to act are critical problems. In the words of one human rights officer, 'the delay in the investigation and processing of complaints is intolerable.' In the words of another, 'dealing with delay is not just a matter of learning to be patient. Justice delayed is justice denied. Cases become more difficult to prove and victimization continues.' Among commission staff, this is the most common concern.

Officials also suggested that in attempting to solve the problem of delays and to expedite the processing of complaints, commissions were entering into dangerous territory. Intake officers were becoming too quick to screen out complaints or dismiss them at an early stage. One respondent commented that 'the commission has shifted to dismissing as many complaints as possible. Dismissals are based on the personal interpretation of the law, even if it flies in the face of Supreme

Court of Canada decisions.' While this focus on screening and dismissals speeds up the process, it may also cause injustice and thereby violate the mandates of the commissions. It was also suggested that the growing reliance on new technologies such as voice mail and 1–800 numbers spelled danger in terms of discouraging legitimate complaints and widening the contact gap between the public and commissions. Finally, in the area of compensation, it was emphasized that compensation levels and penalties were too low, as they did not send a strong enough message about the seriousness of discrimination.

As indicated in Table 5.4, human rights officials are divided on the question of whether the system has improved recently. While 47 per cent expressed the belief that the system was getting better at protecting human rights, 24 per cent felt that it was getting worse. At the very least, this suggests that a substantial number of commission officials, especially front-line staff, doubt whether Canada's human rights delivery is improving.

As revealed in annual reports and discussion papers during the mid to late 1990s, the commissions themselves recognize that further improvements must be made to their procedures and programs. For example, Nova Scotia in 1997 launched a four-phase, stakeholder-centred analysis designed to allow its commission to 'explore ways to improve how the mandate is interpreted through the programs and services that it delivers.'[14] Stakeholders were invited to critique the commission's processes and make recommendations. Similarly, in Alberta in the mid-1990s the government and its commission invited critical feedback (part of which involved the Alberta Human Rights Review Panel) and arranged for a public opinion survey on the question of whether the province's human rights system was effective. Finally, in Saskatchewan in 1996, commission officials produced a special report, *Renewing the Vision*, which recognized problems in the system and recommended major improvements in the complaint process and even a restructuring of the commission.[15] Initiatives such as these three indicate a capacity for self-criticism and a keen awareness of the need for self-improvement – attitudes shared by human rights officials across the country.

In conclusion, human rights systems across Canada do not receive high ratings from advocacy groups, from business organizations, or even from human rights officials. Despite recent reforms, significant concern remains about the performance of commissions. What does this critical outlook bode for human rights protection in Canada?

The Grand Paradox

The fundamental reality of human rights policy and administration is that it exists within a multifaceted paradox. This paradox has been evolving for decades, is interpreted in diverse ways, and has inspired intense debate over how it can be resolved. Before we can thoroughly understand the complexities and dynamics of the paradox, we must carefully review human rights policy and its various contradictory yet interrelated components. To these matters we now turn.

The Paradox, Part 1: Rights Consciousness

As we saw in Chapter 1, the post–Second World War era in Canada was marked by a great and growing societal interest in protecting and promoting human rights. As a result of this concern, governments eventually established human rights legislation and created human rights commissions. This development of equality rights awareness, however, was but a part of a broader social dynamic alive in the country over these years. The evolution of human rights policy was very much influenced by, and influential to, the general evolution of rights awareness in Canada. This development has been one of the most important social and legal currents in modern Canadian history.

Rights consciousness has developed in such a way that it has become embedded in Canadian political culture, Canadian society, and the Canadian state. Opinion surveys and policy analyses indicate that Canadian attitudes toward rights have been deepening and solidifying.[16] Earlier generations tended to view the public good as arising from the interaction of parties, interest groups, and the general public, with governments and legislatures both establishing and defending the rights and interests of citizens. In the past three decades, however, this British parliamentary approach to the public good has come to be superseded by an American-style, legalistic approach. The broad community is no longer perceived as the focus of public action; that focus is increasingly shifting to the individual.

The individual, moreover, increasingly is being seen not simply as an actor in the broad social–political debate on the public issues of the day, but as the fundamental centre of society, around whom all public policy must orbit. And furthermore, the individual now is a bearer of fundamental rights. He or she possesses legal entitlements that all other individuals must respect and that all governments must protect and promote. Certain of these rights – such as fundamental human rights – inhere in individuals simply because they are human beings; other rights – such as rights in criminal law, labour and workers' compensation law, and environmental law – arise through the creation of statutes designed to promote the interests of citizens. Regardless of the legal justification or origin of the right, the result is the same: an individual who possesses a legal entitlement to a particular freedom, privilege, service, or condition, and who can demand that all others respect, honour, and serve that right. Such rights are ordinarily viewed in absolutist terms as conferring special benefits and protections 'as of right' upon individuals, with these rights being non-negotiable and not subject in any way to compromise or bargaining. Logic dictates that rights involve corresponding duties: as the particular individual bears a particular right, governments and all other individuals are morally and legally obliged to uphold that right and to make it manifest within society. This legal obligation is institutionally enforceable, not through Parliament or legislatures but through semijudicial administrative tribunals and ultimately through the courts.[17]

As a result of these developments, the focus of debate respecting the public good has moved away from legislative bodies, political parties, and the interactions of governments and interest groups in the shaping of public policy, and increasingly toward commissions, tribunals, and courts. Rights are legal entitlements to particular services and conditions, with corresponding obligations owed by others; it follows that any perceived infringement on a right becomes a legal as well as a political issue. And increasingly, the vindication and enforcement of rights is sought through judicial institutions. Because these bodies are charged with enforcing rights and remedying wrongs, in a society marked by rights consciousness they become key players. As one result, the discourse of public policy also changes: the language of public interest, collective responsibility, and the common good is replaced by the language of individual rights, individual interests, and public obligations to individual entitlements. And increasingly, this discourse is undertaken not within the confines of a democratically elected and politically responsible assembly but within the courts and other judicial institutions – institutions that, while integral to the democratic process, are nevertheless undemocratic in that they are unelected, as well as not responsible to the public in the traditional meaning of the term. Through the growing recourse to tribunals and courts as the key forums for resolving debates over rights and public policies, we are witnessing the growth of a legalistic approach to the public good at the expense of political approaches. In Peter Russell's apt phrase, we are witnessing 'judicialized politics.'[18]

As this rights consciousness has become embedded in Canadian society, so too has it become embedded in the state through state-centred forces. Human rights codes, the federal Bill of Rights, and the Canadian Charter of Rights and Freedoms are only the most direct manifestations of this. Since the Second World War, Canadian governments have increasingly embraced the discourse of rights as a mark of progress and good government. The Charter is extolled as a high point of Canadian civilization, while human rights are promoted by all governments and by all major political parties as fundamental to democratic government. Beyond this, Canada's courts have strengthened and entrenched the principles of human rights and administrative law within the workings of Canadian governments and their semijudicial administrative agencies. Furthermore, governments have enhanced rights consciousness by, for example, providing financial support for rights advocacy groups, establishing ombudsman's offices designed to protect citizens' rights vis-à-vis governments, and elaborating citizens' rights in ordinary legislation across the panorama of governmental responsibilities. Through these measures and many others, Canadian governments have signalled not only that they are aware of rights consciousness but also that they support its fundamental ideals.

An important component to rights consciousness, as suggested above, is that of legal rights consciousness and the growing public respect for and expectation of legal due process in so much of public administration. Legal rights to 'due process' or 'natural justice' (in the traditional administrative law parlance) entail specific legal entitlements borne by citizens with respect to state actions. When the state – through its departments, agencies, boards, or commissions – takes actions that directly affect the legal rights of individuals, groups, or corporations, it must do so in accordance with the set rules of administrative law. These rules, which are related to notice, hearings, legal representation, examination, written reasons, and freedom from bias (see Chapter 2), establish clear procedural entitlements to citizens while imposing strict procedural obligations on governmental decision-making bodies.

In recent decades these fundamental rules of due process have grown in scope and strength, as a result of the litigation of aggrieved individuals, groups, and corporations as well as the legal sensibilities of lawyers and judges. The end result has been that formal rules of due process have become entrenched in all Canadian administrative law decision making, with this process being ultimately sanctioned and supported by the Supreme Court of Canada. As Evans, Janisch, and Mullan have long argued, a quiet revolution has taken place in Canadian administrative law involving a distinct legalization of process and action within state agencies responsible for applying law and policy within society.[19]

In this process, the values of administrative due process have become embedded within both society and the state. Among individuals, groups, and corporations dealing with state agencies, rights are now viewed as 'de rigueur' – as the necessary preconditions for any legitimate form of state decision making. As the term suggests, these rights are now seen as 'natural' when thinking of 'justice,' as being 'due' in any form of semijudicial 'process.' And as these ideals have become entrenched in society, so too have they been entrenched within the decision making of the state. The rules of administrative law have been sanctioned by the courts, embraced by all regulatory agencies and governmental departments engaged in semijudicial administrative action, and affirmed through legislation. This legislation can take the form of rules of civil procedure, or specific provincial administrative procedure acts, or simply statutory stipulations that the rules of natural justice will be followed in all relevant instances of state action. At all times, state authorities recognize that this legal approach to decision making exists; that it is valid and necessary; that it deserves respect, protection, and promotion; and that the state is obligated to meet these expectations.[20] The result has been the legalization of much of Canadian administrative decision making – a dynamic that has had unintended consequences for the development of human rights policy and procedures.

The Paradox, Part 2: Rights Restraint

The development of a rights-centred culture is one of the most noteworthy features of Canadian society in recent decades. However, this social dynamic has not gone unchallenged. As rights consciousness has emerged as a prominent aspect of modern society it has been subjected to various cross-cutting social and political currents that have had the effect of restricting and even inhibiting the growth of certain aspects of rights consciousness. These are the forces of rights restraint.

The main locus of such restraint, and the longest-lasting one, has been the business community. Yet it is wholly unfair to view the business community as hostile to the broadening of rights consciousness per se; after all, the values associated with individualism, liberty, private property, and the market economy have been closely associated with rights discourse and practice for centuries. The business community has generally supported the concepts of rights policy and rights protection; even so, it has been consistently sceptical of the broadening of human rights policy and the growing power of human rights commissions. A number of criticisms are common within such conservative thought.

One is that rights policy has gone 'too far' in promoting the rights of minorities and special interests, and that it has come to reflect the questionable collective rights of particular pressure groups rather than the broad individual rights of common people.[21] Coupled to this is the criticism that human rights policy has become overwhelmingly statist, in that the commission bureaucracies have become the key players in rights cases, and have thereby divorced rights policy from the common public and from the particular individuals involved in particular cases. This line of reasoning leads to a critique of the procedures and practices of rights commissions. As discussed earlier, commissions are berated for being plagued by caseflow backlogs and delays, which results in increased costs for private legal counsel; commission officers are berated for being unfamiliar with and/or insensitive to the needs and pressures experienced by modern businesses, both large and small; commission staff are berated for being anything from bureaucratically incompetent to idealistic meddlers in business decision-making.

However, criticisms from the business community are most pronounced with respect to the general broadening of rights policy – the 'pushing of the envelope' as endorsed by officials with some commissions. Business groups have been essentially hostile to developments such as affirmative action, employment equity, and systemic investigations. They perceive these approaches as promoting collective over individual rights – an approach to rights policy that they claim is novel and generally unsupported by the public. The business community fully accepts the need for a system of individual rights protection but is leery of any initiatives to promote collective rights and to further such rights through 'systemic' actions. They perceive these approaches as unwarranted state intervention in private enterprise – as unjust in theory and as adding substantially, in practice, to their administrative and financial burden.²²

All of this leaves the general business community in the unsurprising position of being a conservative social force. It accepts the general thrust of traditional rights policy, but insists that this policy must be prudent, sensible, and restrained. Furthermore, it must be enforced in a manner that is sensitive to the needs of business and cognizant of the practical realities of a market economy. Employers must be in a superior position to employees, and the interests of entrepreneurs must be respected.

This critique of human rights policy and administration has its backers in other communities. Analysts such as Manfredi, Knopff and Morton, and Russell have pointed out the negative impact of rights consciousness on Canadian society.²³ Their main contention is that rights consciousness strengthens the rights and interests of individuals at the expense of the interests and welfare of the community as a whole. As Russell has argued, we are increasingly seeing political discourse on the public good being reduced to a legal debate over society's obligations to particular individuals and the limitations to be placed on governments in their dealings with individual citizens. In short, collective interests are circumscribed by individual rights, and private claims to individual entitlements come to 'trump' public claims to social goods. This critique of liberal individualism and rights awareness is not the sole property of conservative analysts. Those on the political left, such as Mandel, Hutchinson and Petter, and Bogart, have said much the same thing, stressing the damage that individual rights consciousness does to the development of collective well-being founded on the broad use of state power.²⁴

Yet neither of these broad approaches to thinking about rights in general necessarily leads to a condemnation of Canadian human rights policy and practice per se. The critics of human rights commissions generally tinker at the edges. More conservative analysts tend to echo business critics in calling for commissions to be more restrained in their approach to rights enforcement; they also tend to stress that individuals should be obliged to bear more personal responsibility for addressing the difficulties they encounter in their lives. More leftist analysts, in contrast, will stress that rights policy has become misaligned, and that governments ought to restructure their rights legislation so that it focuses on more collective rights in specific areas such as income security, job protection, and environmental health.

Clearly, human rights tends to inspire intense debate. This is not to suggest that rights consciousness is not a dominant social force – obviously it is. But it is not a current of thought and action free from all questioning. As a general concept of social ordering, it does confront criticism, and there are at times strong calls for rights policy to be modulated and refined. This is entirely consistent with the broad theory of the embedded state, the existence of which does not preclude significant refinement to the nature and workings of human rights commissions.

Notwithstanding the opposition of the business community and of conservative intellectuals, the key force driving rights restraint has been government financial retrenchment. Over the past two decades, all governments in Canada, regardless of their ideology, and regardless of their electoral pledges and promises, have been forced to bring their deficits under control. This has generally involved spending cuts, privatization, deregulation, the increased resort to user fees for certain public services, and selective tax increases. Reductions in public spending typically resulted in staffing cuts and program 'shrinkage.' In short, governments downsized, and government agencies had to make do with less.

In seeking this end, governments were engaging in what Osborne and Gaebler termed enforced managerial creativity.[25] Given the bureaucratic inertia and institutional complacency so often found in government offices, these authors have stressed that a certain degree of financial restraint can actually benefit an organization if it results in management bringing fresh perspectives to their work and a commitment to seriously consider new approaches. Playing on the theme that necessity is the mother of invention, Gaebler and Osborne stress the benefits that can accrue when officials are compelled to rethink the relationship between ends and means, and are rewarded for developing more economical, efficient, and effective means of attaining desired ends.

In effecting such broad restraint programs, however, most governments – contrary to rational planning theory – adopted the easiest mechanism for reducing spending across a broad menu of programs, all of which possessed well-established bureaucracies and were championed by vocal and defensive client groups. The simplest of negotiating this administrative minefield was to make across-the-board spending cuts whereby all government departments, agencies, policies, and programs were compelled to make do with the same percentage reduction in public funding. When this approach is taken, all policy actors are treated equally, and none can claim that others are receiving special status, and none is able to claim such status. All are forced to 'bite the bullet.' What is lost in attention and sensitivity to special or unique circumstances is more than compensated for by the sheer ease of implementation.

Under this approach, all human rights commissions have felt the impact of spending restrictions. All are encountering declines in funding relative to their workloads, and the tightening up of money for new initiatives, and (usually) the need to reduce or restrict the number of staff they employ. At the same time, these agencies are being pressured to restructure their policies and programs so as to accommodate this restraint. All commission leaderships bemoan the impact of funding restrictions and are being compelled to rethink their operational approaches to rights administration. In effect, they have been ordered to 'do more with less' and to reconfigure themselves. In this way, commissions have been directly confronted with a human rights tension leading to paradox.

The Paradox Constructed: Incompatible Expectations, Limited Capacities

The tensions facing all those interested in human rights policy and administration are complex. The Canadian public is rights conscious, generally supports the expansion of individual human rights policies and protections, and wants governments and commissions to 'take rights seriously.' Rights advocacy groups, moreover, emphasize that rights legislation must be expanded in order to combat the discrimination that still exists in society. They are demanding that codes be strengthened; that individuals be given stronger protections from discriminatory treatment; that rights protections be extended to address collective matters such as affirmative action, employment equity, and systemic discrimination; that commissions be given increased funding to prosecute their work; and that rights procedures be simplified to reduce case delays and improve case handling.

Yet the Canadian public also acknowledges that governments are facing problems. Canadians are generally leery of program initiatives that would increase taxes, and want governments to exercise more restraint in their undertakings. Business advocacy groups as well as some policy analysts, such as Crawford, stress the need for governments and human rights commissions to be much more restrained in how they apply rights policies. These voices call for prudence in the development of rights protections and for the careful management of rights enforcement. They emphasize that governments and commissions should refrain from promoting collective rights that do not have widespread public support and that inflict harm on business. They also contend that commissions should concentrate on their basic tasks – dealing with individual complaints of clearly unjustifiable discrimination – and pay close attention to the rules of due process. Such analysts claim that by holding to this restricted approach to rights enforcement, commissions could do much more with less.

Canadian governments, both federal and provincial, have come to echo these sets of concerns. On the one hand, all governments support rights protection, both in theory and in practice. They extol the importance of human rights society and the role governments play in establishing and maintaining human rights commissions and promoting their work. In the quest to claim credit for a policy that is generally revered while reaffirming the symbolic ideal of rights consciousness, government leaders and officials always come to the fore. No government, no matter how conservative, has ever considered eliminating human rights policy outright. Though BC's Social Credit government abolished its human rights commission in 1983, it maintained a human rights act, albeit of limited form, and replaced the commission with a council. This was the furthest any Canadian government has ever gone in restructuring its human rights policy. Yet even this change could be viewed as change to a superstructure; the essential foundational ideals of state support for human rights were left intact. And a few years later, under a new goverment, BC returned to the mainstream of rights enforcement with its legislative reforms of 1996.

State support for rights policy is most keenly felt within the human rights commissions themselves. All commissions in Canada are animated by an interest in rights advocacy. Senior officials uniformly believe that rights policy is just and proper, that commissions play an integral role in promoting social justice, that rights policy must be more deeply entrenched and more widely expanded, and that commissions should play a leading role in this effort. Most officials recognize that their commissions are facing operational difficulties as a result of diminished resources, and stress the need for increased funding so that they can fulfil their responsibilities.

This latter point, however, highlights that commissions are essentially government programs and face the same administrative realities as other such programs; and here they confront the cross-cutting reality of government restraint. All governments support the general ideal and practice of rights policy, but all governments have also embraced the concepts of financial restraint and the corresponding dynamic of restructuring and downsizing. Given the realities of restraint, governments have been compelled to treat their human rights commissions in the same manner as all other government agencies. Commissions have thus faced funding cut-backs, restraint packages, and the 'streamlining' or 'downsizing' of service levels. Thus, while governments maintain general support for the human rights vision, these very same governments are also forcing rights commissions to endure significant spending restrictions. In a very real sense, over the past decade commissions have been compelled to do more with less.

Viewpoints: 1. Crisis

What are we to make of this evolving tension? One way to interpret it is to deplore it, asserting that the cross-cutting forces of the paradox have thrust the human rights policy field into crisis. We can embrace the values of rights consciousness and the role commissions play in promoting rights protection; we can deplore the growing disparity between the expectations held by rights advocacy groups and the ability of commissions to meet these expectations; and we can then criticize the forces of restraint. We can attack those who call for substantive rights restraint while also criticizing governments for failing to provide sufficient funding to human rights commissions. We can argue that rights policy is fundamentally important to any society that claims to be democratic, that human rights commissions must always be properly and generously funded, and that if financial restraint must be exercised in the public sector, it must be exercised somewhere other than in and through commissions.

This is the approach generally adopted by rights advocacy groups and by defenders of rights commissions, including many commission officials. This approach can be termed the *expansionist* vision, in that it seeks to resolve the paradox by promoting equality rights consciousness while playing down the theoretical and practical significance of restraint.

Yet the tension can be viewed in another way. It is also possible to hold that a crisis is growing in the field of human rights policy, that policy expectations and administrative capabilities are becoming more and more disconnected, and that the theory and practice of rights enforcement must be rethought and restructured. But from this premise – which is essentially shared with the expansionists – it is possible to adopt a directly opposite point of view as to the desired resolution. It can be argued that the tension can best be resolved not through rights expansion, but rather by embracing the policy of restraint: that the crisis can be alleviated by bringing policy more into line with available financial resources and a more prudent, narrow, and restrictive perspective as to the scope of rights to be protected by commissions. This approach can be termed the *contractionist* vision of rights policy, and not surprisingly, it is the position that best captures the perspectives of business advocates and those who are sceptical of rights awareness itself.

Viewpoints: 2. Balance

The tension presented here has tended to result in analysts adopting one of the two crisis approaches mentioned here. Yet there is an entirely different prism through which to view the matter – one that results in a quite different policy prescription. Rather than viewing the conditions of the conflict as creating a crisis, it is possible to view the contending sides as establishing a creative tension that, if well managed, is actually good for the rights policy field. In this respect the tension is not an aberrant and negative condition to be overcome, but rather an expected and positive condition to be welcomed. This is the paradox of human rights policy.

The basic thrust of this understanding is that the conflicting positions here establish important values necessary for optimizing human rights policy. It follows that the tension is not to be resolved through the transcendence of one position over the other, but rather through a heightened awareness of the interrelationships between rights consciousness and rights restraint, and between sound organizational activity and governmental restraint, and through the wise balancing of these contending forces. In this essentially pluralist approach, the claims of both rights expansionists and rights contractionists are to be respected, in that each side speaks to an important aspect of rights awareness. Rights expansionists are correct to advocate for rights consciousness, to stress the importance of broadening rights policies, and to insist that commissions be provided with greater resources. These are all ideas that need to be present in any discussion of human rights policy. But these ideas must be viewed as only a part of the whole. The arguments of rights contractionists also play an important role in the development of rights policy. The principles of rights consciousness, rights protection, and general rights elaboration are not necessarily inconsistent with demands for prudence, restraint, and economy within state bureaucracies. In this respect the voices that call for a reappraisal of rights policy and insist on smaller, less expensive, and more effective rights agencies have an important role to play in enriching the policy and administrative debate respecting how we should structure rights policy and rights commissions for the future.

According to this pluralist perspective, both sides in the debate have significant contributions to make, and the merits of both sets of arguments must be considered when rights policy is fashioned. In this respect both elements of the paradox are valuable, and wise rights policy emerges from the creative dynamic found between these two positions. It is important for those involved in rights policy to contemplate an ideal vision of rights protection, but it is also important for this vision to be grounded in the realities of current governmental spending priorities and limitations. Likewise, while it is important for commissions to be stressing new service delivery methods and searching for more economical means of carrying out their responsibilities, these actions must always be modulated by an awareness that fundamentally, these agencies exist in order to protect and promote a human ideal, and that this makes it necessary for commissions to advance the ideas and practices of human rights within society.

According to this pluralist understanding of rights policy and administration, the key to success is to balance the competing claims of rights expansionists and rights contractionists – to fashion reasonable and viable policies and administrations that blend idealism and realism, vision and prudence, ability and capability. It is at this juncture, of course, that a great debate has always raged – and likely *will* always rage – as analysts both within and outside government assess the merits and demerits of alternative policy directions. Yet this fierce and often bitter debate is not a sign of trouble. On the contrary, it indicates a vibrant policy field enriched by a diversity of opinions and ideas. Within this pluralist perspective we do not look for a 'final resolution' of policy issues. In pluralist theory there is never a moment when a policy issue is settled, when broad social agreement is achieved on desired ends and on the means for reaching them. To be seeking such result is to be asking the wrong question. Rather than outcome oriented, the pluralist perspective is process oriented.[26] Thus, rather than asking what the ideal state of human rights policy in this country would be, the pluralist perspective poses two grand questions: Is the rights system organized so that the voices of leading state and social actors are heard and respected? And is the system organized and managed so that core policy objectives can be met, and so that the system is able to evolve?

The Pluralist Perspective: An Assessment

We believe that the pluralist approach to understanding policy fields in general, and the human rights policy field in particular, is highly valid. We are living in a rights-conscious society, and the development and enforcement of rights policy has been one of the great advances made by Canadian society since the end of the Second World War. Human rights policy and administration has become embedded throughout Canada, with commissions playing a key role in promoting rights awareness, addressing complaints, assessing and resolving disputes, and pushing for a broadening of rights recognition and enforcement. Regarding their primary responsibilities, commissions have been relatively effective, working to advance the cause of human equality, dignity, and respect, while vindicating much of the theoretical and practical work of rights advocacy groups. Commissions are sometimes criticized harshly – sometimes by their own officers – but this should not cloud any historical assessment of them. When commissions and their activities are viewed in terms of process, current criticisms cannot but be moderated by the impact these agencies have had on contemporary social mores. From this perspective, the legacy of the commissions is proud indeed. They have helped to develop rights awareness and to entrench rights policy in the public and private sectors. And, an often overlooked point, they have provided a forum for public debate about Canadian rights policy, and usually provided a warm reception and institutional support for the ideals of rights advocates. All of this is good.

Yet problems do exist. All commissions have faced funding restraint and cutbacks, and this has limited their ability to carry out their mandates. Officials from all commissions have expressed concern about the impact that fiscal restraint is having on their operations. These concerns, in turn, are reflected by rights advocacy groups through their criticisms of commission failures with respect to complaint handling, case management, and sensitivity to complainant needs, and through their more general critique that commission leaders have failed to defend and advance rights policy. There is much merit in these criticisms: commissions have wrestled with problems of case delay and caseflow management for years, and have attributed much of the blame for these problems to financial restraint and the resulting staff shortages. Senior commission officials have also highlighted restraint policies as a leading factor in the decline of their public education and community liaison programs. Commission officials and rights advocates fear that effective rights policy is being sacrificed on the alter of cost efficiency and balanced budgets.

In reflecting on these concerns, it is not hard to find areas where commissions need greater funding. Given the judicially recognized problems of case delay, there is a clear and pressing need for enhanced funding for caseflow management initiatives; money is needed to procure case flow management software and to hire more human rights officers. Commission officers across the country are right to claim that human rights commissions are understaffed as a result of recent cost-cutting measures, and that such understaffing is impeding the ability of commissions to carry out their mandates.

Enhanced funding for certain commission activities will be necessary in order to more closely match resources to responsibilities. At the same time, commissions are finding creative responses to restraint. While it cannot be said that commissions are reinventing themselves, many of them are significantly reforming their operations as they seek ways to stretch their dollars. These reforms have not solved the many problems they face, as the foregoing review on commission reputations has indicated, but neither can they be dismissed as failures. Far from it. From an organizational perspective, and following from the theoretical perspective of Osborne and Gaebler, financial restraint has compelled all commissions to rethink their strategic goals and their operational means of attaining them.

Through this process of reconsideration, commissions have developed a number of innovative approaches: new initiatives on case screening (which includes the downplaying of systemic initiatives); new techniques of caseflow management; new undertakings with respect to permanent tribunals; and new approaches to promoting public education and community contact. While generalized funding cuts cannot be endorsed, it should nevertheless be recognized that funding restraint sometimes results in innovative approaches to policy delivery, and also compels commissions to re-evaluate their core priorities. To this end, various commissions are establishing primary and secondary priorities, and differentiating policy goals with broad public support from those with divided or limited support. In this respect, the general downplaying of systemic investigations and affirmative action policies can be viewed as a positive outcome of restraint policy, in that many commissions are being forced to reassess their priorities and to divert resources away from policies of dubious public support toward those with unmistakable public support – namely, the investigation and resolution of individual rights complaints.

This can be interpreted as commissions being compelled, in a very state-centred manner, to refocus their energies on rights policies that are truly embedded in the Canadian state. One can go so far as to suggest that given the public's ambivalence about systemic discrimination and its remedies, policies of financial restraint have been beneficial, in that they have directed most commissions to concentrate on policy and administrative matters that enjoy strong public support. In essence, commissions have been advised to be cautious, prudent, and restrained in deciding on the amount of time, effort, and resources to expend on policy goals outside of the mainstream of Canadian public opinion. In a similar vein, the courts and the broader legal community have stressed to commissions the crucial importance of the procedural rules of natural justice. Strict attention to procedural rights may be costly and irritating to those seeking the speedy punishment of perceived rights violators; even so, this attention provides commissions with a mantel of professional integrity and with the semijudicial demeanour necessary for the effective exercise of their legal duties.

Other indicators that human rights commissions have been coping rather sucessfully with the challenges they face can be derived from the broader policy environment in which they work. For all the public criticism of their work by rights advocacy groups, complaints have roughly doubled over the past two decades (see Table 3.1). Notwithstanding their concerns about procedural formality and case delay, complainants of alleged discrimination are demonstrating through their willingness to approach commissions that they perceive the human rights enforcement system as a viable option in their quest for justice. If complainants perceived the system as discredited, they would not be entering it.

In a similar vein, business advocacy groups are highly sensitive to charges of discrimination, and fearful of the public relations consequences of adverse publicity respecting human rights investigations and charges. While this behaviour may be self-serving, it nonetheless indicates a general change in the attitude of the business community. Through the work of commissions, public sensitivity to rights policy has increased, to the point that businesses realize that discriminatory behaviour is not only a public wrong, and thus subject to legal sanction, but also now a private business liability that is detrimental to their own operations and reputations.

All these reforms, activities, and understandings should not be read either as endorsements of restraint per se or as full acclaim for the work of governments and commissions in coping with restraint. While commissions have wrought important reforms through their struggles with the pressures of restraint, these reforms have been generally achieved through a policymaking system that is quite closed and élitist. The numerous reforms to rights policy and administration over the past decade have generally been achieved through a highly state-centred approach in which commissions rethink and restructure themselves with little to no involvement of other stakeholder groups or the general public. While this approach can achieve good results, it leaves much to be desired in a democracy, and especially in a policy field that is meant to promote the individual rights held by all people in this society.

Given the importance of the issues, and given the strength of rights consciousness within this society, and given the interest that diverse social groups have in rights policy and administration, it would be desirable for commissions and their responsible governments to be more open when they undertake human rights reform, and to invite more public participation. As we have seen, these reforms have been substantial. Given that all Canadians have a stake in human rights policy, a proper respect for the 'public interest' would entail much greater public involvement in decision making. Greater involvement in turn would entail greater consultation with stakeholder interest groups, greater interaction with interested members of the public, and greater liaison with the media in keeping the public apprised of reform initiatives. And there would be substantive benefits to such participative action. Apart from the legitimate due process such an approach evokes, new policy and administrative outcomes are more likely to be well conceived, well structured, and well balanced, and thus more easily implemented and more easily embedded in the workings of the rights system. In recent years commissions have been spending much of their time coping with the stresses of restraint policies, and it is clear that their relations with their stakeholder groups have been strained by this. All commissions need to mend the rapport they have with interest groups concerned with their work, and this can best be achieved by increasing public participation in the work of commissions reform.

Conclusion: The Paradox Continues

As we began with a paradox, so must we conclude, for the tension between rights consciousness and rights restraint is unresolvable. In paradoxical fashion, this is one of the great strengths of the human rights system. Rights consciousness has been one of the great social forces of our time. This is altogether good and desirable, and enhances the democratic nature of Canadian society. Rights advocacy groups are key players in the rights policy field, persistently pushing society in general and governments in particular to broaden and deepen this society's rights protections. This also is good, and a sign of a vibrant policy field. But rights policy does not exist in an absolutist world in which there is only one acceptable perspective on human rights. We live in a pluralistic society in which rights policy is subject to a number of divergent analytical perspectives. Thus we have seen business groups adopting quite critical perspectives on rights policies, and the very concept of individual rights consciousness has become the subject of much debate and re-evaluation. This too is good, and a sign that the broad policy field is alive to divergent voices, with policymakers possessing a range of choices as to how to develop and advance future policy.

As these diverse groups raise divergent policy prescriptions, governments and commissions find themselves caught in the middle, playing a major leadership role (thus demonstrating the relevance of state-centred theory) while seeking some form of balance between these contending points of view. Governments throughout this country are committed to the principles of rights consciousness and to maintaining core human rights programs that are in broad symmetry with mainstream public understanding of desirable rights policy. Yet we also know that governments always have other major policy goals and that these other objectives may run counter to the specific interests of the rights policy field. This is clearly the case with policies of financial restraint. Governments must strive to achieve a balance: to maintain

The Paradox of Human Rights Policy 167

core rights policy objectives while limiting government spending. It follows that governments instruct commissions to attain both goals, however distasteful this task may be for commission staff.

As a result, commissions find themselves in a 'no man's land.' They must deal with a society that is, at core, rights conscious. They must also deal with a variety of strong interest groups capable of articulating powerful points of view. They must also deal with governments intent on securing financial restraint. And they must also work within a framework of procedural legalities and due process. It is a devilish task, and one that is rarely appreciated in this society. In attempting to strike the balance, commissions have engaged in some highly innovative, state-directed initiatives aimed at delivering rights programming more efficiently and effectively. There have been some successes here (see Chapter 4), and other initiatives deserve careful scrutiny in the future.

Two unmistakable impacts of these developments bear repetition. One is that selective programs of financial restraint can inspire creative management and administration as commissions confront the need to do more with less. The other is that programs of restraint compel commissions to prioritize their policy objectives – to emphasize core responsibilities and allow secondary concerns to fade into the background. In this respect we have seen commissions emphasizing individual rights complaints and downplaying their systemic discrimination and affirmative action policies. As these priorities tend to reflect those of the broader public, it can be argued that financial restraint has actually connected commissions more closely to the general public interest. While rights advocates and certain officials within commissions may not like this logic, this dynamic may serve to keep commissions attuned to the needs and concerns of common Canadians in these very turbulent times. This may prove to be a silver lining to the cloud of restraint.

The paradox guarantees that debates about rights policy will always be energetic, and enlivened by sharply contrasting theoretical and practical visions as to what human rights policy and administration should be. It also ensures that governments maintain a strong commitment to rights policy, while insisting that such policy be modulated and conditioned by prudence, reason, caution, and (if necessary) restraint. Commissions, in turn, are required to balance all these contending and contrasting forces; they seek not some final resolution of the paradox, but rather a system of management that will enable rights policy and programming to remain an effective part of social life while being responsible to the needs of both governments and the broader public. To this end, commissions must work in the long-term interests of the public. That advocacy groups on both sides of the paradox are often critical of commissions is no surprise, as the operational goals of these groups and the commissions are quite different. The ultimate mark of success for Canada's human rights commissions as they manage rights programs and balance interests is that no stakeholder group, no major political party, no government, no major media voice, favours radically restructuring this country's human rights policies or abolishing commissions. In this respect rights policy is, indeed, embedded in this society, as is the place of human rights commissions. The ongoing debate is simply over how we are to manage this reality.

Notes

1 R. Brian Howe, 'The Evolution of Human Rights Policy in Ontario,' *Canadian Journal of Political Science* 24:4 (1991), 787–90. There were exceptions to this. The Liberal Party advocated equal pay legislation for women in 1921 and the CCF urged a Bill of Rights in 1935.
2 Catalogued by Walter Tarnopolsky and William Pentney, *Discrimination and the Law* (Toronto: Carswell, 1994), pp. 1-1 to 1-5.
3 For a discussion of social *laissez-faire* and its influence in Canada, Britain, and the United States, see Ved P. Nanda, 'Racial Discrimination and the Law,' in R.P. Claude (ed.), *Comparative Human Rights* (Baltimore: Johns Hopkins University Press, 1976).
4 Lita-Rose Betcherman, *The Swastika and the Maple Leaf* (Toronto: Fitzhenry & Whiteside, 1975), pp. 50–2.
5 (1940) S.C.R. 139. For a discussion, see Tarnopolsky and Pentney, *Discrimination and the Law*, pp. 1-21 to 1-25.
6 There were exceptions to this. Jewish members of the Ontario legislature in the early 1930s attempted to establish legislation against discrimination in the areas of insurance and signs.
7 Gurston Allen, 'Jewish Occupational Difficulties,' *Report of the Committee on Economic Problems* (Canadian Jewish Congress, 1939).
8 Betcherman, *The Swastika and the Maple Leaf*, p. 50.
9 Walter Tarnopolsky, 'The Impact of United Nations Achievements on Canadian Laws and Practices,' in A. Gotlieb (ed.), *Human Rights, Federalism, Minorities* (Toronto: Canadian Institute of International Affairs, 1970).
10 This was pointed out numerous times during hearings by a special Senate Committee on human rights in 1950. See *Minutes of Proceedings*, Canada, Human Rights and Fundamental Freedoms, Special Senate Committee, 1950.
11 Tarnopolsky and Pentney, *Discrimination and the Law*, pp. 2-2 to 2-3.

12 Walter Tarnopolsky, 'The Iron Hand in the Velvet Glove,' *Canadian Bar Review* 46 (1968), esp. pp. 568–9.
13 The terms 'human rights legislation,' 'human rights codes,' and 'human rights commissions' would not come into use until the early 1960s.
14 Tarnopolsky and Pentney, *Discrimination and the Law*, pp. 2-4 to 2-6.
15 Tarnopolsky, 'The Iron Hand in the Velvet Glove,' pp. 570–71.
16 See Ian Hunter, 'Development of the Ontario Human Rights Code,' *University of Toronto Law Journal* 22 (1972); and T.M. Eberlee and D.G. Hill, 'The Ontario Human Rights Code,' *University of Toronto Law Journal* 15 (1964).
17 A public education function had been performed by the Ontario Anti-Discrimination Commission, created in 1958. But this commission did not handle complaints.
18 Tarnopolsky and Pentney, *Discrimination and the Law*, pp. 2-6 to 2-8.
19 Howe, 'Human Rights Policy in Ontario,' pp. 790–3; and Arnold Bruner, 'The Genesis of Ontario's Human Rights Legislation,' *University of Toronto Faculty of Law Review* 37 (1979) 236–42.
20 Tarnopolsky, 'The Iron Hand in the Velvet Glove,' esp. pp. 572–9.
21 Tarnopolsky and Pentney, *Discrimination and the Law*, pp. 2-6 to 2-7.
22 For a discussion, see Tarnopolsky and Pentney, *Discrimination and the Law*, pp. 2-7 to 2-8; Rainer Knopff, *Human Rights and Social Technology* (Ottawa: Carleton University Press, 1989), ch. 3; and Evelyn Kallen, *Label Me Human* (Toronto: University of Toronto Press), pp. 16–25.
23 William Black, 'Human Rights in British Columbia,' *Canadian Human Rights Yearbook 1984–1985* (Toronto: Carswell, 1985); and R. Brian Howe, 'Human Rights in Hard Times,' *Canadian Public Administration* 35:4 (Winter 1992).
24 Howe, 'Human Rights Policy in Ontario,' p. 792.
25 Russel Zinn and Patricia Brethour, *The Law of Human Rights in Canada: Practice and Procedure* (Aurora: Canada Law Book, 1996, updated 1998), pp. 15-25 to 15-34.
26 Patricia McDermott, 'Pay and Employment Equity: Why Separate Policies?' in Janine Brodie (ed.), *Women and Canadian Public Policy* (Toronto: Harcourt Brace, 1996), pp. 91–5.
27 In New Brunswick, Nova Scotia, and PEI, the legislation is limited to the public sector. In Ontario, it applies to both the public and private sector. In Manitoba, it applies to the public sector with limited application to the private sector.
28 Zinn and Brethour, *Law of Human Rights*, pp. 17-1 to 17-10.
29 Ibid., pp. 16-17 to 16-31.
30 (1980) 1 C.H.R.R.D/155 (Ontario board of inquiry). See Arjun Aggarwal, *Sexual Harassment in the Workplace* (Toronto: Butterworths, 1992), pp. 23–41.

31 (1978) *Froese v. Pine Creek School Div. No. 30* (Manitoba board of adjudication); (1981) *O'Malley v. Simpson-Sears*, 2 C.H.R.R.D/267 (Ontario Bd. of Inquiry); (1985) *Ont. Human Rights Commission and O'Malley v. Simpson-Sears Ltd*, 7 C.H.R.R.D/3102 (S.C.C.). See Beatrice Vizkelety, *Proving Discrimination in Canada* (Toronto: Carswell, 1987), pp. 96–104.
32 (1975) *Gay Alliance Toward Equality v. The Vancouver Sun* (BC board of inquiry). See Ian Hunter, 'The Origins, Development and Interpretation of Human Rights Legislation,' in R. St. J. Macdonald and John Humphrey, *The Practice of Freedom* (Toronto: Butterworths, 1979), pp. 89–90. The board decision later was overturned by the Supreme Court of Canada in 1979.
33 (1976) *University of Saskatchewan v. Saskatchewan Human Rights Commission*, 66 D.L.R. (3d) 561; (1983) *Vogel v. Manitoba*, 4 C.H.R.R.D/1654 (Manitoba board of adjudication).
34 Kallen, *Label Me Human*, pp. 187–91.
35 Vizkelety, *Proving Discrimination*, pp. 36–58.
36 (1971) *Griggs v. Duke Power Co.*, 401 U.S. 424; (1976) *Re A.G. Alba. and Gares*, 67 D.L.R. (3d); (1977) *Singh v. Security and Investigation Services* (Ontario board of inquiry).
37 (1985) *Ontario Human Rights Commission and O'Malley v. Simpson-Sears Ltd*, 7 C.H.R.R.D/3102 (S.C.C.); (1985) *Bhinder and Canadian Human Rights Commission v. C.N.R.*, 2 S.C.R. 561 (S.C.C.).
38 In Ontario's *Code*, it is referred to as constructive discrimination in section 10.
39 Vizkelety, *Proving Discrimination*, chs. 3, 4, and 5.
40 (1977) *Heerspink v. Insurance Corp. of B.C.*, 2 C.H.R.R.D/355 (BC board of inquiry).
41 (1982) 3 C.H.R.R.D/1163 (S.C.C.).
42 (1985) *Winnipeg School Division No. 1 v. Craton*, 6 C.H.R.R.D/3014.
43 (1985) *Ontario Human Rights Commission and O'Malley v. Simpson-Sears Ltd.*, 7 C.H.R.R.D/3102.
44 (1987) *Robichaud v. Treasury Board*, 8 C.H.R.R.D/4326.
45 (1998), *Vriend v. Alberta*, 31 C.H.R.R. D/1 (S.C.C.).
46 These are summarized briefly in Stephen Brooks, 'Public Policy and Policy-Making in Canada,' in Robert Krause and R.H. Wagenberg, *Introductory Readings in Canadian Government and Politics* (Toronto: Copp Clark Pitman, 1991), pp. 228–36. For a fuller discussion, see Robert Alford and Roger Friedland, *Powers of Theory* (Cambridge: Cambridge University Press, 1985).
47 For example, Eric Nordlinger, *On the Autonomy of the Democratic State* (Cambridge: Harvard University Press, 1981).

48 For example, see Alan Cairns, 'The Embedded State: State–Society Relations in Canada,' in Keith Banting (ed.), *State and Society: Canada in Comparative Perspective* (Toronto: University of Toronto Press, 1985).
49 Michael Atkinson, 'Public Policy and the New Institutionalism,' in Michael Atkinson (ed.), *Governing Canada* (Toronto: Harcourt Brace Jovanovich Canada, 1993).
50 See especially W. Peter Ward, *White Canada Forever* (Montreal: McGill-Queen's Press, 1978).
51 Walter Tarnopolsky, 'Discrimination in Canada,' in Walter Tarnopolsky, Joyce Whitman, and Monique Ouelette, *Discrimination in the Law and the Administration of Justice* (Canadian Institute for the Administration of Justice, 1993), p. 13.
52 Ronald Inglehart, *The Silent Revolution* (Princeton: Princeton University Press, 1977).
53 Abraham Maslow, *Motivation and Personality* (New York: Harper and Row, 1954).
54 *Census of Canada*, 1941, 1961, and 1981.
55 Augie Fleras and Jean Elliott, *Multiculturalism in Canada* (Scarborough: Nelson Canada, 1992), pp. 28–30.
56 Statistics Canada census data. See Susan MacDaniel, 'The Changing Canadian Family,' in Sandra Burt, Lorraine Code, and Lindsay Dorney (eds.), *Changing Patterns: Women in Canada* (Toronto: McClelland & Stewart, 1988), pp. 108–13.
57 Howe, 'The Evolution of Human Rights Policy in Ontario,' 790–3; Arnold Bruner, 'The Genesis of Ontario's Human Rights Legislation,' *University of Toronto Faculty of Law Review* 37 (1979), 237–42.
58 Doris Shackleton, *Tommy Douglas* (Toronto: McClelland & Stewart, 1975), pp. 198–9.
59 (1986) 7 C.H.R.R. D/3529.
60 See *Statutes of Ontario*, 1986, c. 64.
61 Knopff, *Human Rights and Social Technology*, p. 87.
62 This was the case up to 1996. See Table 1.4 and Table 1.5.
63 Alan Cairns, 'The Embedded State,' and Stephen Brooks, 'Public Policy and Policy-Making,' pp. 235–6.
64 A point made by Knopff, *Human Rights and Social Technology*, p. 87.

2. The Public Administration of Human Rights

1 John Willis, 'Three Approaches to Administrative Law,' *University of Toronto Law Journal* 1 (1935), 53.

2 See ibid.; and John Willis, 'Statutory Interpretation in a Nutshell,' *Canadian Bar Review* 16 (1938), 1; J.A. Corry, 'Administrative Law and the Interpretation of Statutes,' *University of Toronto Law Journal* 1 (1936), 286; and Paul Weiler, In *The Last Resort: A Critical Study of the Supreme Court of Canada* (Toronto: Carswell, Methuen, 1974).

3 Weiler, *In The Last Resort*, 135–6, and Harry Arthurs, 'Protection Against Judicial Review,' in *Judicial Review of Administrative Rulings* (Montreal: Institute for the Administration of Justice, 1983), pp. 157–8.

4 John Willis, 'McRuer Report: Lawyers' Values and Civil Servants' Values,' *University of Toronto Law Journal* 18 (1968) 351, 353–5; and Weiler, *In The Last Resort*, pp. 131–50.

5 Walter Tarnopolsky and William Pentney, *Discrimination and the Law*, (Toronto: Carswell, 1994), pp. 2-1 to 2-8.

6 See Willis, 'McRuer Report: Lawyers' Values and Civil Servants' Values,' 353–5; J.A. Corry, The Genesis and Nature of Boards,' in John Willis (ed.), *Canadian Boards at Work* (Toronto: Macmillan of Canada, 1941); Philippe Nonet, *Administrative Justice* (New York: Russell Sage, 1969); and K.C. Davis, *Discretionary Justice* (Baton Rouge: Louisiana State University Press, 1969).

7 Willis, 'Three Approaches to Administrative Law' (1935).

8 Nonet, *Administrative Justice*, 1969.

9 Willis, 'Three Approaches to Administrative Law' (1935); and 'Statutory Interpretation in a Nutshell' (1938).

10 Lord Hewart, *The New Despotism* (London: E. Benn, 1929).

11 John Evans, Hudson N. Janisch, and David J. Mullan, *Administrative Law: Cases, Text, and Materials*, 4th ed. (Toronto: Emond Montgomery Publications, 1995), pp. 18, 27–31, 813–16.

12 Tarnopolsky and Pentney, *Discrimination and the Law*, pp. 2-6 to 2-8, 2-12 to 2-19.

13 F.R. Scott, 'Expanding Concepts of Human Rights,' in F.R. Scott, *Essays on the Constitution: Aspects of Canadian Law and Politics* (Toronto: University of Toronto Press, 1977); and Walter Tarnopolsky, *The Canadian Bill of Rights*, 2nd rev. ed. (Toronto: Macmillan of Canada, 1978).

14 See the Senate of Canada, *Minutes of Proceedings, Human Rights and Fundamental Freedoms*, Special Senate Committee, 1950, pp. 24–5, 46–7, 90. See also F.R. Scott, 'Dominion Jurisdiction over Human Rights and Fundamental Freedoms,' *Canadian Bar Review* 27 (1949).

15 Walter S. Tarnopolsky, 'The Iron Hand in the Velvet Glove: Administration and Enforcement of the Human Rights Legislation in Canada,' *The Canadian Bar Review* 46 (1968).

16 See Scott, 'Dominion Jurisdiction over Human Rights,' pp. 535–6; and 'Administrative Law,' *Canadian Bar Review* (1948).
17 Tarnopolsky and Pentney, *Discrimination and the Law*, pp. 2–8.
18 Note that we are using the term 'semijudicial' in contrast to the term 'quasi-judicial.' In general political science usage, both terms connote an executive blending of adjudicative and administrative functions; the creation of an institution that possesses an admixture of roles ranging from the purely administrative through to the assessment of legal rights and duties and the adjudication of disputes relating to such rights and duties. We have refrained from using the term 'quasi-judicial' in the body of the text, in that this term has a narrower meaning within administrative law discourse. To avoid confusion between the political science and legal understandings of the term, we have used the more generic term 'semijudicial.' For a brief legal assessment of the term, see David P. Jones and Anne S. de Villars, *Principles of Administrative Law*, 2nd ed. (Toronto: Carswell, 1994), pp. 77–9.
19 We will note later the different constitutive arrangement with respect to the federal commission.
20 Tarnopolsky and Pentney, *Discrimination and the Law*, p. 2-4.
21 *Amber v. Leder* 1970 (Ontario board of inquiry).
22 *Bell v. Ontario Human Rights Commission*, [1971] S.C.R. 756.
23 Tarnopolsky and Pentney, pp. 2-4 to 2-8.
24 Ibid., pp. 14-1 and 14-2.
25 Ibid., p. 14–2.
26 Ibid.
27 See Chapter 1, pp. 28–31, 47–8.
28 Tarnopolsky and Pentney, *Discrimination and the Law*, p. 14-2.
29 Ibid.
30 Ibid.
31 William W. Black, *Reassessing Statutory Human Rights Legislation Thirty Years Later: Human Rights Enforcement in British Columbia: A Case Study* (Ottawa: Human Rights Research and Education Centre), pp. 19, 25–7.
32 Tarnopolsky and Pentney, *Discrimination and the Law*, p. 14-3.
33 Ibid.
34 Canadian Human Rights Commission, *Annual Report*, 1996; Ontario Human Rights Commission, *Annual Report*, 1997; Quebec Human Rights Commission, *Annual Report*, 1995.
35 Ontario, Human Rights Code, R.S.O. 1990, c. H.19.
36 Ontario Human Rights Commission, *Annual Report* 1997, p. 65.
37 Ibid, p. 66.
38 Ibid.

39 Ibid., p. 67.
40 Ontario, Human Rights Code, R.S.O. 1990, c. H.19, ss. 33, 34.
41 Ibid., s. 33(1)
42 Ibid., s. 33(1)
43 Ibid., ss. 33, 43.
44 Ibid., ss. 39, 40, 41; and Tarnopolsky and Pentney, *Discrimination and the Law*, ch. 15.
45 Ontario, Human Rights Code, S.O. 1994, c. 27. These revisions to the code have had the effect of superseding the system of ad hoc panel adjudication that had been the norm in case adjudication since the inception of the code. For a description of the old process, see Zinn and Brethour, *The Law of Human Rights in Canada* (Aurora: Canada Law Book Inc., 1996).
46 Ibid., ss. 39, 40, 41, and Tarnopolsky and Pentney, *Discrimination and the Law*, ch. 15.
47 Russel W. Zinn and Patricia P. Brethour, *The Law of Human Rights in Canada: Practice and Procedure*, pp. 18-6 to 18-26.
48 Zinn and Brethour, *The Law of Human Rights in Canada*, pp. 16-7 to 16-8, 16-34 to 16-35, 18-3.
49 Ibid., pp. 17-1 to 17-10.
50 Canada, Canadian Human Rights Act, R.S. 1985, c.H-6, amended by R.S., c. 1985, c. 31 (1st Supp.), R.S., c. 1985, c. 32 (2nd Supp.).
51 Tarnopolsky and Pentney, *Discrimination and the Law*, pp. 2–12 to 2–13.
52 Canadian Human Rights Commission, *The Canadian Human Rights Act: A Guide*, 1993.
53 Canada, Canadian Human Rights Act, S.C. 1976–77, c. 33, s. 39.
54 *MacBain v. Canada (Canadian Human Rights Commission)*, [1985] 1 F.C. 856, 16 Admin. L.R. 109, 11 D.L.R. (4th) 202 (C.A.).
55 Canada, Canadian Human Rights Act, 1985, s. 48.2.
56 Ibid., ss. 16–21, 27.
57 Ibid., s. 32.1.
58 Canada, Canadian Human Rights Commission, *Annual Report, 1996* (Ottawa: Minister of Public Works and Government Services Canada, 1997), p. 100.
59 Quebec, *Charter of Human Rights and Freedoms*, S.Q. 1989, c. 51, ss. 1–4.
60 Ibid., ss. 71(6), (7), and (8).
61 Ibid., ss. 57–8.
62 Ibid., ch. 52.
63 Such 'supremacy clauses' are found in most other provincial human rights acts, and elevate human rights law above all other provincial laws. But the effect of the clause in the Quebec charter is greater, since the scope of the legislation is so much greater.

64 Quebec, *Commission des droits de la personne, 1995 Annual Report*, p. 14. Prior to the amendments of 1995, the structure of the commission was unitary and did not provide for a division of policy and program interest between commissioners.
65 Quebec Human Rights Commission, *Annual Report* (Quebec: Government of Quebec, 1995), pp. 49–53.
66 Ibid., p. 18.
67 Tarnopolsky and Pentney, *Discrimination and the Law*, p. 15–66.
68 Quebec Charter of Rights and Freedoms, 1989, ss. 101, 103.
69 Ibid., ss. 125–32.
70 Ibid., s. 62.
71 British Columbia Human Rights Act, S.B.C. 1984, ch. 22, s. 10(1).
72 William W. Black, *Reassessing Statutory Human Rights Legislation Thirty Years Later: Human Rights Enforcement in British Columbia: A Case Study*, pp. 11–12.
73 Ibid., pp. 19–22.
74 Ibid., pp. 21–2.
75 Ibid., p. 22. In 1994, William W. Black produced a very similar report directly for the BC government with respect to the reform of provincial human rights policy. See William W. Black, 'Report on Human Rights in British Columbia' (Victoria: Government of British Columbia, 1994).
76 Ibid., pp. 73–4.
77 Ibid., pp. 90–9, 103–5.
78 British Columbia Human Rights Code, S.B.C., 1996, c. 210.

3. Fiscal Restraint

1 Walter Tarnopolsky and William Pentney, *Discrimination and the Law* (Toronto: Carswell, 1994), p. 2–6.
2 Dorene Jacobs, *The Ontario Human Rights Commission: A History* (Toronto: Ontario Human Rights Commission, 1970), p. 45.
3 Ontario Human Rights Commission, *Annual Reports*, 1978–79 and 1995–96.
4 Tarnopolsky and Pentney, *Discrimination and the Law*, pp. 8-2 to 8-6.
5 *Vriend v. Alberta* (1998), 31 C.H.R.R. D/1 (S.C.C.).
6 From data in commission annual reports.
7 Based on commission annual reports.
8 From commission annual reports.
9 Ontario Human Rights Commission, *Annual Reports*, 1980–81 and 1990–91.
10 From commission annual reports.
11 Rainer Knopff and Thomas Heilke, 'Human Rights Litigation, 1956–1984,' *Canadian Human Rights Reporter* 8 (February/March 1987).

Notes to pages 75–80   177

12 Statistics made available by the *Canadian Human Rights Reporter* based on its 1998 *Revised Consolidated Index*, 1980–97. The figures do not always reflect the date of decision, only the year published.
13 From the *Canadian Human Rights Reporter*.
14 Ontario Human Rights Commission, *Life Together* (Toronto: Queen's Printer, 1977).
15 *Life Together*, pp. 86–91.
16 From the early 1980s to the mid-1990s, human rights spending as a percentage of provincial spending fell in BC from .02 to .01, in Alberta from .01 to <.01, in Saskatchewan from .03 to .01, in New Brunswick from .02 to .01, and in Nova Scotia from .03 to .02. The percentage in Manitoba remained at .02 and in Newfoundland at <.01. From the early 1990s to the mid-1990s, the percentage fell in Ontario from .03 to .02, in Quebec from .02 to .01, and in PEI from .04 to .01.
17 R. Brian Howe, 'Human Rights in Hard Times: the Post-War Canadian Experience,' *Canadian Public Administration* 35:4 (Winter 1992), 476–7.
18 See Doris Anderson, 'Human Rights Take a Beating across Canada,' *Toronto Star*, 28 July 1984; June Callwood, 'Human Rights Legislation Still Plagued by Wrongs,' *The Globe and Mail*, 1 August 1985; June Callwood, 'Human Rights Commissions Uncertain Avenue of Redress,' *The Globe and Mail*, 22 October 1986.
19 On Ontario, Matt Maychak, 'Human Rights Boss Demands Staff,' *Toronto Star*, 19 January 1987, and Andrew Cardozo, 'Human Rights Take a Backward Step,' *Toronto Star*, 9 December 1992; on Alberta, Canadian Press, 'Strengthen Rights Body, Alberta Told,' *The Globe and Mail*, 1 July 1994; on Saskatchewan, Geoffrey York, 'Prairie Rights Groups to Be Reduced,' *The Globe and Mail*, 20 June 1987; on Manitoba, Aldo Santin, 'Funding, Politics Cited for Agency's Fading Role,' *Winnipeg Free Press*, 14 August 1990; and on Nova Scotia, Dave Sullivan, 'Protecting Rights Comes at a Cost,' *Halifax Chronicle-Herald*, 3 December 1990.
20 For example, Doris Anderson, 'Lets' Look at Our Own Human Rights Record,' *Toronto Star*, 12 December 1987.
21 For example, Shelagh Day, 'The Process of Achieving Equality,' in Ryszard Cholwinski (ed.), *Human Rights in Canada* (Ottawa: Human Rights Research Centre, 1990); Ken Norman, 'Problems in Human Rights Legislation and Administration,' in Sheilah Martin and Kathleen Mahoney (eds.), *Equality and Judicial Neutrality* (Toronto: Carswell, 1987); and R. Brian Howe and Malcolm Andrade, 'The Reputations of Human Rights Commissions in Canada,' *Canadian Journal of Law and Society* 9:2 (1994).
22 As reported in the editorial page of the *Toronto Star*, 26 November 1986.

23 Ontario, *Special Report of the Ontario Ombudsman Following Her Investigation into the Ontario Human Rights Commission*, July 1993, p. 3.
24 Alberta, Office of the Ombudsman, *Annual Report*, April 1995.
25 Mary Cornish, Rick Miles, and Ratna Omidvar, *Achieving Equality: A Report on Human Rights Reform* (Toronto: Ministry of Citizenship, 1992).
26 Howe and Andrade, 'The Reputations of Human Rights Commissions,' pp. 7–15.
27 (1986), 8 C.H.R.R. D/3712 (Q.B.); revd [1989] 5 W.W.R. 1, 10 C.H.R.R. D/16305.
28 (1989), 11 C.R.R.R. D/240 (Q.B.).
29 For example, *Nisbett v. Manitoba Human Rights Commission* (1993), 101 D.L.R. (4th) 744, 19 C.H.R.R. D/504 (Man. C.A.).
30 (1988), 10 C.H.R.R. D/5968.
31 (1990), 12 C.H.R.R. D/285 (Ontario board of inquiry).
32 (1989), 9 C.H.R.R D/4537 (Ontario board of inquiry).
33 (1990), 13 C.H.R.R. D/158 (Ontario board of inquiry).
34 For a comparison between 1980–81 and 1993–94, see R. Brian Howe and David Johnson, 'Variations in Enforcing Equality: A Study of Provincial Human Rights Funding,' *Canadian Public Administration* 38:2 (Summer 1995), 242–62.
35 For example, Paul Sniderman, Joseph Fletcher, Peter Russell, and Philip Tetlock, *The Clash of Rights* (New Haven: Yale University Press, 1996), pp. 80–119.
36 A discussion of revenue availability in comparison to other theories is in Irene Ip, *Big Spenders: A Survey of Provincial Government Finances* (Toronto: C.D. Howe Institute, 1991).
37 For a summary of pluralist and public choice theory, see Stephen Brooks, *Public Policy in Canada*, (Toronto: Oxford University Press, 1998), pp. 25–32.
38 Statistics Canada, *Canadian Social Trends* (Autumn 1993), cat. no. 11-008.
39 Brooks, *Public Policy in Canada*, pp. 25–6.
40 This was part of a larger survey on the reputations of human rights commissions among concerned interest groups. The survey was done in 1993. For general findings, see R. Brian Howe and Malcolm Andrade, 'The Reputations of Human Rights Commissions in Canada.'
41 Of 80 randomly selected groups, 50 returned questionnaires, 26 from the highest-funding provinces (Ontario, Nova Scotia, and PEI), 24 from the lowest (Alberta, BC, and Newfoundland).
42 Colin Campbell and William Christian, *Parties, Leaders, and Ideologies in Canada* (Toronto: McGraw-Hill Ryerson, 1996).
43 See Sniderman et al., *The Clash of Rights*, pp. 103–19.

44 Under consideration here are only premiers who served more than one year in office between 1980 and 1996. We consider 23 premiers in total.
45 See George Perlin, 'Party Democracy in Canada: An Introduction to the Issues,' in George Perlin (ed.), *Party Democracy in Canada: The Politics of National Party Conventions* (Scarborough: Prentice-Hall Canada, 1988); Joseph Wearing, 'Can an Old Dog Teach Itself New Tricks? The Liberal Party Attempts Reform,' in Alain Gagnon and Brian Tanguay (eds.), *Canadian Parties in Transition: Discourse; Organization; Representation* (Scarborough: Nelson Canada, 1989); and Reg Whitaker, 'Party and State in the Liberal Era,' in Hugh Thorburn (ed.), *Party Politics in Canada*, 6th ed. (Scarborough: Prentice-Hall Canada, 1991).
46 Campbell and Christian, *Parties, Leaders, and Ideologies*; and Gad Horowitz, 'Conservatism, Liberalism, and Socialism in Canada,' *Canadian Journal of Economics and Political Science* 32 (1966).
47 For analysis at the federal level, see Andrew Johnson and Andrew Stritch (eds.), *Canadian Public Policy: Globalization and Political Parties* (Toronto: Copp Clark, 1997).
48 For a review and critical analysis of this belief, see Warren Magnusson, William Carroll, Charles Doyle, Monika Langer, and R.B.J. Walker (eds.), *The New Reality* (Vancouver: New Star Books, 1984); and Daniel Drache and Meric Gertler (eds.), *The New Era of Global Competition* (Montreal: McGill-Queen's University Press, 1991).
49 For a short review of the problems flowing from public debt, see Brooks, *Public Policy in Canada*, pp. 107–11.
50 For the development of this belief at the federal level, see Peter Leslie, 'The Economic Framework: Fiscal and Monetary Policy,' in Johnson and Stritch, *Canadian Public Policy*, pp. 24–52.
51 Eli Teram and Pamela Hines, 'The Case for Government Involvement in the Management of Cutbacks by Public Service Organizations,' *Canadian Public Administration* 28:4 (Winter 1985), 513–30.
52 Howe, 'Human Rights in Hard Times,' pp. 467–70; and Sniderman et al., *Clash of Rights*, pp. 103–19.
53 Howe, 'Human Rights in Hard Times,' pp. 470–7.
54 For discussion, see Joe Chidley, 'Reduced Expectations,' *Maclean's*, 30 December 1996/6 January 1997, pp. 22–5.
55 Abraham Maslow, *Motivation and Personality* (New York: Harper and Row, 1954).
56 Sniderman et al., *The Clash of Rights*, pp. 148–55. In the Sniderman survey, 68 per cent of Canadians were found to be opposed to affirmative action for women in large companies.

4. Coping with Restraint

1 David Osborne and Ted Gaebler, *Reinventing Government: How the Entrepreneurial Spirit is Transforming the Public Sector from Schoolhouse to State House, City Hall to Pentagon* (Reading: Addison-Wesley, 1992); Sandford Borins, 'The New Public Management Is Here to Stay,' *Canadian Public Administration*, 38:1 (Spring 1995), 122–32; and Bryne Purchase and Ronald Hirshhorn, *Searching for Good Governance* (Kingston: School of Policy Studies, Queen's University, 1994).
2 Donald J. Savoie, 'What Is Wrong with the New Public Management?' *Canadian Public Administration*, 38:1 (Spring 1995), 112–21; Michael J. Trebilcock, *The Prospects for Reinventing Government* (Toronto: C.D. Howe Institute, 1994); and Paul G. Thomas, 'Coping with Change: How Public and Private Organizations Read and Respond to Turbulent External Environments,' in F. Leslie Seidle (ed.), *Rethinking Government: Reform or Reinvention?* (Montreal: Institute for Research on Public Policy, 1993).
3 The chapter represents an elaboration and enhancement of empirical and analyical material on provincial commissions. See David Johnson and R. Brian Howe, 'Human Rights Commissions in Canada: Reform or Reinvention in a Time of Restraint?' *Canadian Journal of Law and Society* 12:1 (Spring 1997).
4 A significant amount of information for this chapter was obtained through personal interviews with various senior officials from each provincial human rights agency as well as the federal commission. All interviewees were guaranteed anonymity. The schedule of interviews was as follows: Newfoundland Human Rights Commission, St John's (1 September 1995); Prince Edward Island Human Rights Commission, Charlottetown (17 August 1995); Nova Scotia Human Rights Commission, Halifax (4 August 1995); New Brunswick Human Rights Commission, Fredericton (14 August 1995); Quebec Human Rights Commission, Montreal (30 August 1995); Ontario Human Rights Commission, Toronto (12 June 1995); Manitoba Human Rights Commission, Winnipeg (15 May 1995); Saskatchewan Human Rights Commission, Saskatoon (17 May 1995); Alberta Human Rights Commission, Edmonton (19 May 1995); British Columbia Human Rights Council, Victoria (24 May 1995); Canadian Human Rights Commission, Ottawa (15 December, 1996).
5 Osborne and Gaebler, *Reinventing Government*, p. 25.
6 Ibid., pp. 16–20.
7 Borins, 'The New Public Management Is Here to Stay,' pp. 122–3.
8 Purchase and Hirshhorn, *Searching for Good Governance*, p. 43.
9 Ibid., pp. 46–54.

10 See, for example, Peter F. Drucker, 'Really Reinventing Government,' *The Atlantic Monthly*, February 1995, p. 52.
11 Savoie, 'What Is Wrong with the New Public Management?' pp. 114–19.
12 Trebilcock, *The Prospects for Reinventing Government*, p. 6.
13 Alan Cairns, 'The Embedded State,' in Keith Banting (ed.), *State and Society: Canada in Comparative Perspective* (Toronto: University of Toronto Press, 1985).
14 Trebilcock, *The Prospects for Reinventing Government*, pp. 68–73.
15 Thomas, 'Coping with Change,' p. 55.
16 Ibid.
17 Ibid., p. 57.
18 Ibid., pp. 57–8.
19 Ontario, Ontario Human Rights Code Review Task Force, *Achieving Equality: A Report on Human Rights Reform* (The Cornish Report) (Toronto: Policy Services Branch, Ministry of Citizenship, 1992), p. 1.
20 Ibid., p. 21.
21 Ontario, Ontario Human Rights Code Review Task Force, *Achieving Equality*, p. 20.
22 Ibid.
23 Ibid., p. 2.
24 Ibid., pp. 2–7.
25 Charles Ferris, *Towards a World Family: A Report and Recommendations Respecting Human Rights in New Brunswick* (Fredericton: 1989); Saskatchewan, Saskatchewan Human Rights Commission, *Renewing the Vision: Human Rights in Saskatchewan* (Saskatoon: Saskatchewan Human Rights Commission, 1996); Alberta, Alberta Human Rights Commission, *Equal in Dignity and Rights: A Review of Human Rights in Alberta by the Alberta Human Rights Review Panel* (Edmonton: Alberta Human Rights Commission, 1994); William W. Black, Report on Human Rights in British Columbia (Victoria: BC Human Rights Commission, 1995). See also William W. Black, *Reassessing Statutory Human Rights Legislation Thirty Years Later: Human Rights Enforcement in British Columbia: A Case Study* (Ottawa: Human Rights Research and Education Centre, 1995).
26 Interviews, British Columbia Human Rights Council, Alberta Human Rights Commission, Manitoba Human Rights Commission, Ontario Human Rights Commission, Quebec Human Rights Commission, New Brunswick Human Rights Commission, Nova Scotia Human Rights Commission, Newfoundland Human Rights Commission.
27 Saskatchewan, Saskatchewan Human Rights Commission, *Renewing the Vision: Human Rights in Saskatchewan*, p. 34.
28 Interviews, Nova Scotia Human Rights Commission, New Brunswick

Human Rights Commission, Ontario Human Rights Commission, Alberta Human Rights Commission.
29 Interviews, Nova Scotia Human Rights Commission, Quebec Human Rights Commission, Ontario Human Rights Commission, Manitoba Human Rights Commission, British Columbia Human Rights Council.
30 Interviews, Ontario Human Rights Commission, New Brunswick Human Rights Commission. See also the Ontario Human Rights Code Review Task Force, *Achieving Equality: A Report on Human Rights Reform* (the Cornish Report) (1992), pp. 20–2, 46; and Ontario Human Rights Commission, Annual Report 1995–1996, p. 1.
31 R. Brian Howe and Malcolm Andrade, 'The Reputations of Human Rights Commissions in Canada,' in *Canadian Journal of Law and Society* 9:2 (Fall 1994), 2, 10–11.
32 Alberta, Alberta Human Rights Commission, *Equal in Dignity and Rights*, p. 49.
33 Interviews, Manitoba Human Rights Commission, Nova Scotia Human Rights Commission, Ontario Human Rights Commission.
34 Charles Ferris, *Towards a World Family: A Report and Recommendations Respecting Human Rights in New Brunswick*, p. 207.
35 Michael G. Crawford, 'Human Rights Commissions: Politically Correct Predators?' *Canadian Lawyer* (October 1991), pp. 16–23.
36 Interviews, Nova Scotia Human Rights Commission, Quebec Human Rights Commission, Ontario Human Rights Commission, Manitoba Human Rights Commission, Alberta Human Rights Commission. See also New Brunswick Human Rights Commission, *Annual Report 1992–1993*, pp. 7–8; and Manitoba Human Rights Commission, *Annual Report* 1992, pp. 1–2.
37 Tarnopolsky and Pentney, *Discrimination and the Law*, pp. 15-8.10 to 15-24.
38 Interview, Nova Scotia Human Rights Commission.
39 Interview, Saskatchewan Human Rights Commission.
40 Interview, Manitoba Human Rights Commission.
41 Interviews, Quebec Human Rights Commission, Saskatchewan Human Rights Commission. See also Quebec, *Commission des droits de la personne, 1994 Annual Report*, pp. 18–23, 40–3; and Saskatchewan Human Rights Commission, *Annual Report, 1992*, pp. 5–16.
42 Interviews, Alberta Human Rights Commission, Newfoundland Human Rights Commission. See also Alberta Community Development, *Our Commitment to Human Rights*, 1995, pp. 21–2; and Newfoundland Human Rights Commission, *Annual Report 1993*, pp. 6–7.
43 Interviews, Newfoundland Human Rights Commission, New Brunswick

Human Rights Commission, Quebec Human Rights Commission, Ontario Human Rights Commission, Manitoba Human Rights Commission, British Columbia Human Rights Council.
44 Walter S. Tarnopolsky, 'The Iron Hand in the Velvet Glove: Administration and Enforcement of Human Rights Legislation in Canada,' *Canadian Bar Review* 46 (1968), 565.
45 Interview, Ontario Human Rights Commission.
46 Interviews, Newfoundland Human Rights Commission, Nova Scotia Human Rights Commission, New Brunswick Human Rights Commission.
47 Personal interviews, Manitoba Human Rights Commission, Alberta Human Rights Commission, British Columbia Human Rights Council. See also Manitoba Human Rights Commission, *Annual Report 1993*, pp. 1–2; and British Columbia Council of Human Rights, *Annual Report 1991–1992*, pp. 9–12.
48 Ronald Dworkin, *Taking Rights Seriously* (Cambridge: Harvard University Press, 1978), pp. 88–90.
49 Interviews, New Brunswick Human Rights Commission, Prince Edward Island Human Rights Commission, Ontario Human Rights Commission, Saskatchewan Human Rights Commission, Alberta Human Rights Commission.
50 Howe and Andrade, 'The Reputation of Human Rights Commissions in Canada,' pp. 12–14.
51 Saskatchewan, Saskatchewan Human Rights Commission, *Renewing the Vision: Human Rights in Saskatchewan*, p. 33.
52 With respect to the courts, see Perry S. Millar and Carl Baar, *Judicial Administration in Canada* (Kingston and Montreal: McGill-Queen's University Press, 1981).
53 Personal interviews, Nova Scotia Human Rights Commission, New Brunswick Human Rights Commission, Ontario Human Rights Commission, Alberta Human Rights Commission, British Columbia Human Rights Council. See also Ontario Human Rights Commission, *Annual Report 1995–1996*, pp. 8–9; Nova Scotia Human Rights Commission, *Annual Report 1995*, p. 9; Alberta Community Development, *Our Commitment to Human Rights*, 1995, p. 9; and John McEvoy and Constantine Passaris (eds.), *Human Rights in New Brunswick: A New Vision for a New Century*, pp. 119–20.
54 Maureen Solomon, Douglas K. Somerlot, *Caseflow Management in the Trial Court: Now and For the Future* (Chicago: American Bar Association, 1987).
55 Interview, Quebec Human Rights Commission.
56 Interview, New Brunswick Human Rights Commission.
57 Interview, Ontario Human Rights Commission.

58 Interviews, Newfoundland Human Rights Commission, Prince Edward Island Human Rights Commission, Quebec Human Rights Commission, Ontario Human Rights Commission, Saskatchewan Human Rights Commission, Alberta Human Rights Commission.
59 See the Cornish Report, p. 17; and BC Human Rights Commission, *Annual Report 1996–97* (Victoria: BC Human Rights Commission, 1997) p. 7.
60 Newfoundland Human Rights Commission, Prince Edward Island Human Rights Commission, Ontario Human Rights Commission, Manitoba Human Rights Commission. Alberta Human Rights Commission, British Columbia Human Rights Council.
61 Interview, Prince Edward Island Human Rights Commission. See also Prince Edward Island Human Rights Commission, *Annual Report 1993*, pp. 13–15.
62 Interviews, Manitoba Human Rights Commission, Saskatchewan Human Rights Commission.
63 Interview, Newfoundland Human Rights Commission.
64 Interviews, New Brunswick Human Rights Commission, Prince Edward Island Human Rights Commission.
65 Newfoundland Human Rights Commission, New Brunswick Human Rights Commission, Ontario Human Rights Commission, Manitoba Human Rights Commission, Saskatchewan Human Rights Commission.
66 Quebec, S.Q., *Charter of Human Rights and Freedoms*, 1989, c. 51, ss. 62, 101, 106, 110, 114–24.
67 Interview, Quebec Human Rights Commission. See also Quebec, *Commission des droits de la personne, 1992 Annual Report*, ch. 3.
68 Ontario, Ontario Human Rights Code Review Task Force, *Achieving Equality*, pp. 108–9.
69 Ontario, Statutes of Ontario, 1995. Bill 175, An Act to Amend the Statutes of Ontario with Respect to the Provision of Services to the Public, the Administration of Government Programs and the Management of Government Resources.
70 Interview, Ontario Human Rights Commission.
71 Alberta, *Our Commitment to Human Rights: The Government's Response to the Recommendations of the Alberta Human Rights Review Panel* (Edmonton: Department of Community Development, 1995), p. 9; and Alberta, Human Rights, Citizenship and Multiculturalism Act, S.A., 1996, C.25.
72 Alberta, *Our Commitment to Human Rights*, p. 9.
73 Saskatchewan, Saskatchewan Human Rights Commission, *Renewing the Vision: Human Rights in Saskatchewan*, pp. 51–52.
74 Ferris, Towards a World Family: A Report and Recommendations Respect-

ing Human Rights in New Brunswick, pp. 223–5.
75 Interviews, Newfoundland Human Rights Commission, Nova Scotia Human Rights Commission.
76 Interviews, Newfoundland Human Rights Commission, Nova Scotia Human Rights Commission. See also Newfoundland Human Rights Commission, *Annual Report 1993*, pp. 8–11; and Nova Scotia Human Rights Commission, *Annual Report 1995*, p. 30.
77 Interviews, New Brunswick Human Rights Commission, Ontario Human Rights Commission, Manitoba Human Rights Commission, British Columbia Human Rights Council. See also, Ontario Human Rights Commission, *Annual Report 1995–1996*, p. 31; New Brunswick Human Rights Commission, *Annual Report 1992–1993*, pp. 19–22; Manitoba Human Rights Commission, *Annual Report 1992*, pp. 12–13.
78 Interviews, Alberta Human Rights Commission, Saskatchewan Human Rights Commission, Manitoba Human Rights Commission, New Brunswick Human Rights Commission, Nova Scotia Human Rights Commission.
79 Interview, New Brunswick Human Rights Commission. See also McEvoy and Passaris, *Human Rights in New Brunswick*, p. 119.
80 Interviews, Quebec Human Rights Commission, Ontario Human Rights Commission, Nova Scotia Human Rights Commission.
81 Interview, New Brunswick Human Rights Commission.
82 Interview, Quebec Human Rights Commission. See also Quebec, *Commission des droits de la personne, 1994 Annual Report*, pp. 48–54, and *Rapport annuel 1995*, pp. 59–65.
83 Quebec, *Commission des droits de la personne, 1995 Annual Report*, pp. 56–8.
84 Interview, Quebec Human Rights Commission.
85 Interviews, Newfoundland Human Rights Commission, Nova Scotia Human Rights Commission, Quebec Human Rights Commission, Ontario Human Rights Commission, Manitoba Human Rights Commission, British Columbia Human Rights Council.
86 Interviews, Nova Scotia Human Rights Commission, Quebec Human Rights Commission, Ontario Human Rights Commission, Alberta Human Rights Commission. See also, Manitoba Human Rights Commission, *Annual Report 1992*, p. 12; Nova Scotia Human Rights Commission, *Annual Report 1995*, pp. 34, 41–2; and Ontario Human Rights Commission, *Annual Report 1995–1996*, pp. 9–11.
87 Interviews, Prince Edward Island Human Rights Commission, New Brunswick Human Rights Commission.
88 Interview, Ontario Human Rights Commission. See also Ontario Human

Rights Code Review Task Force, *Achieving Equality: A Report on Human Rights Reform*, 1992, pp. 27, 47–9.
89 Interviews, British Columbia Human Rights Council, Saskatchewan Human Rights Commission, Manitoba Human Rights Commission, Quebec Human Rights Commission, New Brunswick Human Rights Commission, Nova Scotia Human Rights Commission, Prince Edward Island Human Rights Commission. See also, Saskatchewan Human Rights Commission, *Annual Report 1992*, p. 14; and New Brunswick Human Rights Commission, *Annual Report 1992–1993*, p. 22.
90 Saskatchewan, Saskatchewan Human Rights Commission, *Renewing the Vision: Human Rights in Saskatchewan*, p. 96.
91 Canadian Human Rights Commission, *Annual Report 1996*, p. 63.
92 Canadian Human Rights Commission, *Annual Report 1996*, p. 63.
93 Canadian Human Rights Commission, *Annual Report 1997*, p. 59–60.
94 Interview, New Brunswick Human Rights Commission.
95 Interviews, Nova Scotia Human Rights Commission, Prince Edward Island Human Rights Commission, Manitoba Human Rights Commission, Ontario Human Rights Commission.
96 Ontario Human Rights Commission, *Annual Report, 1995–1996*, p. 3.
97 Interviews, Newfoundland Human Rights Commission, Nova Scotia Human Rights Commission, New Brunswick Human Rights Commission, Quebec Human Rights Commission, Ontario Human Rights Commission, Manitoba Human Rights Commission, Alberta Human Rights Commission, British Columbia Human Rights Council.

5. The Paradox of Human Rights Policy

1 An example of this view is Kathleen Ruff, 'A Critical Survey of Human Rights Acts and Commissions in Canada,' in Walter Tarnopolsky, Joyce Whitman, and Monique Ouelette (eds.), *Discrimination in the Law and the Administration of Justice* (Canadian Institute for the Administration of Justice, 1993).
2 This business view is expressed by Michael Crawford, 'Human Rights Commissions: Politically Correct Predators?' *Canadian Lawyer* (October 1991).
3 The methodology is the same as in an earlier study of advocacy groups only. See R. Brian Howe and Malcolm Andrade, 'The Reputations of Human Rights Commissions in Canada,' *Canadian Journal of Law and Society*, 9:2 (Fall 1994), 1–20.
4 This was also noted by Howe and Andrade, 'The Reputations of Human Rights Commissions,' pp. 8–9.
5 Kathleen Ruff, 'A Critical Survey of Human Rights Acts,' p. 33.

6 Shelagh Day, 'The Process of Achieving Equality,' in Ryszard Cholewinsky (ed.), *Human Rights in Canada: Into the 1990s and Beyond* (Ottawa: Human Rights Research and Education Centre, 1990), p. 23.
7 Margaret Philp, 'Human Rights: Drowning in Grievances,' *The Globe and Mail*, Saturday, 6 December 1997, p. D1.
8 *The Financial Post*, editorial, 5 May 1994, p. 51.
9 *Report of the Auditor General of Canada to the House of Commons* (September 1998), ch. 10.
10 U.S. Department of State, *Canada: Country Report on Human Rights Practices for 1996*, in Department of State Human Rights Country Reports (February 1997).
11 Michael Crawford, 'Human Rights Commissions,' p. 16.
12 James Carlisle, 'Accused Employers Could Face Double Trouble,' *The Financial Post*, 15 February 1994, p. 16.
13 Ted Byfield, 'B.C. Government Seems Bent on Going Down in Flames,' *The Financial Post*, 24 June 1995, p. 20.
14 Nova Scotia Human Rights Commission, *Strategic Planning Objectives* (Halifax: Nova Scotia Human Rights Commission, 1997).
15 Saskatchewan Human Rights Commission, *Renewing the Vision: Human Rights in Saskatchewan* (Saskatoon: Saskatchewan Human Rights Commission, 1996).
16 Paul M. Sniderman, Joseph Fletcher, Peter H. Russell, and Philip E. Tetlock, *The Clash of Rights* (New Haven: Yale University Press, 1996); Alan Cairns, 'The Embedded State: State–Society Relations in Canada,' in Keith Banting, research co-ordinator, *State and Society: Canada in Comparative Perspective* (Toronto: University of Toronto Press, 1986); Rainer Knopff and F.L. Morton, *Charter Politics* (Toronto: Nelson Canada, 1992); Michael Mandel, *The Charter of Rights and the Legalization of Politics in Canada* (Toronto: Wall & Thompson, 1989); Peter H. Russell, *Constitutional Odyssey: Can Canadians Be a Sovereign People?* (Toronto: University of Toronto Press, 1992); and Ian Greene, *The Charter of Rights* (Toronto: Lorimer, 1989).
17 Ronald Dworkin, *Taking Rights Seriously* (Cambridge: Harvard University Press, 1978), chs. 6, 7.
18 Peter H. Russell, 'The Political Purposes of the Canadian Charter of Rights and Freedoms,' *Canadian Bar Review* (March 1983), pp. 30–54.
19 John Evans, Hudson N. Janisch, David J. Mullan, *Administrative Law: Cases, Text, and Materials*, 4th ed. (Toronto: Emond Montgomery Publications, 1995), ch. 1.
20 Ibid.; David P. Jones and Anne S. de Villars, *Principles of Administrative Law*, 2nd ed. (Toronto: Carswell, 1994), ch. 1.

21 Ian Hunter, 'Liberty and Equality: A Tale of Two Codes,' *McGill Law Journal* 29 (1983).
22 Michael Crawford, 'Human Rights Commissions,' pp. 16–23.
23 Christopher P. Manfredi, *Judicial Power and the Charter: Canada and the Paradox of Liberal Constitutionalism* (Toronto: McClelland & Stewart, 1993); Knopff and Morton, *Charter Politics*; and Peter H. Russell, 'The Effect of a Charter of Rights on the Policy-Making Role of Canadian Courts,' *Canadian Public Administration* (Spring 1982), pp. 1–33.
24 Mandel, *The Charter of Rights and the Legalization of Politics in Canada*; A. Hutchinson and A. Petter, 'Private Rights? Public Wrongs: The Liberal Lie of the Charter,' *University of Toronto Law Journal* 38 (1988), 278; Bogart, *Courts and Country: The Limits of Litigation and the Social and Political Life of Canada* (Toronto: Oxford University Press, 1994).
25 David Osborne and Ted Gaebler, *Reinventing Government* (Reading: Addison-Wesley, 1992), ch. 1.
26 Classic defences of this pluralist perspective are to be found in Robert A. Dahl, *A Preface to Democratic Theory* (Chicago: University of Chicago Press, 1956); Robert A. Dahl, *Pluralist Democracy in the United States* (Chicago: Rand McNally, 1967); and Sidney Hook, *Pragmatism and the Tragic Sense of Life* (New York: Basic Books, 1974).

Index

adversarial system, 40, 44
advocacy group views, 142–5
affirmative action, 15, 74, 79, 100, 136–7, 154, 157, 167
Alberta, Human Rights Commission, 110, 133, 149; human rights legislation, 15, 23, 25, 33, 50–1, 58, 108, 118, 128; Ombudsman's office, 80; and public education, 122, 124; and resources, 76–8, 83–4; and systemic discrimination, 113, 115; and tribunal, 119–20
Amber case, 47
Andrade, Malcolm, 80
Asian Canadians, treatment of, 4, 26

Bell case, 47
Bennett, William, 93
Bhinder case, 24
Bill of Rights (Canada), 34, 152
Bill of Rights (Saskatchewan), 7, 12, 29
black Canadians, treatment of, 4–5
Black, William, 66–7
Blakeney, Allan, 93
boards of inquiry, 11, 15, 22–3, 30–1, 35, 116–18

Bogart, William, 155
Borins, Sandford, 102, 104, 128
British Columbia, Human Rights Commission, 13, 15, 67, 133; and boards of inquiry, 23, 117; and caseloads, 71, 74–5; Human Rights Council, 13–14, 36, 65–6, 132; human rights legislation, 13–15, 29, 33, 36, 50–2, 58, 65–7, 71, 73, 96, 108, 118, 128, 147, 158; model of rights administration, 65–8, 132; and public education, 74, 121; and resources, 76–8, 83–4; and systemic discrimination, 74, 67, 125; and tribunal, 67–8, 119
Buchanan, John, 93, 95
business views, 10–11, 145–7, 154–5

Cairns, Alan, 33–4, 105
Callbeck, Catherine, 93
Cameron, Donald, 93, 95
Campbell, Colin, 91
Campbell, Kim, 93
Canadian Association of Statutory Human Rights Agencies, 36
Canadian Human Rights Advocate, 80, 144

Canadian Human Rights Commission, 15, 58–9, 61, 75, 93, 145; and caseloads, 71–5; and resources, 76–80; and systemic discrimination, 125; and tribunal, 59–60, 109, 118
Canadian Human Rights Reporter, 36, 75, 144
caseflow delay, 79–82, 110–11, 114, 142, 144–5, 148–9, 154, 157, 163
caseflow management, 43, 47, 109, 111, 115, 117, 163
case screening, 112–13, 148–9
C.D. Howe Institute, 97
Charter of Rights (Canada), 24, 31–2, 34–5, 56, 81–2, 89, 95, 136, 143, 152
Charter of Rights (Quebec), 30, 62, 73
Cherie Bell case, 22
Chrétien, Jean, 76, 93, 96
Christian, William, 91
Christie case, 5
civil law standard of proof, 9, 46–8, 57–8
civil liberties associations, 29, 87, 138
code of civil procedure (Quebec), 63–4
Cornish Report, 80–1, 108, 117, 119, 125, 133
Corry, J.A., 39
Craton case, 24
Crawford, Michael, 147, 157
criminal law standard of proof, 7, 47
courts: critique of, 39–42; role of, 7, 22–5, 30–2, 35, 81–2

Day, Shelagh, 80, 144
Dennis case, 82
Douglas case, 81
Douglas, T.C., 29
Dworkin, Ronald, 114

Eberlee, Thomas, 11
embedded state theory, 33–6, 96, 105, 152, 156, 165, 168
Employment Equity Act (federal), 60, 125
Employment Equity Act (Ontario), 125
equal pay, 14
equal pay acts, 8
equal pay for work of equal value, 15
Evans, John, 153

fair practices legislation, 7–9, 12
federal Auditor General, 145
federal human rights legislation, 15, 22, 30, 49–52, 58–9, 118
federal model of rights administration, 58–61, 133
Ferris, Charles, 111, 120
financial restraint, 109, 115, 157–9
Fraser Institute, 97
Froese case, 22
Frost, Leslie, 11

Gaebler, Ted, 102–3, 106, 128, 156, 163
Gares case, 23
Gay Alliance case, 23, 73
gay and lesbian rights, 23–5, 30, 32, 73
Getty, Donald, 93, 95
Gohm case, 82
Griggs case, 23
Grossman, Allan, 11

Harcourt, Michael, 93
Harris, Mike, 115, 127
Heerspink case, 24
Hirshhorn, Ronald, 102, 104, 128
Howe, R. Brian, 80
human rights commissions: adminis-

trative rationale for, 42–4; and *contractionist* vision, 160–1; and crisis, 159; and *expansionist* vision, 159–60; legal rationale for, 44–8; and organizational design, 48–51, 127–34, 157–66; and pluralist perspective, 161–6. *See also* individual provinces and territories, and Canadian Human Rights Commission
human rights report card, 138–49
human rights staff views, 147–9
Hutchinson, Alan, 155

immigration, patterns of, 10, 28–9
Indian Act, 4
Inglehart, Ronald, 27–8
inquisitorial system, 44
interest groups, 10, 25–6, 28–36, 79–81, 86–8, 98–100, 136–45
investigation and conciliation, 113–15

Janisch, Hudson, 153
Japanese Canadians, 6
Jewish community, 5–6, 29, 87

Keynesian consensus (policy), 30, 96
Klein, Ralph, 76
Knopff, Rainer, 155
Kodellas case, 81

law, role of, 39–42, 44–8, 128–31, 150–3, 160–2, 165–6
Lord Hewart, 41
Lougheed, Peter, 95
Lutz case, 82

MacBain case, 59
MacLeod, Alexander, 11

Mandel, Michael, 155
Manfredi, Christopher, 155
Manitoba Human Rights Commission, 110, 112, 117; and affirmative action, 74; and boards of adjudication, 22–3; and caseloads, 74; human rights legislation, 15, 23, 33, 50, 58, 73; Ombudsman's office, 110; and public education, 74, 121–2; and resources, 77–8, 83–4; and systemic discrimination, 125–6
Maslow, Abraham, 27, 99
Morton, Ted, 155
Mullan, David, 153
Mulroney, Brian, 93, 96

native groups, 34, 85–6, 138, 140
New Brunswick Human Rights Commission, 15, 110, 133; and affirmative action, 15; and case-flow management, 116; and caseloads, 71, 74; human rights legislation, 33, 50–1, 58, 108, 111, 120; and investigation and conciliation, 114; and public education, 121–2; and resources, 77–8, 83–4; and systemic discrimination, 115, 125–6
Newfoundland Human Rights Commission, 73, 117; and caseloads, 71; human rights legislation, 22, 33, 50–1, 58, 120; and investigation and conciliation, 114; and public education, 121; and resources, 77–7, 83–4; and systemic discrimination, 113
New York, human rights legislation, 6–7
Nonet, Philippe, 41
Norman, Ken, 80

Northwest Territories, human rights legislation, 11–12, 23, 25
Nova Scotia Human Rights Commission, 110, 112, 149; human rights legislation, 15, 50–1, 58; and investigation and conciliation, 114; Ombudsman's office, 110; and public education, 121–2, 124; and resources, 77–8, 82–4; and systemic discrimination, 74, 113, 115, 125–6
O'Malley case, 23–4
Ontario Human Rights Commission, 9, 15, 52, 54, 71, 76, 110, 115, 143, 145; and affirmative action, 74; Auditor General, 80; and boards of inquiry, 22–3, 56–7, 117; and caseflow delay, 54, 115; and caseflow management, 53, 116; and caseloads, 71–6; and case procedure, 54; human rights legislation, 9–11, 15, 22–4, 29, 32–3, 47, 49–52, 56–58, 73, 108, 118, 127–8; and investigation and conciliation, 114; model of rights administration, 59–60, 132–3; Ombudsman's office, 80, 110, 144–5; and public education, 74, 121–2, 124; and resources, 76–8, 83–4; and screening process, 55, 113; and systemic discrimination, 74; and systemic investigation, 113, 125–7; and tribunal, 119
Osborne, David, 102–3, 106, 128, 156, 163

pay equity, 15
Peckford, Brian, 93, 95
Pentney, William, 50
Perlin, George, 94

Petter, Andrew, 155
pioneering legislation, 6–9, 30
primacy clause, 24, 95
Prince Edward Island Human Rights Commission; and caseloads, 71; human rights legislation, 23, 25, 33, 51, 58; and resources, 77–8, 83–4; and systemic discrimination, 113, 125–6
public education, 9, 35, 74, 120–4
Public Service Employment Act (federal), 61
Purchase, Bryne, 102, 104, 128

Quebec Human Rights Commission, 15, 61–3; and affirmative action, 63; and caseflow management, 116; and caseloads, 71; human rights legislation, 12, 15, 22–3, 49–52, 58, 63–4, 67, 73, 118, 128; model of rights administration, 61, 119–20, 132–3; and public education, 121–4; and resources, 77–8, 83–4; and systemic discrimination, 113, 125; and tribunal, 64–5, 109, 119

Racial Discrimination Act, 7
Rae, Bob, 93
reasonable accommodation, 22–3, 30
reasonable cause, 13–14
Re Blainey case, 31–2
reforming government, 102, 106, 127–32, 134, 165
reinventing government, 102–4, 106–7, 130–1
rights consciousness, 3, 26–7, 31, 34–5, 74, 99, 109, 150–4, 157–8, 165–7
rights restraint, 75–84, 96–100, 153–7, 166; and administrative structure,

89–90; and influence of ideology, 91–2, 94–5, 96, 100; and interest group pressures, 86–8; and legal constraints, 68–9, 128–31, 153–6; political party in office, 91–2, 96, 100; and revenue availability, 84; and size of minorities, 84–6; and women ministers, 90–1
Robarts, John, 11
Robichaud case, 24
Romanow, Roy, 76
Ruff, Kathleen, 144
Russell, Peter, 152, 155

Saskatchewan Human Rights Commission, 15, 110, 112, 117, 133, 149; and affirmative action, 15, 74; and caseflow management, 116; and caseloads, 74–5; human rights legislation, 15, 22, 29, 33, 50–1, 58, 108, 118, 128; and public education, 74, 122; and resources, 76–8, 83–4; and systemic discrimination, 113, 125; and tribunal, 119–20
Savoie, Donald, 102, 104–6, 128
Scott, Frank, 42
Singh case, 23
social and economic rights, 12, 27
social *laissez-faire*, 4–5, 26–7, 31, 34, 41
society-centred theory, 25–6, 83, 86–7
Solomon, Maureen, 116
Somerlot, Douglas K., 116
state-centred theory, 25–6, 83, 93–5

systemic discrimination, 15, 23–4, 30, 74, 79–80, 108, 113, 124–7, 137–8, 154, 157, 163–4, 167

Tabar case, 82
Tarnopolsky, Walter, 11, 26, 42–3, 50, 113
Thomas, Paul, 102, 105–6, 128
Trebilcock, Michael, 102, 105–6, 128
Trudeau, Pierre, 93
Turner, John, 93

United States, human rights developments, 6, 23, 27, 30
Universal Declaration of Human Rights, 6
University of Saskatchewan case, 23

Van Der Zalm, William, 93
Vogel case, 23
Vriend case, 24–5, 32, 73

Wearing, Joseph, 94
Wells, Clyde, 93
Whitaker, Reg, 94
Willis, John, 39, 41
Wilson, James Q., 104
women in workforce, 10, 26, 28–9

Yaremko, John, 11
Young Offenders Act (Quebec), 62
Youth Protection Act (Quebec), 62
Yukon Human Rights Commission, 15; human rights legislation, 23, 73